ART ON TRIAL

ART/
ON TRIAL/From Whistler
/to Rothko

LAURIE ADAMS

WALKER AND COMPANY ● NEW YORK

First published in the United States of America in 1976 by the Walker Publishing Company, Inc.

Published simultaneously in Canada by Fitzhenry & Whiteside, Limited, Toronto.

ISBN: 0-8027-0517-0

Library of Congress Catalog Card Number: 75-36535

Printed in the United States of America.

10 9 8 7 6 5 4 3 2 1

An excerpt* of a trial held before the Holy Tribunal of the Inquisition: Venice, July 18, 1573. Paolo Veronese, one of Italy's leading painters has been accused of heresy. He included certain figures unacceptable to the authorities in a painting entitled *Feast in the House of Simon*, i.e., *The Last Supper*.

Q: In this Supper . . . what is the significance of the man whose nose is bleeding?

A: I intended to represent a servant whose nose was bleeding because of some accident.

Q: What is the significance of those armed men dressed as Germans, each with a halberd in his hand?

A: We painters take the same license the poets and the jesters take and I have represented these two halberdiers, one drinking and the other eating nearby on the stairs. They are placed here so that they might be of service because it seemed to me fitting, according to what I have been told, that the master of the house, who was great and rich, should have such servants.

Q: And that man dressed as a buffoon with a parrot on his wrist, for what purpose did you paint him on that canvas?

A: For ornament, as is customary.

Q: Who are at the table of Our Lord?

A: The Twelve Apostles.

Q: What is St. Peter, the first one, doing?

A: Carving the lamb in order to pass it to the other end of the table.

Q: What is the Apostle next to him doing?

A: He is holding a dish in order to receive what St. Peter will give him.

Q: Tell us what the one next to this one is doing.

A: He has a toothpick and cleans his teeth. . . .

Q: Does it seem fitting at the Last Supper of the Lord to

Literary Sources of Art History: An Anthology of Texts from Theophilus to Goethe, ed. Elizabeth Gilmore Holt (copyright 1947, © 1975 by Princeton University Press): Paolo Veronese "Trial before the Holy Tribunal," pp. 246-48. Reprinted by permission of Princeton University Press.

paint buffoons, drunkards, Germans, dwarfs and similar vul-
garities?

A: No, milords.

Q: Do you not know that in Germany and in other places
infected with heresy it is customary with various pictures full
of scurrilousness and similar inventions to mock, vituperate,
and scorn the things of the Holy Catholic Church in order to
teach bad doctrines to foolish and ignorant people? . . .

The judges gave Veronese three months to amend his
picture. Instead, he changed the painting's title to *The Feast
in the House of Levi*, thereby satisfying the Holy Tribunal
that the Lord's Last Supper had not been defiled.

CONTENTS

ACKNOWLEDGMENTS

The material on the trials has, for the most part, been taken directly from the original transcripts. In *Whistler* v. *Ruskin,* however, I have relied primarily on Stanley Weintraub's *Whistler* and H. Montgomery Hyde's *Their Good Names* for the actual testimony. For the Van Meegeren chapter, the main sources are Lord Kilbracken's two books, *Master Forger* and *Van Meegeren: Master Forger.* I am particularly grateful to Lord Kilbracken for his permission to use the English translation of the trial transcript as it appears in those earlier books.

Assistance and helpful suggestions have come from the art world as well as from the legal and criminal justice professions. In particular I would like to thank John Adams, Stanley Arkin, Robert Callagy, John Cronin, Jack Flam, Wilson Gathings (my editor), Sidney Geist, Richard Green, Theodore Kaplan, Joan Lapham, Larry Loeb, Judith McQuown, Ben van Meerendonk, Matthew Neary, Stephen Radich, George Schneider, Ginger Seippel, J.R. Voûte, Henry de Vries, and Tom Wolfe.

I am also grateful for the assistance of Carlton Kelsey of the Amagansett Free Library, Mary Schmidt of the Columbia Fine Arts Library, and Hubbard Balloo of the photographic reproduction department at Columbia.

INTRODUCTION / Tom Wolfe

"When art goes on trial," says Laurie Adams, "strange things happen." Strange, and then some. At the outset we are treated to some marvelous bureaucratic vaudeville. Edward Steichen, the photographer, goes to France in 1926 and buys a piece of abstract sculpture for $1500 from a young artist named Brancusi and ships it back to New York. It's called *Bird in Space.* At dockside in New York, the customs officers take a look at this slender, slightly spiraled length of polished bronze and decide that it does not fit the category Art Object (which is duty free) but falls under Kitchen Utensils, Hospital Supplies, and Other Manufactured Metal (duty: forty percent).

What sniggers and horselaughs the U.S. Customs gets from *le tout New York* over that! A socialite, Mrs. Harry Payne Whitney, puts up the money for Steichen and Brancusi to fight the case. Frank Crowninshield of *Vanity Fair* and an impeccable procession of art experts come to Federal court in the name of Brancusi and the Modern Movement. The grand sum of six hundred dollars in duty charges is at stake. Yet the Feds fight it out to the finish, using three lawyers and art experts of their own. Why? Is it a case of dismal workadaddy civil servants instinctively hating abstract art— this lump of metal some greaser had the audacity to polish up and ask fifteen hundred for? Or do they really think that unscrupulous rack-jobbers are going to import job-lots of corkscrews from Japan and exhibit them as art objects on the docks of San Pedro, California, thereby evading millions in duty before unloading them on housewives in the Sanitary Stores?

Here, of course, we have our old fall guys, the philistines —the Customs Service lifers, the public prosecutors, assorted lawyers, and the like. But then the plot of Laurie Adams' chronicle begins to take some subtle twists. The art world turns out to have some utterly Mad Nit notions of its own. And the stakes become much grander. (For example, by 1974 another Brancusi piece, less well known than *Bird in Space*, has sold for $750,000.)

Not only grander, but positively Byzantine . . . In New York in the 1970s we see the American art world wrestling over the ghost of that great peekaboo hermit of Upper Bohemia, Mark Rothko; or, more precisely, over his ghost and several hundred Abstract Expressionist paintings he left behind when he committed suicide. A righteous band of art experts steps forth in court. How noble of them! They're here to defend Rothko's children against the sly designs of his dealer and his executors. But soon a subplot develops: could it be that this great Lincoln Brigade of experts has really closed ranks to shore up the sinking reputation—and collapsing price structure—of Abstract Expressionism itself? In the end the court is left with this skullcrusher: how much money, how many *millions* of dollars, are hundreds of paintings in an out-of-date style by a dead painter with a Big Recent Reputation worth—when there have never been enough sales to establish a true market value in the first place? As if to add the final perfect loony note, the court actually reaches a conclusion on this point.

The art experts! What a marvelous breed! In courtroom after courtroom. But first I should emphasize that Laurie Adams, an art historian, is generally sympathetic to the predicaments of art lovers, artists, critics, connoisseurs and other art worldlings when they wind up in the grip of the law. She regards the art world as a serious and important sphere with special customs and consideration (e.g., the imponderable called *taste*), which the law should take into account and generally doesn't. But above all, she is a scholar with a gift for narrative. The result is rich material in which the prospector can find unexpected delights. And for me it is the spectacle of the "art expert" that becomes fascinating as her saga progresses. Irresistible, in fact!

In Amsterdam in 1945, for example, Dutch authorities arrest a fifty-seven-year-old small-time artist and good-time charlie named Han van Meegeren and charge him with treason—for selling a Dutch national treasure, Vermeer's *Christ and the Woman Taken in Adultery*, to Hermann Goering three years earlier. "Fools!" says van Meegeren. Vermeer, he insists, never painted a picture called *Christ and the Woman Taken in Adultery*. He, van Meegeren, painted it—which makes him not a traitor but a forger; and not only that, a forger who put a big one over on the Nazi enemy. But he has also put a big one over on the art world—whose own experts have certified *Christ and the Woman Taken in Adultery* as a real Vermeer—and for this he is *not* forgiven. Moreover, the art world soon learns that van Meegeren has in fact painted 0000 of the 0000 "known" Vermeers!

In Laurie Adams' skillful recounting, the story of van Meegeren and the fake Vermeers is more than a detective story, a courtroom drama, and an *opéra bouffe*. It also raises some profound questions about the nature of art in the 20th century. For a start, the question of just what is valued in a painting. Why should van Meegeren's Vermeers have any less value than Vermeer's Vermeers—if not even the experts could tell the difference?

As Aldous Huxley pointed out in a similar context, the answer is simple and primitive: the art world believes in magic. The hand of the Old Master and his charisma—i.e., his gift from God—touched the one canvas and not the other. This is magic primordial, magic by proximity. It is precisely the same magic that for four centuries animated a furious debate within Christendom over which of three clumps of indistinguishable dried oyster-white bones, buried in three different places in the world, were actually Christopher Columbus's.

The religion of the 19th century, said Jacob Burckhardt,

was "rationalism for the few and magic for the many." In our own day we can turn that dictum around. The religion of the 20th century is rationalism for the many and magic for the few. Over the past hundred years the belief of the "many" in folk magic, in witches, horned devils, spells, amulets, lucky beans, and the like, has declined steadily. The folks have gone in for rationalism and now believe in computers, polls, pills, chemical adjustments, sex therapy, and market surveys. But a belief in magic—art magic—has grown just as steadily among "the few," which is to say those who come out of the leading universities. Today they *believe* in art, with a blind faith, in a way that has no parallel in history. It is no exaggeration to say that art has become literally, not metaphorically, the religion of the educated classes in the West in the last quarter of the 20th century.

Both Nietzsche and Max Weber predicted as much nearly a century ago as a corollary to "the death of God" and "the demystification of the world." Weber predicted that aesthetics would replace ethics as the standard by which educated people make moral judgments. So it is that the intellectual today no longer sees his devil figures as evil. Instead they are sick (Nixon) or philistine (Wallace). And so it is that the intellectual today uses art to perform the age-old social function of religion, i.e., to separate Me and My Mates from the mob (known today as "the middle class") and to project Our Values up onto the dome of the sky, where they are perceived as God, who is known today as "culture." Culture is abetted by his holy spirit, known as "creativity," which he breathes into certain favored mortals as his charisma, or holy gift, so that they become the sons of God, who are known as "geniuses."

It should come as no surprise, then, to learn that art experts today are not experts in the sense in which that term is used in medicine, engineering, or other sciences. They are, rather, like Medieval Scholastics. Their learning is presumed to be great, but their power comes not from learning but from their faith and their non-rational gifts (from Above). Nor should it come as any surprise to find that art experts are usually (and doggedly) sectarian.

One of Laurie Adams' most revealing cases is the suit a woman named Andrée Hahn brings against the art dealer nonpareil, Sir Joseph Duveen, in 1920. Mrs. Hahn is a Frenchwoman who has just married an aviator from Missouri. She announces that she has inherited an original Leonardo, *La Belle Ferronnière*, and that she is bringing it from France to Kansas City, with every intention of selling it for a fortune. A New York newspaper reporter asks the great Duveen for a comment, and he obliges. Without setting eyes on Mrs. Hahn's prize, he pronounces it a fake.

Mrs. Hahn sues for $500,000, charging that Duveen has slandered her painting and rendered it unsaleable. The litigation goes on for years. At the outset Duveen seems in absolute command. He musters the inevitable experts. All testify that Madame Hahn's *La Belle Ferronnière* is a copy, and a dismal copy, at that, of the real article, which hangs in the Louvre.

But just at this point we are treated to one of those surprises that make this book so instructive. We see Mrs. Hahn's lawyer, a man with the terrifically floriferous name of Hyacinthe Ringrose, reduce the expertise of Duveen's art connoisseurs to hash . . . at least in the eyes of the jury.

A connoisseur is, of course, "one who knows," and Ringrose hammers away at the single question, "Yes, but *how* do you know?" This simple strategy quickly reveals that art experts possess very little in the way of analytical techniques, next to nothing on the order of a scientific method, and absolutely nothing in the line of rigorous concepts (a condition, incidentally, that has scarcely changed in the half century since then). One of Duveen's experts, Robert Douglas, director of the National Gallery of Ireland, is finally reduced to saying that he *knows* when a picture is genuine because he has a "flair" for knowing such things. Even the connoisseur of all the connoisseurs, Bernard Berenson, is led at last by the tireless Mr. Hyacinthe Ringrose to saying that he *knows* because he has a "sixth sense" for knowing.

"A *flair*?" says Ringrose. "A *sixth sense*?" And he lets the offending words shiver in all their nudity before the court.

This took me back all at once to my newspaper days, to

the courthouse beat, to those bewildering occasions on which religious sects wound up in the clutch of the law. Some upland West Virginia snakehandler and his wife would be accused of holding off the County Health Officer with coon dogs and twelve-gauge guns as he sought to deliver the rattle-snake-bite serum into the veins of their mortally ill child. Invariably the trial would reach the point where the snake-handler patriarch is backed into a corner and has to deliver his bottom-most argument: namely, that he has done what he has done because he has been so instructed by the Lord.

At this juncture the prosecutor always pauses.

"The Lord?" he says.

"Yes," says the True Believer.

"I see."

Another pause . . . and here the prosecutor tries to remove all obvious overtones of doubt, irony, snobbery, or cynicism from his voice as he delivers his clincher: "And would you care to tell us, sir, just how the Lord transmitted these instructions to you?"

And the True Believer opens his mouth to tell the court *precisely* how the Lord has done so—but in that very moment he realizes what a hopeless trap he is in right now, in the here and now, in this temporal court of law . . . even though on The Day of *Final* Judgment the tables will be turned, for "he that believeth not shall be damned" (Mark 16:16). He starts to open his mouth—and not a word comes out. Instead, he shoots his interrogator a murderous look that says: "*How*? He *spoke* to me, you ninny! There's no way I can explain that to the lost and damned of your courtroom —but it's perfectly obvious to *those of us who know*."

Likewise, the bottom-most argument of the experts whose performances decorate this book so richly . . . "It's all perfectly obvious . . . to *those of us who know*."

This article of faith is finally put into so many words for us by an art critic, Hilton Kramer, who testifies as an expert in a 1966 case in which a dealer named Radich is charged with exhibiting sculpture that defiles the American flag. In court Kramer maintains an urbane and fireproof aplomb.

But afterwards the frustration of the True Believer before the bar bursts into flames.

"Suddenly," he writes, "complicated questions of esthetic intention and artistic realization—questions that require a certain specialized intelligence and taste even to be properly phrased, let alone answered—were cast into an alien legalistic vocabulary that precluded the very possibility of a serious answer."

Which is to say: "There's no way I can explain it to the lost and the damned of your courtroom—but it's all perfectly obvious to *those of us who know.*"

This belief that taste is an absolute value, rather than an amusing side of human nature, is what creates much of the eccentric atmosphere of the great art trials. One may regard it as merely droll. Or one may regard it as a serious matter for the courts to take into account, as Laurie Adams does. But all must agree on one point: millions of dollars now change hands as a result of just such ineffable considerations.

What a golden swamp! What fabulous fogs! What a mist rises over El Dorado! Behold, ye who believe not—the very miasma of the modern faith in art generates something quite concrete . . . which is to say, fortunes! . . . something quite objective . . . which is to say, money! . . . money in the bank! the real goods! emminently spendable! Easy Street, U.S.A.! The Rothko case is proof, if further proof is needed.

But was it not ever so with the great modern religions? The greater the faith, the fuller the coffers . . . Not exactly the Apostles' Creed, but certainly the deacons' . . . We have but to ask the shades of Otto the Great, Pope Urban II, the Mighty Khan, Father Divine, and Daddy Grace.

FOREWORD

We generally think of people—not objects—as going on trial. Nevertheless, there have been a number of legal cases in which works of art have dominated the courtroom proceedings. Indeed, the very outcome of such trials depends on the nature of the art object. This phenomenon is not so unusual as it appears. The work of art is a man-made object with qualities unique unto itself. Each work of art—like each human being—is one of a kind. It has historical as well as aesthetic significance. These factors, together with substantial financial considerations, have involved works of art in numerous litigious situations.

The trials that have resulted are interesting from several points of view. Usually the characters involved are colorful personalities. They have included figures of immense financial power, those with twisted mental conditions, prominent art experts, and, directly or indirectly, the artists themselves. The assembly of such figures in a courtroom, arguing out their conflicts, provides dramatic confrontation of a most revealing and often entertaining kind.

The six trials chosen for examination in this book cover a fairly wide range of both legal and artistic considerations. The libel trial of *Whistler* v. *Ruskin* pitted artist against critic in the late nineteenth century. Some fifty years later, another accusation of libel resulted in the courtroom confrontation between Sir Joseph Duveen, the great art dealer, and Mme. Andrée Hahn, the owner of a so-called Leonardo da Vinci. In 1927 Edward Steichen went to court to prove that an imported statue by Brancusi was a work of art in order to avoid paying U.S. customs duty on it. Immediately following World War II in Holland, Han van Meegeren was accused of treason for trafficking with the Nazis and ended up on trial for forgery. During the Vietnam war and the political upheavals in the United States in the late 1960s and early 1970s, a New York art dealer accused of flag desecration became involved in legal proceedings lasting seven years. In the 1970s, a number of legal problems arose concerning various aspects of the estate of artist Mark Rothko. When the Rothko case went to trial in New York Surrogate Court, the public became aware of the incredible international struggle for power and money going on behind the scenes of the contemporary art world.

Trials are often microcosms of more general issues in the public eye. Each of the art trials discussed reflects certain larger conflicts of its era; political, social, psychological, aesthetic. Usually all these elements appear to some degree. Taken separately, each case presents an artistic window on its times. Taken together, they provide a developmental picture of the work of art as a facet of Western society. The work of art thus builds up a backlog of legal credentials as each trial establishes some new aspect about art. In England and America, this is especially true because the legal systems are based on precedent as well as statute.

A close examination of the most famous art trials of the last hundred years is important for two reasons. On the one hand, it mirrors certain historical aspects of art as a developing process. On the other, it focuses attention on art as a practical reality. Contrary to much popular belief, art need not be either inaccessible or lofty, reserved for an elite group. Art actually embodies the whole of life; as is never more persuasively evident than in the legal wrangles over one or another aspect of a particular object.

On another more philosophical level, an examination of the testimony given when art is on trial reveals something of the elusive nature of art when it is subjected to verbal precision. "What is art?" is a question that philosophers and aestheticians have debated over the centuries. Interestingly, the same question often arises in the course of these trials. Regardless of the original impetus for the trial, in order to prove its case, one side or the other usually feels impelled to prove that something is or is not art. This process, though often bizarre, nevertheless provides a glimpse into different aspects of the art world and highlights the basic absurdity of subjecting the aesthetic nature of art to legal scrutiny. The six trials presented on the following pages are by no means the only art trials that have achieved notoriety in the last hundred years, but they are, I believe, the most intriguing and those with the greatest historic significance. Each one gives us a new insight into the endlessly tantalizing world of artistic creation.

CHAPTER ONE

THE BRUSH / OR THE PEN?/Whistler v. Ruskin

> For Mr. Whistler's own sake, no less than for the protection of the purchaser, Sir Coutts ought not to have admitted works into the gallery in which the ill-educated conceit of the artist so nearly approached the aspect of wilful imposture. I have seen, and heard, much of Cockney impudence before now; but never expected to hear a coxcomb ask two hundred guineas for flinging a pot of paint in the public's face.

This statement, written in 1877 by John Ruskin, the renowned Victorian art critic, led to one of the most celebrated trials in nineteenth-century England. Ruskin, Slade Professor of Art at Oxford, published the remarks in his monthly pamphlet pretentiously entitled *Fors Clavigera*—"hammer-bearing fate." As the mouthpiece for Ruskin's personal philosophy, *Fors Clavigera* tended to extoll the past and the virtues of hard work while regretting the deterioration of the modern industrial age. Clearly, for Ruskin, certain types of modern art were symptomatic of a widespread cultural disintegration afflicting late-nineteenth-century society.

Whistler disagreed. He promptly sued Ruskin for libel. Although Ruskin had criticized Whistler on previous occasions, he had never been as explicit or as personal in his attacks as when referring to the picture displayed at the open-

FIGURE 1. James Abbott McNeill Whistler (1834-1903), *Nocturne in Black and Gold: The Falling Rocket*. c. 1875, American. Purchase, The Dexter M. Ferry Jr. Fund. Courtesy The Detroit Institute of Arts.

ing of London's Grosvenor Gallery. Founded by the wealthy banker Sir Coutts Lindsay in May 1877, the gallery exhibited modern French and English painting and spearheaded a break with the official art of London's Royal Academy. Whistler showed nine paintings at the opening, only one of which was for sale. The price: two hundred guineas. Entitled *Nocturne in Black and Gold: The Falling Rocket* (fig. 1), the painting depicted Whistler's impression of fireworks in the public gardens at Cremorne.

The root of the burgeoning controversy, in fact, seems to have been the very impressionistic quality of Whistler's painting. As such, his libel suit against Ruskin would present a microcosmic capsule of events and controversies then raging in the art world of Western Europe. From around 1850, when the most avant-garde painters of France began producing work in the style that came to be pejoratively referred to as Impressionist, the more academic establishment had railed against this modern movement. The hub of the movement was in France, and artists came to Paris from all over to participate in it and to learn from it. Whistler had come from America to study in France, but later preferred to settle in London, where Pre-Raphaelitism reigned supreme in matters of taste. Socially, Whistler soon found himself moving in Pre-Raphaelite circles, which included some of the most prominent celebrities of the day.

The Pre-Raphaelite movement was an extremely complex one. It embodied social and moral elements as well as aesthetic aspects. In 1848 the Pre-Raphaelite Brotherhood was formed and itself had constituted a rebellion against the prevailing artistic establishment. Among the original members were men who would become some of Whistler's closest friends: William Holman Hunt, John Everett Millais, Dante Gabriel Rossetti, and his brother William Michael Rossetti. Later, Edward Burne-Jones would join the group. They were young men who enthusiastically embraced their new ideals and frequently allowed youthful élan to dictate behavior. One example of such behavior was their conspiratorial vow of secrecy. And, as if needing a password for admission to the group, they decided to inscribe its initials on all of their paintings. The PRB, which then became the trademark of their canvases, resulted predictably in various jokes. Thus, "the initials were said to stand for 'Please Ring Bell' or, in the case of Rossetti, 'Penis Rather Better.' "[1]

Inseparable from the Pre-Raphaelite painters and their movement was the art criticism, thought, and influence of John Ruskin. His strict moral sense, which probably derived from his excessively austere Scottish background, seemed to have endowed him with a taste for pictures with social messages. With respect to the artists themselves, Ruskin admired technique and precision—"workmanship"—especially as perceived among Renaissance painters like Giotto and Botticelli, who preceded Raphael. For Ruskin, technique became a moral as well as an aesthetic virtue. On the whole, Ruskin and the Pre-Raphaelites disliked classical and baroque art and felt themselves akin to the direct approach to nature they believed to be characteristic of the Italian Quattrocento. The Pre-Raphaelite working procedure was meticulous (fig. 2). The artist first outlined the general composition on the canvas and then applied a smooth, thin coat of white. The outline would show through the white and guide the painter during the picture's entire execution. He would work slowly with small brushes to ensure the clarity of the finest detail, while the white underpaint would produce an unusual brightness of color.

Artistically, Whistler had little in common with the Pre-Raphaelites. On a social level, however, the American painter was a poseur and a dandy. His stylish, narcissistic exhibitionism was entirely in tune with the members of the Pre-Raphaelite group. A constant social performer, Whistler costumed himself for the part of the strutting peacock. His outrageous and frequently witty sartorial habits ranged from wearing pink ribbons on his shoes to walking the streets of London with two umbrellas. So obtrusive was Whistler's personal flamboyance that it sometimes overshadowed his own paintings. "In the end," wrote art critic Denys Sutton, "it

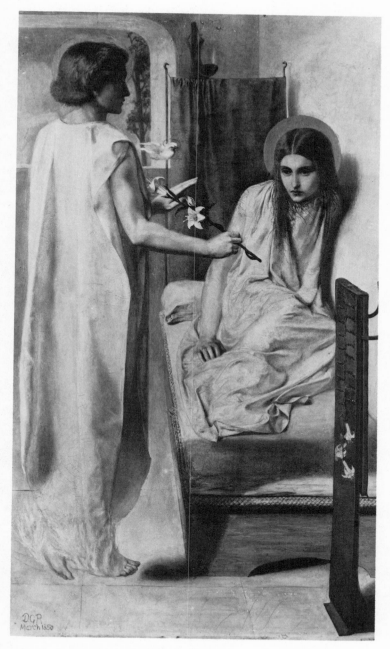

FIGURE 2. Dante Gabriel Rossetti (1828-82), *Ecce Ancilla Dei*. The
Tate Gallery, London.

was Whistler the man, not Whistler the artist, who stole the thunder."[2]

Whistler's close conscious identification with his self-image as social butterfly is evidenced by the change in his signature during the 1870s. Instead of the JMW monogram he had previously used, he now signed his paintings with a butterfly—and *butterfly* quickly became his epithet in the London press. But the fluttering, elegant insect so appropriate to Whistler's outward projection of himself was not restricted to his paintings; it appeared on his stationery and his linen. It became, wrote Roy McMullen, "his totem and heraldic symbol."[3]

In addition to minute attention to his own social image, Whistler had another preoccupation which was a side effect of his flair for the colorful and the exotic and which, to some extent, deflected attention from his art. He was an interior decorator. At certain periods of his life, he spent so much time on interior decoration that he was considered a professional. Reflecting the general taste of the times, Whistler was enamored of things oriental, a preference which considerably influenced his style of decoration. He collected oriental furniture, Chinese porcelain, Japanese prints, screens, and fans. Up to a point, this preoccupation was characteristic of the Impressionist painters and, like them, Whistler endowed a number of his pictures with Japanese elements. Nevertheless, despite the aura of superficiality which surrounded Whistler's social life and the energy which he poured into this and other peripheral activities, he remained a hard-working, industrious, and original painter.

Whistler lived at what is now 101 Cheyne Walk in Chelsea with views of the Thames and of Battersea Bridge, both of which would become subjects of some of his most controversial paintings. A report sent from *The New York Times* London correspondent on May 23, 1878, lauded Whistler's courage in making London his home. That Whistler lived most of his adult life as an expatriate increased the theatricality of his existence. He was not at home and could thus throw himself into his various social roles with greater abandon than if he had remained immersed in his childhood culture. "It is a creditable fact," wrote the correspondent, "for an American to come to London, and, making his way through insular prejudices into the very heart of intellectual circles, to hold his own there." Whistler, he wrote, was indeed a "shining light in the art world of this metropolis," although—referring to the artist's well-known temperamental nature—he was "sometimes more daring than discreet."[4] Despite Whistler's social preference for London, however, his artistic sympathies lay with the French Impressionists.

Whistler made several trips to France, keeping in constant contact with developments in Impressionism. It was during a visit to Paris in 1862 that he acquired the Impressionist taste for Japanese art, and in the following year he exhibited *The White Girl* (fig. 3) at the Salon des Refusés. In many ways *The White Girl* is a painting typical of the early Impressionist style. The subject represented is an ordinary person, the artist's mistress Jo, and not the heroic, historical, or aristocratic subject preferred by the prevailing French establishment, which the neoclassical artists were likely to paint. The French neoclassical artists enjoyed a dominant position similar to that of the Pre-Raphaelites in England. Both embodied the prevailing—and therefore officially accepted—taste of the day. Unlike a neoclassical portrait, Whistler's *White Girl* is not grand or particularly imposing; in fact, Jo's drooping shoulders emphasize her rather slouched posture. The clear, crisp outlines typical of such neoclassical artists as Ingres and David are gone. Whistler's are fuzzy, and his brushstrokes are visible; a characteristic that would become a most prominent mark of Impressionism. Certain forms are slightly blurred at the edges, as where Jo's hair blends with the background paint. Also characteristic of Impressionism is the interest in pattern evident in the representation of the floor and the taste for silhouetting in the placement of the model's dark hair against a light background.

In light of Whistler's natural inclination toward Impres-

FIGURE 3. James Abbott McNeill Whistler, *The White Girl* (*Symphony in White, No. 1*). National Gallery of Art, Washington. Harris Whittemore Collection.

sionism, it is interesting that he was not without his own conflicts about that style. Whistler had been consistently admired for his abilities as a draftsman, and his talent for etching had been frequently compared with that of Rembrandt and other Old Masters. Before leaving America, he had worked as a draftsman in Washington and had, in fact, been making drawings and caricatures since childhood. At the same time, however, Whistler was attracted by the vibrant and seemingly spontaneous use of color characteristic of Impressionism. It might be said that his puritanical background was associated in his mind with the controlled medium of drawing while color was associated with sensuality. That this was indeed the case seems clear from a letter that Whistler wrote to Fantin-Latour in 1867, in which he discussed his own change in taste from Courbet to the linear control of Ingres: "Drawing, by God! Color is vice, although it can be one of the finest virtues. When controlled by a firm hand, well-guided by her master, Drawing, Color is then like a splendid woman with a mate worthy of her—her lover but also her master—the most magnificent mistress possible. But when united with uncertainty, with a weak drawing, timid, deficient, easily satisfied, Color becomes a bold whore, makes fun of her little fellow, isn't it so?"[5] In other words, the sensual (and for Whistler, feminine) nature of color must be kept under control by the masterful (masculine) art of drawing.

Such conflicts seem to have been a recurrent theme in Whistler's life. His father had been a military engineer, and, in 1851, as a young man, Whistler entered West Point. As might be expected, he rebelled against military routine and was eventually expelled. Later, during his employment as a draftsman in Washington, his creative exuberance impelled him to draw over the walls of the room where he lived as well as on the walls outside his office at work. Such deceptively childish behavior reveals Whistler's inner struggle between control and spontaneity. The conflict is clear: on the one hand, he worked as a draftsman—in line—while on the other he sought a release from the confining boundaries of line.

When Whistler finally decided to make art his career, his Calvinist mother tried to dissuade him; she would have preferred her son to enter the clergy. What little artistic encouragement Whistler received came from his father who, militarily minded though he was, was a much more colorful personality than his wife. He was musical and artistic and had a taste for travel and adventure. Nevertheless, Whistler's mother would soon become reconciled to her son's career, even providing her steady support and boasting of his successes to her friends. "God has given the talent," she would say many years later, "and it cannot be wrong to appreciate it."[6]

At twenty-one, Whistler left the United States for Europe, where he seriously studied art. But even as an expatriate, Whistler was not to escape his mother's presence. Whistler's witty, colorful personality and life-style were bohemian. His mother eventually went to live in London, where she tried to provide a stabilizing influence on her son. Her arrival, toward the end of 1863, sent his mistress, Jo, in search of other living arrangements. Although the separation had no discernible effect on their relationship, the disapproval of Whistler's mother may be imagined from a description of her provided by one of the artist's London contemporaries as a "very religious lady [who] used to say that she liked being up in her bedroom because there she felt nearer her Maker."[7] As a result of his mother's presence, Whistler was continuously in a position of trying to maintain the delicate balance between the strictures of her puritan conditioning and his own preference for the flamboyant bohemianism of his friends. Beneath his veneer of successful social management, Whistler was nevertheless in his mother's grip; although not averse to mistresses, he did not marry until the relatively advanced age of fifty-four, after his mother's death.

The year 1867 was the time of Whistler's letter to Fantin-Latour on drawing as the "master of color," and it was also the year in which he began giving his paintings the musical titles that would soon cause great controversy. Still another aspect of the conflict within the artist himself, the decision to use musical titles was a clear statement in favor of the modern Impressionist style of painting. Some of these titles, such as *Symphony in White No. 3*, applied to new paintings, while others were new names for older paintings. Thus, *The White Girl*, which had been exhibited at the Salon des Refusés, was retitled *Symphony in White No. 1*.

In addition to Symphonies in color, Whistler now painted Arrangements, Harmonies, Variations, and Nocturnes. The latter, usually applied to night scenes, had actually been suggested to Whistler by his patron, Frederick Leyland, a self-made Liverpool shipper who also patronized many of the Pre-Raphaelite painters. Critical reaction to the paintings with musical titles was generally negative and, for the most part, Whistler earned his living by painting portraits on commission. When, for example, the *Symphony in White No. 3* was exhibited, an article appeared in the June 1867 issue of the *Saturday Review*, pointing out the inaccuracy of the title.[8] The painting, complained the reviewer, had yellow, red, blue, green, and flesh colors, and therefore could not reasonably be entitled *Symphony in White*. Whistler, famous for his acerbic wit, had harsh words for the reviewer. "*Bon Dieu!*" he wrote from Chelsea, "did this wise person expect white hair and chalked faces? And does he then, in his astounding consequence, believe that a symphony in F contains no other note but shall be a continued repetition of F, F, F? . . . Fool!"[9] But, regardless of critical misunderstanding, these musical titles precisely suited Whistler's impressionistic intentions. They reflected his taste, shared with the Impressionists, for the representation of atmospheric conditions, the illusion of spontaneity in the use of color, and the rejection of both neoclassical and Pre-Raphaelite insistence on narrative content.

To illustrate his rejection of narrative content, (i.e., story *line*), Whistler described the solitary, silhouetted figure in his *Harmony in Grey and Gold* as follows: "I care nothing for the past, present or future of the black figure, placed there because the black was wanted at that spot. All that I know is that my combination of grey and gold is the basis of the picture. Now this is precisely what my friends cannot grasp."[10] Interesting, in view of Whistler's emotive associations with color, is the familiar painting of his mother, which he titled—as if referring to her somber puritanism—*Arrangement in Grey and Black*. The artist was apparently very satisifed with this painting and—shades of Leonardo and the *Mona Lisa*—he told his mother that "he could not let it out of his sight."[11]

Some of Whistler's identification with his mother is evident from his self-portrait, *Arrangement in Grey* (fig. 4). Despite the telltale butterfly and a slightly self-conscious allusion to Rembrandt's self-portraits, little of Whistler's flamboyance has penetrated the pictorial representation of himself. Contrary to his social outfits, in the picture, set against a brown background, he wears black and grey. For all his outward posturing, when it came to painting, Whistler was as serious as the black and grey tones of his self-portrait. As if reflecting his very puritanical attitude toward his pictures—and the strenuous efforts he poured into making them—his studio, too, was black and grey.

One of Whistler's favorite subjects was the Thames, which provided him with the opportunity to study and paint the effects of water and fog on light. Monet, the leading French Impressionist, was also fascinated by the Thames as well as by the Seine and the waterways of Venice. In choosing the Impressionist style with its interest in color, spontaneity of vision, and prominent brushstrokes that usually blurred the edges of forms, Whistler was virtually rejecting the clear outlines and narrative emphasis of prevailing taste in both England and France. He was also, of course, moving toward a resolution of his own stated conflict between line and color.

In challenging Ruskin in the courts, Whistler's litigious personality led him into one of the most celebrated trials involving works of art. Although Ruskin had indeed made the libelous comments and had undeniably called the artist a "Cockney coxcomb," it was Whistler who actually brought

FIGURE 4. James Abbott McNeill Whistler, *Self-Portrait*. Bequest
of Henry Glover. Courtesy The Detroit Institute of Arts.

the libel to the attention of the general public. Ruskin's monthly pamphlet had a small audience, and had Whistler not felt impelled to bring the lawsuit, the remarks would most probably have gone unnoticed. Whistler's tendency toward violence erupted into physical fights on several occasions throughout his lifetime, but the trial that Whistler instigated became a battle between opposed intellectual principles. On one level, the puritanical views of Ruskin would be pitted against the more modern views of Whistler, and there is irony in the fact that Whistler had had to struggle against the very puritanism within himself that he would now be fighting in court. On another level, the new Impressionist style would be on trial against London's artistic establishment as canonized by the Royal Academy. Even more universal in the world of creativity was the opposition of artist and critic. As Whistler himself said, it was a trial "between the Brush and the Pen."

That simple phrase evokes a number of associations that go far deeper than its surface reference to artist and critic. Impressionism was very much a style of the Brush, while the Pen suggested the linear qualities of neoclassical and Pre-Raphaelite painting. And again, while on the surface the trial would pit Brush against Pen, it would mirror the old conflict within Whistler's own development as an artist, his progressive rejection of the linear and his assumption of impressionistic use of color. Finally, on an even deeper psychological level, the erotic symbolism of Brush and Pen can hardly escape notice. If one is to believe Whistler's own statement in his 1867 letter to Fantin-Latour, he certainly associated the Brush, and its reference to color, with sensuous female qualities, while the Pen had the obvious masculine significance of control and mastery.

After a delay of over a year, caused in part by Ruskin's mental illness, the trial began. It lasted for two days—from November 25 to November 26, 1878. Sir John Walter Huddleston and a special jury heard the case in the Court of Exchequer in Westminster. Whistler's case was prepared by Anderson Rose, who had handled the artist's constant financial problems, and it was argued by counsel Mr. Serjeant Parry and Mr. William Petheram. Burne-Jones, the Pre-Raphaelite painter, handled Ruskin's case since the critic had suffered a breakdown several weeks before the trial opened.

Ruskin's spell of madness was but one stage in a steady march toward mental decline. As early as 1874, he referred to periods of confusion and despondency, and the following year, he broke down before his students during an Oxford lecture. Starting in the 1860s, Ruskin had recorded terrifying erotic dreams in his diaries. There is considerable poetic justice and psychological truth in the fiercely moralizing Ruskin's hallucinations, shortly before the trial, in which Satan assumed the form of a black cat and commanded him to perform various obscene acts.[12] The Satanic cat leaped at Ruskin from behind a *mirror*, thus confirming that the critic himself was ordering this distinctly unpuritanical form of behavior. As might be expected under the circumstances, Ruskin's doctor forbade him to appear in the courtroom.

Attorney General Sir John Holker, and his junior counsel, Charles Bowen, argued Ruskin's case. Both sides had difficulty in persuading artists to testify. Eventually, each produced three witnesses. In addition, Whistler testified in his own behalf.

At 11:00 A.M. Monday, November 25, the trial began. For the theatrically inclined Whistler, the court setting must have indeed been a stage. The courtroom was crowded with an audience of celebrities. On the surface the case was a libel suit dealing with the matter of Whistler's wounded vanity. In fact, however, it dealt with a far more complex set of issues.

Serjeant Parry opened the case for Whistler on a rather tentative note:

> I speak for Mr. Whistler, who has followed the profession of an artist for many years, while Mr. Ruskin is a gentleman well known to all of us, and holding perhaps the highest position in Europe or America as an art

critic. Some of his works are destined to immortality, and it is the more surprising, therefore, that a gentleman holding such a position could traduce another in a way that would lead that other to come into a court of law to ask for damages. The jury, after hearing the case, will come to the conclusion that a great injustice has been done. Mr. Whistler. . . . is not merely a painter, but has likewise distinguished himself in the capacity of etcher, achieving considerable honors in that department of art. He has been an unwearied worker in his profession, always desiring to succeed, and if he had formed an erroneous opinion, he should not have been treated with contempt and ridicule. . . .

Mr. Ruskin pleaded that the alleged libel was privileged as being a fair and *bona fide* criticism upon a painting which the plaintiff had exposed to public view. But the terms in which Mr. Ruskin has spoken of the plaintiff are unfair and ungentlemanly, and are calculated to do, and have done him, considerable injury, and it will be for the jury to say what damages the plaintiff is entitled to.[13]

On the other hand, the Attorney General's opening statement for Ruskin was a forceful apology for the critic's philosophy of life and defense of his art criticism. What would become of the arts without criticism as an inspiration and a spur to excellence? This was the thrust of his opening remarks. Unfortunately, continued the Attorney General, Ruskin would be unable to appear in his own defense owing to illness:

> That gentleman, it is well known, has devoted himself for years to the study of art. From 1869 he has been Slade Professor at Oxford: he has written much on art, and judging from his works it is obvious that he is a man of the keenest susceptibility. He has a great love and reverence for art and a special admiration for highly finished pictures. His love for art almost amounts to idolatry, and to the examination of the beautiful in art he has devoted his life.

Rightly or wrongly, Mr. Ruskin has not a very high opinion of the days in which we live. He thinks too much consideration is given to money-making, and that the nobility of simplicity is not sufficiently regarded. With regard to artists, he upholds a high standard and he requires that the artist should possess something more than a few flashes of genius. He requires a laborious and perfect devotion to art, and he holds that an artist should not only struggle to get money, but also to give full value to the purchaser of his production. It was the ancient code that no piece of work should leave the artist's hands which his diligence or further reflection could improve, and that the artist's fame should be built upon not what he received but upon what he gave. . . .

In the present mania for art it had become a kind of fashion among some people to admire the incomprehensible, to look upon the fantastic conceits of an artist like Mr. Whistler, his "nocturnes," "symphonies," "arrangements" and "harmonies," with delight and admiration; but the fact was that such productions were not worthy of the name of great works of art. This was not a mania that should be encouraged; and if that was the view of Mr. Ruskin, he had a right as an art critic, to fearlessly express it to the public. . . .

Let them examine the *Nocturne in Blue and Silver*, said to represent Battersea Bridge. What was that structure in the middle? Was it a telescope or a fire-escape? Was it like Battersea Bridge? What were the figures at the top of the bridge? And if they were horses and carts, how in the name of Fortune were they to get off? Now, about these pictures, if the plaintiff's argument was to avail, they must not venture publicly to express an opinion, or they would have brought against them an action for damages. . . . As to these pictures, they could only come to the conclusion that they were strange fantastical conceits not worthy to be called works of art. . . .

If Mr. Whistler disliked ridicule, he should not have subjected himself to it by exhibiting publicly such productions. If a man thinks a picture is a daub he has a right to say so, without subjecting himself to the risk of an action. . . .

Mr. Ruskin says, through me as his counsel, that he does not retract one syllable of his criticism, . . . The libel complained of said . . . "I never expected to hear a coxcomb ask two hundred guineas for flinging a pot of paint in the public's face."

What is a coxcomb? It comes from the old idea of the licensed jester who wore a cap and bells with a cock's comb in it, who went about making jests for the amusement of his master and family. If that is the true definition, then Mr. Whistler should not complain, because his pictures have afforded a most amusing jest! . . .

Mr. Ruskin believes he is right. For nearly all his life he has devoted himself to criticism for the sake of the art he loves, and he asks you, gentlemen of the jury, not now to paralyze his hands. If you give a verdict against him, he must cease to write. It will be an evil day for the art of this country if Mr. Ruskin is to be prevented from indulging in proper and legitimate criticism, and pointing out what is beautiful and what is not, and if critics are to be all reduced to a dead level of forced and fulsome action.[14]

Following this sermonizing depiction of Ruskin as England's true prophet of the beautiful, the witnesses were called to the stand. Whistler was the first to testify, and, under cross-examination by the Attorney General, he gave his views on critics and art criticism:

"You know," questioned the Attorney General, "that many critics disagree with your views as to these pictures?"

"It would be beyond me to agree with the critics."

"You don't approve of criticism?"

"I should not disapprove in any way of technical criticism by a man whose life is passed in the practice of the science which he criticizes; but for the opinion of a man whose life is not so passed, I would have as little regard as you would, if he expressed an opinion on law."

"You expect to be criticized?"

"Yes, certainly, and I do not expect to be affected by it until it comes to be a case of this kind."

The single most important issue in the trial revolved around the relationship of Whistler's musical titles to the paintings themselves. "What is your definition of a nocturne?" Whistler's own counsel asked him.

"I have perhaps meant rather to indicate an artistic interest alone in the work," replied the artist, "divesting the picture of any outside anecdotal sort of interest which might have been otherwise attached to it. It is an arrangement of line, form, and color first; and I make use of any incident of it which shall bring about a symmetrical result. Among my works are some night pieces, and I have chosen the word *Nocturne* because it generalizes and simplifies the whole set of them."

After this perfectly reasonable explanation, several of Whistler's paintings were introduced as exhibits, including a portrait of Henry Irving as Philip II of Spain, as an *Arrangement in Black*, and the *Nocturne in Black and Gold: The Falling Rocket* (fig. 1), which had been the object of Ruskin's attack, and several other *Nocturnes*. One of these slipped and, to the amusement of the crowd, hit an elderly spectator on the head. The canvas nearly fell from its frame. "Is that your work, Mr. Whistler?" asked Parry.

"Well, it was," snapped the artist, "but if it goes on much longer in that way, I don't think it will be."

Then the Attorney General cross-examined. "You have sent pictures to the Academy which have not been accepted?"

"I believe that is the experience of all artists," replied Whistler.

"Why do you call Mr. Irving an *Arrangement in Black*?"

"All these works are impressions of my own; I make them my study. I suppose them to appeal to none but those who may understand the technical matter."

At a later point in the cross-examination, the judge asked Whistler what his *Nocturne in Blue and Silver: Old Battersea Bridge* (fig. 5) was supposed to represent.

"It represents Battersea Bridge by moonlight," came the obvious reply.

FIGURE 5. James Abbott McNeill Whistler, *Nocturne in Blue and Silver: Old Battersea Bridge*. The Tate Gallery, London.

"Is this part of the picture at the top Old Battersea Bridge?" persisted the judge.

"Your lordship is too close at present to the picture to perceive the effect which I intended to produce at a distance. The spectator is supposed to be looking down the river towards London."

"The prevailing color is blue?"

"Yes."

"Are those figures on the top of the bridge intended for people?"

"They are just what you like."

"That is a barge beneath?"

"Yes, I am very much flattered at your seeing that. The picture is simply a representation of moonlight. My whole scheme was only to bring about a certain harmony of color."

Still later the Attorney General asked about *The Falling Rocket: Nocturne in Black and Gold*.

"What is the subject of the *Nocturne in Black and Gold*?"

"It is a night piece," Whistler replied, "and represents the fireworks at Cremorne."

"Not a view of Cremorne?"

"If it were a view of Cremorne, it would certainly bring about nothing but disappointment on the part of the beholders. It is an artistic arrangement."

"How long did it take you to paint that?"

"One whole day and part of another."

"You have made the study of art your study of a lifetime. What is the peculiar beauty of that picture?"

Throughout the trial, the conflict between concrete and abstract raged, and it was embodied in this exchange between Whistler and the Attorney General. Each held firmly to his position as Whistler described the impossibility of answering the last question.

"It is as impossible for me to explain to you the beauty of that picture as it would be for a musician to explain to you the beauty of a harmony in a particular piece of music if you have no ear for music."

Of course the introduction of musical titles emphasized the abstract qualities of Whistler's painting, thereby further arousing the hostilities of tastes that were inclined toward narrative content.

"Do you think that anybody looking at the picture might fairly come to the conclusion that it had no particular beauty?" persisted the Attorney General.

"I have strong evidence that Mr. Ruskin did come to that conclusion," Whistler pointed out facetiously.

"Do you think it fair that Mr. Ruskin should come to that conclusion?"

"What might be fair to Mr. Ruskin I cannot answer. But I do not think that any artist would come to that conclusion. I have known unbiased people express the opinion that it represents fireworks in a night scene." Thus, in his reply, Whistler again raised the issue of artist versus critic.

The first witness called on Whistler's behalf was William Michael Rossetti, art critic and brother of the Pre-Raphaelite painter Dante Gabriel Rossetti. He testified reluctantly, since he was a friend of both Ruskin and Whistler. According to Rossetti, the *Nocturne in Blue and Silver* was "an artistic and beautiful representation of a pale but bright moonlight." He appreciated Whistler's use of musical titles but did not admire his pictures without exception. *The Falling Rocket* was not one he admired.

"Is it a gem?" the Attorney General asked Rossetti.

"No," replied the artist.

"Is it an exquisite painting?"

"No."

"Is it very beautiful?"

"No."

"Is it eccentric?"

"It is unlike the work of most other painters."

"Is it a work of art?"

"Yes, it is."

Having introduced the question of eccentricity, the Attorney General pursued the point in his examination of the next witness. Albert Moore was a rather minor member of the Pre-Raphaelite school and a painter who, like Whistler, had not been admitted to the Royal Academy.

"Is the picture with the fireworks an exquisite work of art?" queried the Attorney General.

"There is a decided beauty in the painting of it," replied Moore.

"Is there any eccentricity in this picture?"

"I should call it originality. What would *you* call eccentricity in a picture?" With this response, Albert Moore succeeded in deflecting some of the Attorney General's hostility toward Whistler. For, if anything, Whistler was widely regarded as eccentric in his dress as well as in his behavior. So why not imply, reasoned Ruskin's attorney, that Whistler's paintings were also eccentric, thereby suggesting a lack of artistic substance? By taking *eccentric* to mean original, rather than odd, Moore's answer enhanced Whistler's stature as an artist.

Whistler's last witness, William Gorman Wills, was a playwright and portrait painter. He described Whistler's pictures as "artistic masterpieces painted by a man of genius. . . . Mr. Whistler," he said, "looks at nature in a poetical light and has a native feeling for color."

These words of praise for Whistler were countered from the opposing side on the issue of "finish" versus "atmosphere." This is essentially the same as the conflict between line and color, narrative content and Impressionism. Edward Burne-Jones, a leading Pre-Raphaelite artist, testified that in his opinion, "complete finish ought to be the object of all artists. A picture ought not to fall short of what has been for ages considered complete finish."

Asked about Whistler's *Old Battersea Bridge*, Burne-Jones replied that it was better than *The Falling Rocket* in color but not in composition, detail, or form. "It is formless," he tried to explain. "It is bewildering in form."

"And as to composition and detail?"

"It has none whatever. A day and a half seems a reasonable time within which to paint it."

"Does this picture show any finish as a work of art?"

"No, I should call it a sketch. I do not think Mr. Whistler intended it to be regarded as a finished picture. It shows no finish—it is simply a sketch."

"Now, take the *Nocturne in Black and Gold*. Is that in your opinion a work of art?"

"No, I cannot say it is," Burne-Jones replied. "It is only one of a thousand failures that artists have made in their efforts to paint night."

Ruskin's counsel illustrated his meaning of "finish" by comparing Whistler's work with Titian's *Portrait of Doge Andrea Gritti*, a painting of the Italian Renaissance.

"It shows finish," Burne-Jones said of the Titian. "It is a very perfect sample of the highest finish of ancient art. The flesh is perfect, the modeling of the face is round and good. That is an 'arrangement in flesh and blood!' "

And of Whistler's style, Burne-Jones continued, "Mr. Whistler gave infinite promise at first, but I do not think he has fulfilled it. I think he has evaded the great difficulty of painting, and has not tested his powers by carrying it out. The difficulties in painting increase daily as the work progresses, and that is the reason why so many of us fail. We are none of us perfect. The danger is this, that if unfinished pictures become common, we shall arrive at a stage of mere manufacture and the art of the country will be degraded."

Finally, however, Burne-Jones would admit that in spite of Whistler's "lack of finish," he did have "an unrivaled sense of atmosphere."

Also regretting the absence of finish in Whistler's painting was Tom Taylor, editor of *Punch* and a noted art critic. In a review written for the *Times*, Taylor had already declared that the *Falling Rocket* was not a serious work of art. He read his own review in court, concluding that "all Mr. Whistler's work is unfinished. It is sketchy. He, no doubt, possesses artistic qualities, and he has good appreciation of qualities of tone, but he is not complete, and all his works are in the nature of sketching. I have expressed, and still adhere to the opinion, that these pictures only come 'one step nearer pictures than a delicately tinted wallpaper.' "

The comparison with wallpaper is one which becomes

more and more familiar in art criticism as paintings become progressively more abstract. Considering that a great deal of wallpaper design is representational, the comparison is perhaps more facetious than accurate.

Testifying before Taylor was the Royal Academician William Powell Frith, who agreed that the *Falling Rocket* was not serious. Of *Old Battersea Bridge*, he said, "There is a pretty color which pleases the eye, but there is nothing more. To my thinking, the description of moonlight is not true. The color does not represent any more than you would get from a bit of wallpaper or silk. . . . Composition and detail are most important matters in a picture. In our profession men of equal merit differ as to the character of a picture. One may blame, while another praises, a work."

Under cross-examination by Serjeant Parry, Frith agreed that Whistler had "very great power as an artist."

The impression that Whistler's paintings were quickly executed without sufficient organization, composition and detail led his detractors to raise the related issues of time and money.

"Did it take much time to paint the *Nocturne in Black and Gold*? How soon did you knock it off?" the Attorney General asked.

"I beg your pardon."

"I was using an expression which was rather more applicable to my own profession. How long did you take to knock off one of your pictures?"

"Oh, I knock off one possibly in a couple of days—one day to do the work and another to finish it."

"And that was the labor for which you asked two hundred guineas?"

"No," replied Whistler firmly, "it was for the knowledge gained through a lifetime."

The judge continued this line of questioning:

"How long did it take you to paint that picture?" he asked, referring to the *Nocturne in Blue and Silver*.

"I completed the work in one day, after having arranged the idea in my mind."

"After finishing these pictures, do you hang them up on

the garden wall to mellow?" the Attorney General interjected.

"I should grieve to see my paintings mellowed. But I do put them in the open air that they may dry as I go on with my work."

Ruskin's attack on Whistler had been considerably motivated by the asking price of 200 guineas for the *Falling Rocket*. In this, Ruskin's moral stance that an artist should not only struggle to make money, but also to give full value to the purchaser of his work was adopted by Whistler's opposition. In the light of Whistler's consistently poor financial condition compared with Ruskin's personal (and unearned) wealth, the emphasis on this point is more than a little hypocritical. In an attempt to demonstrate that Whistler had indeed suffered financial loss as a result of Ruskin's criticism, Petheram asked the artist whether he had sold a *Nocturne* since. "Not by any means at the same price as before," replied Whistler.

On cross-examination, the Attorney General pursued the financial point. "Is two hundred guineas a pretty good price for an artist of reputation?"

"Yes," agreed Whistler.

"It is what we who are not artists would call a stiffish price."

"I think it very likely it would be so."

"Artists do not endeavor to get the highest price for their work irrespective of value?"

"That is so, and I am glad to see the principle so well established." In this reply, Whistler asserted that artists, like most people, work for money.

The popular notion that artists produce works of art for love and are thus more reconciled to material hardship than members of other professions is an interesting one. It probably derives from a romantic tendency to endow art with religious significance. Part of this is historical, since most of the monumental art of Europe was inseparable from religion until the seventeenth century. Even from that time, however, the work of art occupied a special, somewhat mystical place in society. Art is characteristically elevated to a sphere above the ordinary so that, in some circles, it seems to be the last of the great religions. This is never more evident than in the social distinction between the rich man who collects nothing and the rich man who collects "art." Culture, with a capital C, is considered something of a moral virtue and has been for centuries.

Ironically enough, these attitudes are more apt to occur among the patrons of art than among the artists themselves. Certainly the vast majority of artists, writers, and all varieties of performers, work for money and fame. Whistler himself, especially in his later years, resented the success of his contemporaries. "Poverty," said Whistler, "may induce industry, but it does not produce the fine flower of painting. The test is not poverty, it's money. . . . If I had had, say, three thousand pounds a year, what beautiful things I could have done."[15]

For Ruskin, on the other hand, an artist was not entitled to a single farthing for which he had not struggled furiously. His attorney hammered away on this issue: "You offer that picture to the public as one of particular beauty, as a work of art, and which is fairly worth two hundred guineas?"

"I offer it as a work which I have conscientiously executed and which I think is worth the money," Whistler replied flatly. "I would hold my reputation upon this, as I would upon any of my other works."

Rossetti testified that in his view 200 guineas "is the full value of the picture," while Burne-Jones disagreed, "seeing how much careful work men do for much less." Again the amount, rather than the quality of the work, was emphasized.

Thus the celebrated libel trial between Whistler and Ruskin became a vehicle for the expression of opposing philosophies of art and art criticism. In the summation for Whistler, Serjeant Parry concluded:

> His [Ruskin's] decree has gone forth that Mr. Whistler's pictures were worthless. He has not supported

that by evidence. He has not condescended to give reasons for the view he has taken, he has treated us with contempt, as he treated Mr. Whistler. He has said: "I, Mr. Ruskin, seated on my throne of art, say what I please and expect all the world to agree with me." Mr. Ruskin is great as a writer, but not as a man; as a man he has degraded himself. His tone in writing the article is personal and malicious.

Mr. Ruskin's criticism of Mr. Whistler's pictures is almost exclusively in the nature of a personal attack, a pretended criticism of art which is really a criticism upon the man himself, and calculated to injure him. It was written recklessly, and for the purpose of holding him up to ridicule and contempt. Mr. Ruskin has gone out of his way to attack Mr. Whistler personally and must answer for the consequences of having written a damnatory attack upon the painter. That is what is called pungent criticism—but it is defamatory, and I hope that you, gentlemen of the jury, will mark your disapproval by your verdict.[16]

Ruskin's counsel closed by saying that the critic had given his opinion of Whistler's painting and that he held that opinion still.

The judge's final words to the jury left no doubt that Whistler had been libeled. The jury's task would be to assess the amount of damages, although here, too, the judge made his own feelings eminently clear:

There are certain words by Mr. Ruskin, about which I should think no one would entertain a doubt: those words amount to a libel. It is of the last importance that a critic should have full latitude to express the judgments he has honestly formed, and for that purpose there is no reason why he should not use ridicule as a weapon; but a critic should confine himself to criticism, and not make it the veil for personal censure, nor allow himself to run into reckless and unfair attacks merely for the love of exercising his power of denunciation. The question for the jury is, did Mr. Whistler's ideas of art justify the language used by Mr. Ruskin? And the further question is whether the insult offered—if insult there has been—is of such a gross character as to call for substantial damages. Whether it is a case for merely contemptuous damages to the extent of a farthing, or something of that sort, indicating that it is one which ought never to have been brought into court, and in which no pecuniary damage has been sustained; or whether the case is one which calls for damages in some small sum as indicating the opinion of the jury that the offender has gone beyond the strict letter of the law.[17]

The jury found for Whistler. Damages to be awarded: one farthing. The judge, in turn, refused to assess costs. This decision presented little financial problem for Ruskin, but for Whistler it proved to be a considerable hardship; he would soon find himself bankrupt. Ruskin reacted to his moral defeat by resigning his Slade Professorship at Oxford, as Whistler had said he should. "Let him resign his present professorship," declared the artist, "to fill the chair of Ethics at the University. As master of English literature, he has a right to his laurels, while, as the populariser of pictures he remains the Peter Parley of painting."[18]

George Bernard Shaw, in his usual down-to-earth way, offered a sobering comment on the case. Whistler, he said, should have based his case on commercial damage rather than artistic conscience. "In talking about his artistic conscience," Shaw declared, "he could only raise a farthing—that being all conscience is worth in the eyes of the law!"

For Whistler, however, the trial remained a matter of principle, reflecting the characteristic conflict between artist and critic. As he wrote later: "Over and over again did the Attorney General cry out aloud, in the agony of his cause, 'what is to become of painting if the critics withhold their lash?'

"As well might he ask what is to become of mathematics under similar circumstances, were they possible. I maintain that two and two the mathematician would continue to make four, in spite of the whine of the amateur for three, or the cry of the critic for five."[19]

Editorial pages devoted a great deal of space to the trial (fig. 6). On Sunday, December 15, 1878, two lengthy articles appeared in *The New York Times*. One, entitled, "Flinging Paint in the Public's Face,"[20] provided a heated commentary on Whistler, Ruskin, and the general state of "modern art." On the one hand, began the article, Ruskin's anger was unseemly and inexplicable. Had it been directed at the public's complacency, one could understand it, even excuse a sensitive man "suffering from the provocation of seeing these things paraded and admired, and extreme violence of language" if directed at the pictures or the deluded public. "The world," asserted the writer, "has been much afflicted of late with these slapdash productions of the paint-pot." Nocturnes, Symphonies, Arrangements, and Harmonies, the article continued, are but "exasperating nomenclature which does not belong to the realm of pictorial art." Such titles, the author complained, leave a gap which the observer's imagination has to fill, an unfortunate state of affairs encouraged by Mr. Ruskin himself. Comparing the artists' traditional formal clarity with modern forms, which are but "shadowy and unseen presences," the author declared that the main function of the artist "is shifted to the spectator." And while this might appeal to some observers who felt they had thus contributed to the work, it did not please the author. In his opinion, the artist was supposed to be the interpreter, not the observer. It was the artist's obligation to paint reality as clearly as it was seen: "The vivid imagination of the child or the distempered mind of the invalid may trace strange shapes and scenes in the common place figures of a wallpaper, and see gruesome monsters or forms of fantastic beauty in the pattern of a cambric curtain, but ordinary men and women in a state of health prefer to have their pictures made for them."[21]

True to the Victorian era, the article concluded on a decidedly moralistic note. Taking the example of an East River ferryboat in a fog, the author prescribed that it be clearly painted, not "like a whitewashed wall, with streaks of charcoal suggesting smokestacks and fog whistles, even though it

NAUGHTY CRITIC, TO USE BAD LANGUAGE! SILLY PAINTER, TO GO TO LAW ABOUT IT!

were called a sonata in gray. The public has had a deal of paint flung recklessly in its face, and it was time somebody protested in the name of cleanliness and propriety."[22]

The second article[23] implied that Whistler was most likely angry about being called a coxcomb rather than worried about financial losses resulting from Ruskin's comments. This author also assumed a pious stance. He regretted Whistler's "recent eccentricities" and stressed that he was basically a good artist, especially as an etcher and colorist. The author counseled that Whistler should settle down and paint properly from now on.

The *Morning Adviser* wrote that the verdict would teach the critic moderation and the artist fidelity to his own genius. And to this the *Times* wittily replied, "Has he [Whistler] not a brush to Ruskin's pen? A caricature of Ruskin as an 'arrangement in black and white' would be an immense hit."

A black and white arrangement did, in fact, materialize, but not as a caricature of Ruskin. In May 1879, six months after the trial, Whistler filed a bankruptcy petition which Rossetti laconically labeled "Arrangement in Black and White." The farthing damages awarded Whistler clearly did little to sustain his already deteriorating financial position. Shaw's observation that Whistler would have been better advised to stress money than aesthetics was not far from the truth. Very little was said of the financial hardship Whistler suffered as a result of Ruskin's comments, and even less effort was made to combat Ruskin's basic hypocrisy that artists do not have a right to ask payment for their work.

It would seem, as one of the news reports suggested, that Whistler allowed his case to become sidetracked by the tenor of Ruskin's statement. Aside from protesting the 200 guineas Whistler asked for his painting displayed at the Grosvenor Gallery, Ruskin aimed the majority of his attack at the artist himself. Ruskin focused on a particularly sensitive aspect of Whistler's personality; his flamboyant social narcissism. Ruskin called Whistler ill-educated, conceited, impudent, a Cockney and a coxcomb; he accused him of willful imposture. Whistler himself was adept at scathing verbal attacks on the various people who crossed him; he published a great deal of witty sarcasm criticizing his contemporaries, and on social occasions, he could be counted on for the most devastating comments. Why, then, one might wonder, should he become so exercised by Ruskin's remarks, published in an obscure pamphlet?

The explanation is probably twofold. On the one hand, Ruskin attacked Whistler's social pretensions and, on the other, his paintings. While Whistler was able to separate his outward performing self—his antic disposition—from his more productive and serious creative self, Ruskin combined the artist's two aspects in a single sentence. The coxcomb, he said, had flung paint in the public's face. He accused Whistler the impostor, the impudent and the conceited poseur, of having motivated Whistler the painter. It was this that Whistler would not accept.

Like a Bible-thumping preacher, Ruskin used his position as a critic to denounce the artist, thereby compounding the insult. Obviously Whistler's life-style was a source of great antagonism to the Calvinist piety of the dour Ruskin. This basic opposition between the two men reflected the very conflict inherent in Whistler's own personality: witness his Calvinist mother and his more flamboyant father, his "eccentric" social behavior and his industrious, somber artistic nature. Ruskin's statement must have touched an extremely sensitive nerve in the artist to make him risk litigation against Britain's leading spokesman for the arts. The trial itself touched on these matters only indirectly. The questions and answers revolved around the general opposition of artist and critic and the most absurd issue of all: What is art?

After the trial, insane though he was, Ruskin was still a rich man. Whistler was not. In addition to an extensive backlog of creditors, Whistler owed substantial legal fees. His creditors descended, no longer even willing to accept paintings as collateral, and in May 1879 Whistler was officially bankrupt. The following autumn his house was sold and, in February 1880 Sotheby auctioned off the contents of the house. Everything fetched exceptionally low prices.

In an effort to improve his disastrous financial situation, Whistler accepted a commission for a series of etchings to be produced in Venice and, after a brief period of effort, he returned to his bohemian ways and began borrowing again. It is no doubt of considerable psychological significance that Whistler became artistically blocked around this time. Until his death in 1903, with a few exceptions, he produced only etchings and very tiny oils. He avoided major oil paintings, destroying or leaving unfinished most of those he did begin.

Despite the block of his creative energies, Whistler's artistic reputation took a turn for the better in the last decade of his life. The paintings which had apparently been overshadowed by his social posturings suddenly emerged to claim their birthright. In 1892 New York collector Samuel Untermeyer bought the *Falling Rocket* for 800 guineas and two years later, Charles Freer of Detroit bought 13,000 guineas' worth of pictures from Whistler.

In March 1947, *Art Digest* reported that the "Pot of Paint" had been sold to the Detroit Institute of Arts for approximately $12,000.

CHAPTER TWO

WHAT'S IN / A NAME?/Brancusi v. United States

"What do you call this?"

"I use the same term the sculptor did, *oiseau*, a bird."

"What makes you call it a bird; does it look like a bird to you?"

"It does not look like a bird, but I feel that it is a bird; it is characterized by the artist as a bird."

"Simply because he called it a bird, does that make it a bird to you?"

"Yes, your Honor."

"If you would see it on the street, you never would think of calling it a bird, would you? If you saw it in the forest, you would not take a shot at it?"

"No, your Honor."

"If you saw it anywhere, had never heard anyone call it a bird, you would not call it a bird?"

"No, sir."

Associate Justices Waite and Young are questioning the prominent American photographer Edward Steichen. Justice Waite is presiding at the trial *Constantin Brancusi* v. *United States*, No. 209109, held in U.S. Customs Court, Third Division. The date is October 21, 1927. At issue is whether Brancusi's bronze sculpture, *Bird in Space* (fig. 7), is an original work of art by a professional sculptor and therefore entitled to duty-free entry into the United States.

FIGURE 7. Constantin Brancusi,
Bird in Space. Bronze. Courtesy
Sidney Geist.

Steichen had purchased the sculpture directly from Constantin Brancusi, the Romanian artist living and working in Paris. In 1926 Steichen brought the work from France to New York. It was invoiced as a bronze bird and, as a work of art, assumed by the importer to be free of duty. Duty-free importation of works of art is covered by paragraph 1704 of the 1922 Tariff Act, which reads as follows:

> Original paintings in oil, mineral, water, or other colors, pastels, original drawings and sketches in pen, ink, pencil, or watercolors, artists' proof etchings unbound, and engravings and woodcuts unbound, original sculptures or statuary, including not more than two replicas or reproductions of the same; but the terms "sculpture" and "statuary" as used in this paragraph shall be understood to include professional productions of sculptors only, whether in round or in relief, in bronze, marble, stone, terra cotta, ivory, wood, or metal, or whether cut, carved, or otherwise wrought by hand from the solid block or mass of marble, stone, or alabaster, or from metal, or cast in bronze or other metal, or substance, or from wax or plaster, made as professional productions of sculpture only and the words "painting" and "sculpture" and "statuary" as used in this paragraph shall not be understood to include any articles of utility, nor such as are made wholly or in part by stenciling or any other mechanical process; and the words "etchings," "engravings," and "woodcuts" as used in this paragraph shall be understood to include only such as are printed by hand from plates or blocks etched or engraved with hand tools and not such as are printed from plates or blocks etched or engraved by photochemical or other mechanical processes.

Unfortunately for Steichen, the customs officials who dealt with the matter did not agree that *Bird in Space* was covered by that particular paragraph. They preferred to consider the object as manufactured metal and therefore taxable at 40 percent of its value under paragraph 339 of the Tariff Act. As they saw it, the bird was a lump of bronze that fell into the category of:

Articles or wares not specially provided for, if composed wholly or in chief value of platinum, gold, or silver, and articles or wares plated with platinum, gold or silver, or colored with gold lacquer, whether partly or wholly manufactured, 60 per centum ad valorem; if composed wholly or in chief value of iron, steel, lead, copper, brass, nickel, pewter, zinc, aluminum, or other metal, but not plated with platinum, gold, or silver, or colored with gold lacquer, whether partly or wholly manufactured, 40 per centum ad valorem.

The U.S. Customs appraiser announced his decision on the matter in February 1927. He had made a thorough investigation, he reported, and several highly placed figures in the art world had assisted him. Although the appraiser declined to identify his advisers, he quoted one as having said, "If that is art, then I'm a bricklayer," and another, "Dots and dashes are quite as artistic as Brancusi's work." The investigators concluded that Brancusi's sculptures left too much to the imagination, the very same criticism voiced about Whistler's *Nocturnes* fifty years earlier.

A *New York Times* reporter called Brancusi's birds "strange, egg-shaped sculptures without wings." Nor was this the first time Brancusi's works had clashed with traditional American taste. Brancusi had attracted hostility as early as 1913—the year of the Armory Show, the most significant exhibition of the century. He sent a marble statue of a woman—titled *Mlle. Pogany*—to the show. One critic called her "a hard-boiled egg balanced on a cube of sugar" and another published a satirical poem, "Lines to a Lady Egg," in the *Evening Sun*.[1]

By 1927 Brancusi's popularity in official circles had not increased. Not even the protests of artist Marcel Duchamp, art critic Henry McBride, and art editor Forbes Watson impressed the government officials. Those three prominent men made an appointment with a customs representative and tried in vain to persuade him that Brancusi was a serious sculptor and that his intentions, if not his results, were aesthetic rather than utilitarian. The customs man was unmoved. He countered that one Daniel Chester French, an "official" government sculptor favored by Washington's Fine Arts Commission, would not consider Brancusi an artist. And if Daniel Chester French said Brancusi was not an artist, then U.S. Customs said Brancusi was not an artist.

The *Bird in Space* "was finally admitted," Steichen later wrote, "under the classification of Kitchen Utensils and Hospital Supplies, and I was made to pay some six hundred dollars duty on it."[2] When Mrs. Harry Payne Whitney, an active patroness of modern art and a $1,000 contributor to the Armory Show, heard of this, she offered to have her own lawyers take over the case. Steichen agreed and appealed the decision. It was incumbent upon his attorneys, Charles J. Lane and M. J. Speiser, and Thomas Lane of counsel, the attorney who argued the case in court, to establish four points: first, that the article was "original sculpture or statuary"; second, that it was the "professional production of a sculptor"; third, that it was made as the "professional production of a sculptor" and, finally, that it was "not an article of utility."

In order to establish these contentions, the defense called six witnesses who were prominent in the contemporary art world. Edward Steichen, the importer and therefore the plaintiff in the case, was a painter and photographer of considerable distinction. He had been associated with Alfred Stieglitz in the early years of the twentieth century. Both men were dedicated to introducing modern European art into America through the famous New York Photo-Secessionist Gallery at 291 Fifth Avenue. Today Steichen is known primarily for his perceptive photographic portraiture. In the course of his distinguished career, Steichen photographed the leading celebrities of his day, and many of his pictures have become classics of their kind.

Also called were Jacob Epstein, the English sculptor later knighted for his contribution to the development of British art, and William Henry Fox, the director of the Brooklyn Museum. Two editors of respected art publications also testified for the plaintiff—Forbes Watson of *Arts Maga-*

zine and Frank Crowninshield of *Vanity Fair*. Henry Mc-Bride, art critic for the *Sun* and the *Dial*, also testified. Watson and McBride had already made their positions known when they met with the customs official several months earlier. Brancusi was abroad at the time of the trial, and the judge agreed to receive his testimony in writing from Paris.

The defense for the United States was led by Assistant Attorney General Charles D. Lawrence, with special attorneys Marcus Higginbotham and Reuben Wilson, although Higginbotham did most of the actual questioning and cross-examination for his side. They mustered two witnesses—virtually unknown today—who denied all claims of artistic merit to Brancusi's sculpture. Robert Ingersoll Aitken, a New York sculptor who had studied in San Francisco, Rome, and Paris, and whose works were on exhibit throughout the United States, staunchly maintained that Brancusi was no artist and therefore that his productions were not works of art. Thomas Jones, also a New York sculptor, was on the art faculty of Columbia University. Though admitting that Brancusi was "a wonderful polisher of bronze," Jones agreed with Aitken that the bird was not art.

Clearly, then, the primary issue to resolve was whether Brancusi's sculpture was art. To settle such a question about a contemporary work was no easy matter under any circumstances, but to do so in a court of law was even more difficult because the precise terminology characteristic of the law is poles away from the usually vague language of the art critic. Nevertheless the attempt was a fascinating one, and the Brancusi trial revealed aspects of various universal conflicts about the nature of art. It also provided a mirror of the New York and European art worlds in the 1920s, when abstract artists were struggling for general acceptance. That the trial involved the importation of an abstract object into the United States whose officials rejected its aesthetic claims reflected the larger historical situation. Ever since the 1913 Armory Show, the new forms that had been developing in Europe had been gradually making inroads into the American artistic consciousness. Now the American artists were not only influenced by European abstraction, they were inventing new styles of their own. Thus one of the major facets in the trial —as in the art world and even in society at large—was the acceptance or rejection of "modern art."

The trial opened with a certain furor absurd enough to warm the heart of the best-coiffed bald soprano. At issue was the identification of the smooth, elegant object (filed and polished until it assumed something of a banana shape) and its title: *Oiseau*, French for "bird." Offered as the primary exhibit, the bronze bird perched in the courtroom under the scrutiny of justices, lawyers, and witnesses. Would it pass the legal test and become officially a "work of art"? Would the court overrule Customs, which had judged it an "article or ware . . . partly or wholly manufactured" and decide that it contained qualities of aesthetic value?

Having established that *oiseau* was indeed French for "bird" and that that was the name the artist had given his creation, the court proceeded to question the witnesses in turn. The lawyers followed a similar pattern, each beginning with a résumé of the background, professional standing, and artistic qualifications of the witness as he took the stand.

Steichen, the first witness, was a personal friend of Brancusi's and had actually seen him at work on the bird. Once the object's paternity had been established, Steichen described the creative process that produced it. He explained that Brancusi had arrived at the object by steps. First he made a marble figure; then a plaster cast, which he sent to his foundry. The foundry cast the object into bronze and the artist worked on it until it assumed its present shape.

"That is the process it went through," Steichen testified. "I saw that particular bronze there in the process when it was only one-half filed down to its present shape."

"It is not a copy of anything else?" inquired Justice Waite.

"No."

Justice Young asked, "First filed and then polished?"

"Yes. There is no other one in existence in bronze of that shape and size."

This exchange was followed by a discussion of Brancusi's standing as an artist among his peers. As if the bird had to satisfy certain social criteria, the court proceeded to try to establish that its creator was generally considered an artist of high reputation.

"Will you be kind enough to tell the Court the reputation of Constantin Brancusi as an artist?" asked C.J. Lane, attorney for the plaintiff.

"Constantin Brancusi has been in Paris for the last twenty-five years, and he has been exhibiting in all art exhibitions in Europe as well as in America."

"You have seen the exhibitions?" interjected Justice Waite.

"I have seen the exhibitions, yes, in Paris. I have seen them in London and the exhibitions here in New York as well. He is looked upon as one of the most famous of the ultimate school of art."

"Is he represented in any capacity as an artist in America at present?" Lane continued.

"I believe he has one of his bronzes in the Buffalo Museum of Art, and one in Chicago."

Higginbotham objected to the "I believe," and Lane adjusted the question. "Do you know that as a matter of knowledge?"

"I know that; it is a matter of record. He has one also in the Chicago Art Museum."

"Will you name some of the collectors that to your knowledge have copies of his work?"

"Eugene Meyer, Jr., and—I forget the names; there are several others, but I am sorry I don't recall any more that I know of."

"Of your own knowledge, is he represented in galleries in Europe or private collections in Europe?"

"He is represented in the National Gallery of Romania, and in one of the Scandinavian galleries; I don't know whether Norway or Sweden."

"He has been a recognized sculptor, has he not?"

"He has."

Thomas Lane (of counsel) then raised the question of utility, and Steichen replied that he could conceive of no utilitarian purpose that the bird might serve. "Laying aside the title," Lane continued after Steichen's professional credentials had been established, "tell us whether this is a work of art. Has it any underlying aesthetic principle, no matter what its title is?"

"Yes."

"Will you explain, please?"

"From a technical standpoint, in the first place, it has form and appearance; it is an object created by an artist in three dimensions; it has harmonious proportions, which give me an aesthetic sense, a sense of great beauty. That object has that quality in it. That is the reason I purchased it. Mr. Brancusi, as I see it, has tried to express something fine. That bird gives me the sensation of a rushing bird. When originally started, it was not like it is today. For twenty years he has worked on that thing, changing, dividing it until it has reached this stage, where the lines and form express a bird, the lines suggesting it flying up in the sky."

"As I understand it, one would not require great imagination to conceive that this was actually a bird in flight, rising from the ground or in the air?"

"Well, I don't say that it is a bird in flight; it suggests a bird in space."

"I cannot see any necessity in spending time to prove that this is a bird," interjected Justice Waite. "If it is a work of art, a sculpture, it comes under that paragraph. There is no law that I know of that states that an article should represent the human form or any particular animal form or an inanimate object, but is it as a matter of fact within the meaning of the law a work of art, sculpture?"

Justice Waite's comments refer to what antagonizes many people even today: the nonobjective work of art that represents no recognizable form. One's attachment to objects from the environment is seldom more evident than in the frequent hostile reactions to non-objective art. The widespread suspicion that such art is some kind of put-on, that the artist is laughing at the public through his painting or sculpture, is common enough. And, of course, this is a conflict largely restricted to the late nineteenth and twentieth centuries, when cubism broke down traditional ideas about form and space. But, if the artist is serious—hence the court's determination to establish Brancusi's reputation—this is clearly not the case. On the contrary, as the overview of many artists' styles readily indicates, one arrives at abstraction through a long process of change and development. Like the public, the artist is attached to the familiar outlines of his environment and has to work long and hard to free himself from their boundaries. Thus Brancusi spent twenty years on the process of transforming the bird from a figure with recognizable anatomy—head, body, and feet—to a representation of the more abstract *idea* of a bird in space.

Steichen's memoirs describe parts of this process. He first saw the early version—*L'Oiseau d'Or*—in 1909 or 1910 at the Salon des Indépendants in Paris.[3] He bought it for $200, and Brancusi subsequently installed it in the photographer's garden in the South of France. Steichen related that his six-year-old daughter told the artist that the bird's head lay on a horizontal plane and was therefore wrong for singing. (That observation, typical of the concrete thought processes of children, argues against the familiar comment voiced by critics of abstract art that their "six-year-old child could do it.") Brancusi replied that the bird wasn't singing. "It was a mythological bird that, according to legend, guided a Romanian prince through life, and it was talking."[4] By the final version of 1935, Steichen wrote, the artist had "gradually lifted and straightened" the head so that "not only was the movement sharply upward, but the abstract suggestion of an open mouth was also made by an abrupt bias-cut angle at the top."[5]

In his recent study of Brancusi's sculpture, Sidney Geist discusses this development: "Starting with *Pasarea Maiastra* (the Romanian name for the statue), a bird that stands and speaks, Brancusi makes a sequence of *Birds* that are even taller and more slender in proportions; as a result of these changes the *Bird* stretches upward and its open beak now calls to the heavens."[6] And later: "These measurements, relations, and changes in design, their variety and combination, and the number itself of the works chart an intensity of research unparalleled in Brancusi's long effort."[7] Finally, Geist notes the importance of the moment of transition from *Bird* to *Bird in Space*—which corresponds not to natural flight but to the fantasy of "dream flight, in which no effort seems necessary but the slight propulsion afforded by the feet on leaving the earth. . . . The power is that of man's aspirational, ascensional nature which achieves imaginative and nocturnal fulfillment, at once voluptuous and beneficent, in the widely known dream of flight."[8]

The more pedestrian exchange of the cross-examination summed up the same principle. Higginbotham, continually trying to discredit the opposition, addressed Steichen. "You say that for twenty years M. Brancusi has been working on this particular article?"

"Not on that object itself, on various phases of it," Steichen replied undauntedly.

And Justice Waite, who proved to be a breath of fresh air throughout the proceedings, interjected, "He worked on the idea."

The trial followed a similar pattern as each of the witnesses testified. An analysis of the trial's structure reveals that the lawyers concentrated on four or five main points which ultimately influenced the judge's decision. First, the reputations of the witnesses and then that of the artist were examined. The witnesses for Brancusi covered a wider range of art world activity—artists, editors, critics, museum director—than those against, both of whom were conservative sculptors. In retrospect, the former group were far more distinguished than the latter, although that may not have been so evident to the general public in 1927.

All six Brancusi witnesses testified to his prominence

and recognition as a sculptor both in Europe and the United States. Brancusi offered his own credentials in a deposition sent from Paris. He supplied the court with details of his training and exhibitions. This version of the bird, he said, was entirely his idea and production. It was conceived in 1910, and he was only now embarking on the first replica. He began by making a plaster model, which he sent to the foundry together with a formula for the bronze alloy. He pointed out that the foundry molders specialized in doing this type of work for artists. Once Brancusi received the rough cast, he stopped up the air and core holes and polished and filed the bird. He did so entirely alone, without assistants or machinery. Thus, Brancusi asserted that he, a professional sculptor, was the sole conceiver and maker of the object then on trial.

The witnesses for the United States differed on the issue of Brancusi's merit and reputation. Robert Ingersoll Aitken, the New York sculptor, was the most recalcitrant of the witnesses. He did not consider that the witnesses for Brancusi qualified as able art critics. "Have you ever heard of Mr. Brancusi?" Lane asked Aitken.

"Yes," replied the sculptor.

"How long is it since you have heard of him in connection with art?"

"I haven't heard—I haven't read of him for a number of years."

"Where have you read of him?"

"In art publications."

"In books?"

"Art publications."

"Tell us just how many years have you heard of Mr. Brancusi as an artist?"

"Perhaps five years only."

"But you know as a matter of fact, Mr. Aitken, that Mr. Brancusi has done works of art for over twenty-five years, do you not?"

"I do not know that."

And later; "How many works of art made by Mr. Brancusi have you seen?"

"I haven't seen any."

"You have never seen any works by Brancusi?"

"You said 'works of art.' I have not."

"Have you seen any of his works?"

"I have seen works like that," he said, indicating the *Bird in Space*, "but I haven't seen any works of art."

"In other words, you do not regard them as works of art?"

"I do not."

And Thomas Jones, the Columbia University instructor, admitted that one of the books used at the college described Brancusi as "an associate of the cubists and the first sculptor to polish bronze." However, he continued, those paragraphs that so referred to Brancusi, were omitted from the required reading.

The next question—at once the most difficult to resolve and the most important—concerned the nature of art and whether the bird satisfied the necessary criteria to be so considered. As a prelude to this issue, the title again became a matter of discussion.

Higginbotham apparently felt inclined to demonstrate that the title of the sculpture was somehow invalid, thus invalidating the object as a work of art. He asked Steichen, "Now, the Court asked you if you would call this a bird. If Brancusi had called it a tiger, would you call it a tiger, too?"

Lane objected to the question and was sustained by Justice Waite, who observed, "I don't think it makes any difference whether it is called a bird or an elephant. The question is whether it is artistic in fact, in form, or in shape and lines."

Higginbotham took exception and continued. "If he called it an animal in suspense, would you call it an animal in suspense?"

"No."

"You mean you call this a bird because that was the title given by the artist?" Justice Waite interjected.

"Yes, sir."

"If he had given it another title, you would call it by the title he gave?"

"Certainly."

Again Higginbotham persisted. "So, insofar as your artistic training is concerned and your experience, Exhibit One is not a bird in fact."

"No, it is not a bird."

Jacob Epstein replied to a similar set of questions that it was "a matter of indifference what it represents."

In cross-examination, Speiser returned to the problem of the title, asking Epstein to elaborate on the relationship of the title to the content of the sculpture. Epstein did so. "I would, of course, start off with the artist's title, and if the artist called it a bird, I would take it seriously if I have any respect for the artist whatever. It would be my first endeavor to see whether it was like a bird. In this particular piece of sculpture, there are the elements of a bird—certain elements."

Higginbotham took up where Speiser left off. "What elements?"

"If you regard the piece of sculpture in profile, you see there," the English sculptor pointed to the bird's slow, bulging curve, "it is like the breast of a bird, especially on this side."

"All breasts of birds are more or less rounded?"

"Yes."

"Any rounded piece of bronze, then, would represent a bird?"

"That I cannot say."

"Looks more like the keel of a boat, too?" asked Justice Waite.

"If it were lying down," Epstein agreed.

"And a little like the crescent of a new moon?"

"Yes," replied Epstein, satisfied with the associations that the bird aroused in Justice Waite.

"If Mr. Brancusi called this a fish," continued Higginbotham with considerably less subtlety than Justice Waite, "it would be then to you a fish?"

"If he called it a fish, I would call it a fish."

"If he called it a tiger, it would change your mind to a tiger?"

"No."

Asked about Brancusi's place in the world of art, Epstein offered a historical comparison. "He is related to a very ancient form of sculpture, I should say even to the Egyptian. He does not stand absolutely alone. He is related to the fine ancient sculpture, like the early Egyptian, three thousand years old. If you would like to bring into court a piece of sculpture—ancient sculpture—which I have, I can illustrate for you." Epstein left the stand and returned with the sample.

"What is that piece you have there?"

"That is a hawk . . . an ancient Egyptian hawk, three thousand years old."

"You can see some similarity in form, with what you understand to be a hawk?" asked Justice Waite, still absorbed by the bird's relationship to nature.

"An ornithologist might not find it," admitted Epstein. "I see the resemblance to a bird. The feathers are not shown. The feet are not shown."

"The wings and the feet are not shown," Waite agreed. "Still you get the impression it is a hawk."

"Yes."

Frank Crowninshield of *Vanity Fair* described the similarities between the sculpture and a bird, though he pointed out the relative unimportance of the title. "It has," he said, "the suggestion of flight, it suggests grace, aspiration, vigor, coupled with speed, in the spirit of strength, potency, beauty, just as a bird does. But just the name, the title, of this work, why, really, it does not mean much. . . . In a way the title has very little to do with the work of the sculptor. It does not affect at all the aesthetic quality of the work as a work of art if it has proportion, balance, workmanship, and design."

William H. Fox, director of the Brooklyn Museum, testified that the sculpture did not suggest a fish to him.

"If he called it a tiger in flight?" persisted Higginbotham.

"No."

"Does it suggest a lion or other animal?"

"It is possible that the quality of flight might appeal to

me as an abstract quality, just simply as part of the qualities, but not really that of a realistic tiger or lion."

In short, then, as Justice Waite finally said, "We are laying great stress on calling it a bird. I cannot see any point in the question whether it is called a bird."

In the course of the trial, lawyers, witnesses—even the judges—eventually considered the crucial question: what is a work of art? Each witness had something to say on the matter, which he applied to the bird so that it was either admitted into, or rejected from, the category of art. Below are the opinions of the witnesses for Brancusi, as summarized in the plaintiff's brief of argument:

> *Edward Steichen:* It is a work of art because it has form and balance; form is something that is achieved in the mind of the sculptor, and balance is in length, breadth, and thickness. Balance is the relationship of these forms to each other. The whole of it has harmonious lines; the base is very good in proportion to the top. It has proportion, that is, harmony.
>
> *Jacob Epstein:* It is a work of art because it pleases my sense of beauty; gives me a feeling of pleasure; made by a sculptor; it has to me a great many elements, but consists in itself of a beautiful object.
>
> *Forbes Watson:* It is a work of art because of the form, the balance, the beautiful sense of workmanship, and the pleasure it gives me to look at it.
>
> *Frank Crowninshield:* It appeals to me [as a work of art] because of its proportions, its form, its balance, the design and workmanship.
>
> *William Henry Fox:* . . . . It has expression, form, registering an idea, probably suggested by a flight of a bird, but merely suggesting the flight of a bird.
>
> *Henry McBride:* [Considers it a work of art because of what all the previous witnesses have said and that] it excites in me a sense of beauty and appeals to my imagination.

These statements, though made in all sincerity, reveal the difficulty in applying satisfactory verbal descriptions to objects. At the same time, however, the trial testimony demonstrated that certain practical consequences may indeed result from the seemingly vague language of aesthetics and these, together with certain other considerations, were elicited by the persistence of Higginbotham. Edward Steichen's convictions inspired him to purchase the bird in the first place and eventually go to court to prove them. Mrs. Harry Payne Whitney's convictions prompted her to finance Steichen's case. Higginbotham tried to invalidate the purchase by interjecting a personal element. "Did you buy this?" he asked Steichen.

"I bought that, yes," Steichen replied.

"For what purpose?"

"Because I considered it a work of art, liked to put it in my home."

"If somebody came to buy, would you sell it?"

"No."

"Do you sell other works of art?"

"My own works, yes."

"But you bought this for your own private collection because of the fact that you were a close personal friend of Mr. Brancusi and liked his work?"

"Not because I was a close personal friend, but because I liked the thing."

"But he is a personal friend?"

"No personal element in it whatsoever."

"That did not enter into it at all?"

"Not at all."

With Epstein, the unsinkable Higginbotham raised the question of the mechanic versus the artist, reduced in this trial to a bird and a brass rail. "So if we had a brass rail," Higginbotham asked, "highly polished, curved in a more or less symmetrical and harmonious circle, it would be a work of art?"

"It *might* be a work of art," allowed Epstein.

"Whether it is made by a sculptor or made by a mechanic?"

"A mechanic cannot make beautiful work," the sculptor asserted.

"Do you mean to tell us that that Exhibit One if formed up, that a mechanic, that is a first-class mechanic, with a file and polishing tools could not polish that article up?"

"He can polish it up, but he cannot conveive of the object. That is the whole point. He cannot conceive those particular lines, which give it its individual beauty. That is the difference between a mechanic and an artist—he cannot conceive as an artist."

And Justice Waite, with his refreshing good sense and basic understanding of the issues added, "If he can conceive, then he would cease to be a mechanic and become an artist?"

"Would become an artist; that is right."

Justice Waite closely questioned William H. Fox about his own role as director of the Brooklyn Museum in connection with the bird. Under Lane's earlier examination, Fox had indicated his wish to buy the bird or some similar work by Brancusi for the museum. He would have done so, he stated, but for lack of funds. "You are a curator of something, you say?" Justice Waite asked.

"I am director at the museum."

"The object of the museum is to furnish the public an opportunity to see works of art?"

"Yes."

"To educate people along that line?"

"Yes, sir."

"That is to say, you seek to put into your place works of art, beautiful and artistic things?"

"Yes, sir."

"If you were sent out by somebody to buy a work of art to put in the institution and educate the people, would you have selected this as a work of art?"

"Yes, sir. I would select that as the work of an artist I esteem as an artist."

"You would have selected it more as a curiosity?"

"No, sir, I would not. I would select it because of its appeal to me as an object of art, as a beautiful piece, because of its beauty, its symmetry, its quality that gives me pleasurable emotion."

"Do you think the rank and file of people who visit your museum would be educated by that form?"

"I hope they will be, sir. I think they will appreciate its beauty."

"Do you think there would be more than one in ten thousand that would think it was a bird?"

"I think more than one in ten thousand would say it was a beautiful object."

The two witnesses against Brancusi also used the art critic's characteristically vague language when attempting to define art. In their case, however, the words were intended to exclude the *Bird in Space* from that category. "How do you define art?" Thomas Lane asked Robert Aitken under cross-examination.

"I don't define art," he replied.

"You mean art cannot be defined?"

"I would not say it cannot be defined, but—"

"Have you ever thought of a definition of art that you can give?"

"Yes, I have."

"What would be your definition of art?"

"Broadly speaking, it would be something created by man, which would arouse an unusual emotional reaction."

"And if it did not create an unusual emotional reaction, you would say it is not art?"

"Well, that emotional reaction should be along the lines of aesthetics only."

"But if it did not arouse an unusual emotion, would you say it is not art?"

"Unusual emotion? I will qualify that. I should say stirred the aesthetics, the sense of beauty." And clearly, in Aitken's sense of aesthetic beauty, there was no room for Brancusi's sculpture.

Lane then tried to reduce the impact of Aitken's views

on the court by implying that the New York sculptor disliked all modern art. By this he meant works of art whose relationship to nature is not easily recognizable. But it was not until he questioned the other New York sculptor, Thomas Jones, that Lane was given a direct answer to this point. Brancusi's bird, Jones testified, is "too abstract and a misuse of the form of sculpture." It did not arouse his sense of beauty.

Later, Higginbotham returned to the issue of mechanical skill versus artistic creation. Jones had been commissioned to construct a number of civic works; he testified to having representations of *Agriculture* on the Memorial Bridge in Washington, *Dr. Moon* in a Rochester park, and a mausoleum in Rye, New York. Aesthetically such works are a far cry from the kind of forms that interested Brancusi. "In other words," Higginbotham summed up Jones's judgment of the Romanian sculptor, "he is a wonderful polisher of bronze. Any polisher can do that."

The brief for the United States cited two precedents to support its contention that the bird was not entitled to free entry into the country. The first, whose decision had been handed down in 1916 (*U.S.* v. *Olivotti*, 7 Ct. Cust. Appls. 46), involved the importation of a font. It was described as "a plain marble basin, supported by a long, slender, tapering column, which is sustained by a short, round pillar of smaller diameter. The short pillar springs from an angular base which rests on a plain square slab of marble. The surface of the long, tapering column is ornamented by carvings suggestive of leaves." From the outset, however, the font differed from the bird in at least two ways. It could be conceived of as having a utilitarian purpose, and, though the sculptor was a professional, he had copied it from an original in an Italian church.

Interestingly, neither of these two criteria had affected the judge's decision of 1916. "It may be conceded," he wrote, "that it is artistic and beautiful. Nevertheless, those conditions . . . are not sufficient of themselves to constitute a sculpture." His main objection—based on a dictionary definition of sculpture—lay in the absence of any relationship to natural or human form. Although part of the surface had leaves carved in relief, they were considered an incidental ornamentation and therefore not sufficient to render the entire object naturalistic. In the opinion of the judge, the law provided free entry for "only those productions of the artist which are something more than ornamental or decorative and which may be properly ranked as examples of the free fine arts, or possibly that class only of the free fine arts imitative of natural object as the artist sees them, and appealing to the emotions through the eye alone." By this definition, the judge rightly pointed out, other categories are also ruled out—namely, "the potter, the glassmaker, the goldsmith, the weaver, the needlewoman, the lacemaker. . . ."

He was essentially distinguishing between the so-called minor arts and the more monumental arts of large-scale painting and sculpture. However, the problems which might have arisen as a result of this ruling are staggering when one thinks of what artistic masterpieces are excluded by it. What of the pottery, gold, and jewelry uncovered in archaeological sites throughout the world? Would the Scythian gold, highly prized by Leningrad's Hermitage Museum, be barred from free entry into the United States? Coptic textiles are bought and sold regularly as works of art. How, one might wonder, would this ruling have applied to the modern vogue for jewelry made and signed by contemporary artists?

The second case cited only briefly by the defense (U.S. v. Perry 146 U.S. 71 74) involved the importation of glass windows on which prominent artists had represented Christian subjects. In that case, the court found that although artistic and beautiful, the windows fell into the category of decorative and industrial arts. Therefore they could not be considered "fine arts" and were not entitled to free entry. One might wonder what this court would have said of the stained-glass windows of the great Gothic cathedrals, of Chagall's Jerusalem windows, or of those in the Matisse Chapel at St. Paul de Vence.

With these two cases as precedents, the defense argued that the mere fact that Brancusi was a professional sculptor did not guarantee his works free entry. His sculptures, according to the defense, were not the kind of art provided for in paragraph 1704 of the Tariff Act.

The brief for the plaintiff assumed quite a different posture from that of the defense. Steichen's attorneys incorporated a lengthy statement into their brief, amounting to a miniature philosophical treatise. Opening on a historical note, the attorneys for Brancusi pointed to the continual debate over questions of aesthetics through the ages. The greatest philosophical thinkers, from Plato to Ruskin, had wrestled with these issues leaving them still unsolved. "The entire question," wrote the attorneys, "resolves itself into the conception of the artist; into the sincerity of the artist at the time of the creation of the work." They suggested that when the Tariff Act was written into the United States legal structure, it had not been the government's intention to take sides in any debate over particular styles and schools of art. "The theory of the law and the intention of the legislators were to encourage and admit free of duty the sincere efforts of any sculptor or artist which did not have a utilitarian purpose. It was to encourage the importation of art," they asserted patriotically, "for the intellectual and cultural advantage of our own country."

One note of reservation may perhaps be interjected here with regard to the designation of "utility." For there are works of art that, although not planned for utility, are, in reality, utilitarian. Such examples are found in some of the *ready-mades* by Marcel Duchamp, like the *Fountain-Urinal* and the shovel titled *In Advance of a Broken Arm*. It would be an interesting exercise to discover whether a court of law could determine at what point they cease to be what they are in reality and become entitled to admission into the category of art. Of course, Duchamp did not intend his shovel to be used for digging, but rather to be contemplated under the title he gave it. An even more ticklish class of objects is the sarcophagus. In antiquity and during the Renaissance, professional artists made sarcophagi which they intended for use as tombs. Such objects nevertheless are indisputably works of art.

The statement in the defense brief—which resorted to a semipatriotic argument in citing the intellectual and cultural betterment of the United States—underlined that its point held for all works of art, whether ancient or modern. Otherwise limitations would be imposed on the enjoyment of art and, it was implied, on America's cultural development. Finally, as if appealing to the democratic principles of the court and, by extension of the United States, works of art were compared with ideas. Both, the statement concluded, were "entitled to free currency among the nations of the earth, and to fall into the error of bounding 'art' is almost sufficient to destroy the principle of its right to free entrance." Signed "M. J. Speiser, attorneys for the plaintiff," the brief was submitted to the court.

Both sides in the case evidently agreed that the *Bird in Space* was an original, nonutilitarian work by a professional sculptor. The weight of judgment finally focused on a much more important issue; whether the government could dictate taste. The case for Brancusi addressed itself to the general principle that the United States benefited from the free entry of all objects reasonably considered to possess artistic merit. The case against Brancusi, on the other hand, argued that the object must be more naturalistic than abstract. This was the crux of the issue—and it came at a time when the art world itself was torn into similar factions. To some extent, this has been a recurring conflict in art since 1850, when Impressionism broke down the precise outlines and clear forms of the neoclassical establishment in France. The history of artistic style—like politics—is a dynamic process in which progressive and conservative factions are continually at odds.

It was against this background that Justice Waite handed down his historic decision. He, too, indicated that the court's task was to determine whether the bird "conforms to the definition given under law for works of art." He conceded that, according to earlier decisions, the sculpture might well have been rejected as a work of "high art." Justice Waite approached his final judgment with reference to the decision of 1916 on the marble font. He said that since 1916

> there has been developing a so-called new school of art, whose exponents attempt to portray abstract ideas rather than to imitate natural objects. Whether or not we are in sympathy with these newer ideas and the schools which represent them, we think the facts of their existence and their influence upon the art world as recognized by the courts must be considered.
>
> The object now under consideration is shown to be for purely ornamental purposes, its use being the same as that of any piece of sculpture of the old masters. It is beautiful and symmetrical in outline, and while some difficulty might be encountered in associating it with a bird, it is nevertheless pleasing to look at and highly ornamental, and as we hold under the evidence that it is the original production of a professional sculptor and is in fact a piece of sculpture and a work of art according to the authorities above referred to, we sustain the protest and find that it is entitled to free entry under paragraph 1704, supra.
>
> Let judgment be entered accordingly.
Waite, J.

Years later, when Steichen wrote *A Life in Photography*, he discussed the trial. "Because the press had accorded this case all the attention of a scandal," Steichen said, "Brancusi always referred to it as the *brouhaha*. One winter, I made a series of photographs of the bird in my home in Connecticut. I photographed it on the diagonal, with the late afternoon sun playing tricks of light, shade and sparkle with the bronze. I called this series *Brouhaha*."[9]

On May 1, 1974, the Marlborough Gallery sold a sculpture by Brancusi, *La Negresse Blonde II*, for $750,000. This sale set a world record in the auction price for sculpture.

S

CHAPTER THREE

LEONARDO'S / LIBELED LADY/Hahn v. Duveen

He was a man of enormous charisma, energy, charm and self-confidence. Sir Joseph Duveen considered himself the greatest living art dealer. Henry Duveen, his father, had been an art dealer before him. In 1886 he had emigrated from Holland to the city of Hull in the north of England and opened an antique business specializing in oriental porcelain and furniture. Three years later, Joseph was born, and, by his own affirmation, he never made a mistake about a work of art from youth on. He first went to work as a runner in his father's business which had expanded to include branches in New York, London and Paris. Eventually, as president of the Duveen Brothers Corporation, Sir Joseph distinguished himself by selling and buying outstanding works of art at record prices.

In 1901 he paid a record price of over $70,000 for a painting sold at a British auction. In 1906 he bought a major German art collection for $500,000, and, soon afterward, one French collection for $5,000,000 and a second for $3,000,000. With these purchases, Duveen established his basic inventory. "Early in life," wrote S.N. Behrman in his lively biography of the art dealer, "Duveen . . . noticed that Europe had plenty of art and America had plenty of money, and his entire astonishing career was the product of that simple observation."[1]

In the course of his career, Duveen substantially deter-

Leonardo's Libeled Lady / 59

mined the character of most of the great American art collections. He provided Henry Clay Frick with the paintings which would hang in the Boucher and Fragonard rooms of his New York mansion. He acquired Raphael's famous *Cowper Madonna* for Benjamin Altman, who inconveniently died before receiving it. Duveen then sold the picture to P.A.B. Widener, the great Philadelphia collector, for $700,000. Other clients included H.E. Huntington, of California (to whom he sold Reynolds's *Mrs. Siddons* and Gainsborough's *Blue Boy*), E.T. Stotesbury, Andrew Carnegie, Samuel H. Kress, J.P. Morgan, Andrew Mellon, John D. Rockefeller, Jules Bache, and William Randolph Hearst. Throughout his career, Duveen created the impression that a painting purchased from anyone but Duveen was hardly worth having.

On June 17, 1920, a reporter from the *New York World* phoned Duveen to say that *La Belle Ferronnière*, an original painting by Leonardo da Vinci was on its way to Kansas City. Duveen at once pronounced it a fake. The painting (fig. 8), which belonged to a Mrs. Andrée Hahn, had been certified as authentic by French art expert Georges Sortais. The following morning, the newspaper published the dealer's comments. "The picture sent to Kansas City," declared Duveen, "is a copy, hundreds of which have been made of this and other Leonardo subjects and offered in the market as genuine. Leonardo never made a replica of his work. His original *La Belle Ferronière* is in the Louvre. Georges Sortais's certificate is worthless if it really relates to the Kansas City picture."[2] Those comments would lead to one of the most notorious international lawsuits in modern history. Nor was it Duveen's first. He characteristically threw himself into litigation with swashbuckling élan. This case was destined to be his most spectacular.

Mrs. Hahn was determined to go down fighting for the rights of her painting; she had established its provenance entirely to her own satisfaction. Leonardo died in France while in the employ of Francis I, and it was during that period that he painted the portrait of the woman called *La Belle Fer-*

FIGURE 8. *La Belle Ferronnière*, the Hahn version.

ronnière. After Leonardo's death, the painting passed into the French royal collection. Twenty years later, according to Mrs. Hahn's account, the painting began to crack and was transferred from its original panel base to canvas by the royal restorer of Versailles. It remained at Versailles until 1786, when it was given to one of Napoleon's aides. Mrs. Hahn's family was descended from that aide, and an aunt, who was also her godmother, eventually inherited the painting. In 1916 the French art expert Georges Sortais certified the picture while it was in her godmother's possession. Three years later, in 1919, Andrée Lardoux married Harry Hahn, an American aviator, and her godmother gave her the painting as a wedding present. By the following year, the Hahns had settled in Junction City, Kansas, and were preparing to sell their painting through Kansas City art dealer Conrad Hug.

Not unnaturally the Kansas City press gave the prospective arrival of a painting by Leonardo da Vinci a great deal of attention. As early as January 1920, before the painting had even left France, the *Kansas City Star* reported that local art dealers were contracting with a Tulsa oil man for the sale of the painting. The price; $250,000. Subsequently Conrad Hug contacted the president of the Kansas City Art Institute with a view to selling the picture—also for $250,000. The picture itself was much discussed. According to the *Star*, the portrait depicted the wife of Francis I. Conrad Hug declared that during the war the painting had been given refuge in the Louvre and that that alone was proof of its authenticity. "Humbugs," the dealer was quoted as saying, "are not permitted in the Louvre." Nevertheless, "If a Painting Could Talk," an article in the February 1 edition of the *Star* recognized some of the potential problems posed by the picture's arrival. "If the newly announced *La Belle Ferronnière* could speak," mused the author of the article, "would she tell of seeing the ardent eyes of a Leonardo looking into hers as he wielded his brush—as he painted the brown strands of her hair, the rich velvet of her costume, the jewels at her throat and the one set in the center of her lovely forehead, or would she say she is an imposter?" One European Leonardo scholar, Jean Paul Richter, had written that the Louvre painting was by one of the artist's pupils, probably Boltraffio, and that the original was lost. Could the Hahn painting be the lost original, speculated the *Kansas City Star*.

On June 15 the same paper announced that *La Belle Ferronnière* was finally on its way. Two days later without having seen the painting, Duveen pronounced it a fake. Conrad Hug picked up Duveen's gauntlet and prepared to do battle. Again the newspapers rallied around the fray. "Kansas City Art Dealer Insists Famed Painting is One of Ten Originals" ran a headline in the afternoon edition of the *Kansas City Post* on June 19. The same day, the *Kansas City Star* quoted Louvre director M. Marcel as saying: "All our da Vincis date back to the time of Francis I, when they were acquired by the king from the painter himself. No private person could have an opportunity to acquire one legitimately. We hope that the theft of the *Mona Lisa* was the first and last case of its kind. The picture possessed by Mrs. Hahn, not the one remaining in the Louvre, is a clever copy by one of da Vinci's pupils."

No sooner did Hug learn of Marcel's comments than the American dealer declared the painting in the Louvre (fig. 9) a copy. He explained that Napoleon had taken the painting from Italy to France, and the painting had remained in the possession of the same family ever since. "The more they fight, the better pleased I shall be," Hug persisted. He pointed to Richter's statement that the Louvre painting was the work of Boltraffio, Leonardo's pupil, and said that it represented Lucrezia Crivelli. Lucrezia was the mistress of Milan's Lodovico il Moro, who, it was said, loved his wife, Beatrice d'Este, but was under Lucrezia's spell. Her presence and powerful influence at the court of Milan would have been contemporaneous with Leonardo's employment there. Furthermore, Hug informed reporters, Mrs. Hahn had a certificate of authenticity from Georges Sortais bolstered by a letter from the editor of *American Art News* asserting that the French expert was an honest authority.

FIGURE 9. Leonardo da Vinci (1452-1519), *La Belle Ferronnière*.
Louvre, Paris. Cliché des Musées Nationaux.

On June 21 the *Kansas City Post* reported receiving a flurry of letters, telegrams and phone calls about the painting. "The battle of *La Belle* is on," the paper announced. In the same issue, Hug described the painting's lineage once again, adding triumphantly that France would never have let it leave the country. He was, of course, assuming the accuracy of the attribution to Leonardo. The French government had, and still has, a policy that strictly controls the export of works of art and prohibits the departure of any work considered a national treasure.

As for the painting itself, the undisputed facts are few and far between. Whether the Louvre's or Mrs. Hahn's, it was first referred to as Leonardo's in 1642 in Pierre Dan's *Treasure of the Marvels of Fontainebleau*. He called it a portrait of the duchess of Mantua. In 1709 the painting was confused with a portrait in the French royal inventory of the *Belle Ferronnière*, Francis I's mistress. The confusion was compounded by the sixteenth-century meaning of "ferronnière": a ribbon tied around a woman's hair to hold it in place. From 1894, when the traditional attribution to Leonardo was first challenged, there have been two critical schools of thought: those for Leonardo and those who believed the picture to be the work of Boltraffio. A few scholars believed both artists had worked on the painting. Certainly, the Louvre picture which is on poplar rather than canvas, has been restored and modern X rays reveal that the hair did not originally cover the left ear. For a variety of technical reasons they also tend to refute the authorship of Boltraffio.

Another problem is the identity of the woman represented in the picture; she stands out against a dark, almost black, background. She wears a red dress, a necklace, and a headband with a jewel in the center of her forehead. Her representation in three-quarter view, looking out at the observer, is typical of portraiture in the latter part of the Italian Renaissance. She appears to be seated behind, and slightly inclined toward, a horizontal parapet which occupies the bottom of the picture plane.

Suggestions as to her identity are as varied as those

relating to the *Mona Lisa*, Leonardo's most famous mystery woman. Besides Lucrezia Crivelli. *La Belle Ferronnière* has been identified as Beatrice d'Este, Isabella d'Este, Elisabetta Gonzaga, and Cecilia Gallerani. The same names, all referring to women Leonardo probably knew, have also at one time or another been advanced as candidates for the identity of the *Mona Lisa*. Inevitable as is the comparison of *La Belle Ferronnière* with the *Mona Lisa*, it is a particularly tantalizing one. This is partly because the *Mona Lisa* is relatively abstract while *La Belle Ferronnière* is more definitely a specific portrait. The *Mona Lisa* is the representation of a generalized woman although the impetus to make the image was probably triggered by a specific person. It is this general quality of the *Mona Lisa* which is at once the source of her mystery and her almost universal appeal. It is likely that one's sense of Leonardo is so weighted by the impact of *Mona Lisa*'s abstract character, that the individuality of a specific portrait unconsciously jars one's perception of his style and makes it more difficult to accept *La Belle Ferronnière* as Leonardo's without some hesitation.

Indeed, a certain ambivalence has characterized expert judgments of *La Belle Ferronnière*. Many critics who originally believed the picture in the Louvre to be by one of Leonardo's students, later decided that it was by Leonardo himself. Today critical opinion tends to favor the Leonardo attribution although even Kenneth Clark cautions against dogmatic insistence on this point.[3] It would seem that, until such time as a conclusive document turns up, these mysteries will remain unsolved.

Meanwhile Duveen stuck to his guns. When he finally saw a photograph of Mrs. Hahn's picture, he was completely unimpressed. On August 5 he sent a letter from Europe to his New York office in which he wrote the following: "I have in no way changed my opinion about the picture ascribed to Da Vinci, of which you have sent me a photograph. I am convinced that this is an old copy of a picture in the Louvre. I do not think it is contemporary, but is a little later than the Louvre painting."

When it came to determination, however, Mrs. Hahn was firm. All negotiations for the sale of her painting fell through. She promptly hired New York attorney Hyacinthe Ringrose to represent her and to restore her painting's damaged reputation. On November 4, 1921, a summons and complaint was served on Sir Joseph.

Several weeks later, on December 13, a delegation of experts, including Duveen himself, viewed the Hahn painting. On exhibit at Ringrose's Fifth Avenue office, the painting was examined by Princeton professor, Frank Jewett Mather, and the directors of the Worcester Massachusetts Art Museum and Harvard's Fogg Museum. All came independently to the same conclusion. The picture was not by Leonardo. Now in the role of defendant, Duveen served his answer to the complaint on January 21, 1922. In March both sets of attorneys entered into a stipulation allowing depositions to be taken from witnesses in Great Britain, France, Germany, and Italy.

A month later, Mrs. Hahn served an amended complaint. She stated in the amended complaint that her picture had been authenticated by French government expert Georges Sortais in 1916 and that she had published his opinion, thereby increasing the painting's marketability and value. She had established a satisfactory provenance, she said, brought the painting to the United States in order to sell it and had entered into negotiations with the Kansas City Art Institute and other prospective buyers. Duveen "maliciously and knowingly" made "false and reckless" statements to the *New York World* on June 17, 1920, which resulted in substantial financial loss to the plaintiff. Thus, concluded Mrs. Hahn's complaint, her rights of property had been injured, her painting had been slandered and its reputation damaged. She demanded judgment against Duveen of $500,000, plus costs.

Duveen lost no time in replying. He denied the allegations of maliciousness, but admitted having made the remarks to the newspaper. Nor did he regret them since the real Leonardo was still in the Louvre (fig. 9). Included in

Duveen's reply was an extensive justification for his statement. He was, he began with characteristic lack of modesty, president of Duveen Brothers, Inc., probably the world's largest firm of art dealers, and was thoroughly familiar with Leonardo's genuine work. Since none of Leonardo's paintings was in the United States at the time, the dealer declared it would have been a great artistic event if the Hahn picture had been authentic and it was Duveen's duty as a leading and responsible member of the art world to make his opinion known. Furthermore, he elaborated, on stylistic grounds alone, Leonardo could never have painted the Hahn portrait. And by the time he would finish with his analysis, the young lady represented in the painting would sound most unappealing indeed.

Duveen explained:

> The oil painting which is described in the complaint [fig. 8] does not show the consummate skill and grasp of the human structure that is fundamental and inherent in the works of Leonardo; the head is attached on the shoulders in a poor fashion, the plaits of flesh below the chin are not natural; the neck itself is a clumsy cylinder of flesh, and the left hand profile of the neck is out of design; the modeling of the shoulders and breast is crude and primitive. . . . The [Hahn] painting . . . shows a marked absence of gradations of light and color. It shows lack of chiaroscuro. In other words, it changes from light to shade abruptly and not gradually. The coloring is "violent" and does not present "tenderness" and "warmth" as those terms are understood and used by artists and art experts. The cheeks fail to take up or reflect the hue of the bodice of the gown with which the woman is clothed. The form of the face is not brought forth out of subdued light. . . ." [Nor does it] show soft lines, melting gradually into shades. It shows a rigorous "contour" and a very sharp separation of the figure of the subject from its background. It does not appear to have been molded with color and with light. . . . [Leonardo's] portraits do not show a separation of the figure from the background by means of a dark outline. . . .

In his *Treatise on Painting*, Leonardo stated: "On beauty of face: Do not make the lines of muscles too insistent, but allow soft lights to melt gradually into pleasant and agreeable shades. This gives grace and beauty."

And Leonardo followed this in his painting. The oil painting described in the complaint shows none of those characteristics. The eyes are leaden and lifeless. They are not circled with shadows and they seem to lack lashes. The eyebrows do not give the impression that they have sprung from the flesh. . . . The [Hahn] painting shows a hesitancy in drawing which was not present in the work of such a wonderful draftsman as Leonardo. The manner of drapery reveals the cramped brush of a copyist working with a design not his own. There is an entire absence of the psychological depth. The picture is so weak in its structure and in spirit, indeed, so trivial in all its attributes that it falls far short of a work of a man who possessed the complex nature and the mind and imagination, combined with the marvelous versatility, that have been credited to Leonardo. In fact, the portrait described in the complaint has not even been executed by an artist of the first rank;

Whereas the portraits of Leonardo breathe the spirit of live and spiritual power. His works present psychological depth which stamp them with marked superiority. They do not show any hesitancy in drawing. . . .[4]

And, finally, Duveen concluded his stylistic analysis with a few comments on technique:

Leonardo was one of the first of the Italian painters to use oil mixed with colors which, to a great extent, at that time was based upon the Flemish methods. Prior to Leonardo's time the Italian painters did not use oils but painted with "tempera," which was a substance made of eggs. Leonardo did not use "tempera." He prepared the panels for his paintings with "gesso," which is a sort of plaster of paris preparation, mixed with "size" (a thin glue), and this was covered with a coat of white ground in oil. On this the design was outlined and the shadows put in in brown. Over this the colors ground in oil and mixed with varnish were glazed. The painting described in the complaint has an oil priming and is painted on a red ground, neither of which was used in Leonardo's time.[5]

Furthermore, Duveen pointed out, nearly every acknowledged expert agreed with his judgment. As a result, he asked for dismissal of the complaint with costs.

Duveen's eloquence was lost on Mrs. Hahn. She pursued the action across the Atlantic.

LONDON, 1922

Between July and September of 1922, under the stipulation entered into the previous March, attorneys Sherman for the defense and Ringrose for the plaintiff went to London to take the depositions of four experts. All were familiar with the painting in the Louvre and all were prominent as either scholars or connoisseurs. Each had a special interest in the works of Leonardo. None had seen the Hahn picture except through photographs. For the most part, the experts agreed that little could be said about color, pigmentation, glazing, or varnish from a photograph. They were unanimous on one point; the Hahn painting was emphatically not by Leonardo. The plaintiff produced no witnesses to defend the authenticity of her portrait. Her attorney confined himself to cross-examination of defense witnesses.

Captain Robert Langton Douglas, director of the National Gallery of Ireland testified first. "I think, myself," he said, "that the treatment of the drapery, especially over the shoulder, the manner of painting, has not the quality that I look for in a work of Leonardo, especially so in the rather clumsy and superficial way in which the highlights are painted on the ribbons and marks. . . . Of course, I am confined, I admit, by the photograph . . . the woman's left shoulder seems to me to be without sufficient modeling. It is a defect I find in the whole picture—that it is too generalized. That may be due in part to condition, but not entirely."

In other words, the Hahn picture was not sufficiently organic; the points of anatomical transition—as from neck to shoulder—were unconvincing. Leonardo was an avid student of anatomy; he performed dissections and produced numerous and detailed anatomical drawings. He was able to transform his scientific knowledge into pictorial form.

"I may say to you," explained Sherman under direct questioning, "that our trial will be before a jury of gentlemen who presumably are not familiar with the technical language which is used by experts in judging painting, and therefore may I ask you to state what is meant by chiaroscuro, and by the subtlety of modeling which you find lacking . . . ?"

"You see," replied Douglas, "Leonardo suggests various subtle differences of plane in the human countenance by the skillful use of light and shade, and in [the Hahn] case all these planes are flat, too generalized. . . . For instance, that neck looks a great block of stuff. One finds in the neck of a great artist a sense of all various little differences of plane which are due to structure."

Douglas commented on various parts of the Hahn portrait in turn. He could do this, he testified, although he was confined to photographic evidence. The hair, he said, lacked individuality. "It is a great slab of hair with just a few highlights put on above the left temple, but without that living sense of hair. The hair is a vital thing that we especially expect to find in Leonardo, whom we know from tradition had a great feeling for human hair, and a great love of beautiful hair." Indeed, among Leonardo's drawings are many examples of hair, studies of its movement and metaphorical drawings comparing the flow of a woman's hair with the flow of water; others compare hair that is tied in a bun with the forms of certain sea shells. As for the eyes in the Hahn picture, Douglas thought they lacked vitality, the right eye in particular being "very tamely painted."

In short Douglas believed the Hahn picture to be a copy which had been painted in the seventeenth century.

Sir Charles John Holmes, director of London's National Gallery, on the other hand, thought it much later and not even Italian. For a variety of reasons—the pigment, the cracks, the style—Sir Charles pronounced it a nineteenth-century painting from northern Europe, executed in either France or Holland. "The method of drawing the eyes in itself is to me sufficient indication of that date," he declared. "It is a purely nineteenth-century style of drawing the eye." Likewise, the hair was modern and the modeling of the cheek was empty.

Morris Walter Brockwell was the art gallery curator of Doughty House at Richmond in the English county of Surrey. The gallery had a collection of some 400 paintings and was privately owned by Sir Herbert Cook, who also testified for Duveen. Brockwell was primarily a cataloger and, in establishing his expertise, explained his duties. Cataloging involved a thorough examination of the picture, its pedigree, its style and measurements. "The word 'catalog' really means, I think, that you put your views into a definite and concise form, together with the measurements of the picture, with a view to publication."

Brockwell was eloquent in explaining his rejection of the Hahn picture. "The features are pulpy and lack definition. The eyes have no life; the hair is wiglike; the contour is misleading; . . . the line of the parting of the hair, if continued, would go straight through the lady's eye and not in the direction of her nose, . . . The line which seeks to show the relationship between the chin and the upper portion of the neck is obviously wrong in nature. . . . I do not think that the eyes match. The whole picture is lacking in that sense of life and the qualities which stand for the work of Leonardo. . . . The costume, as here rendered, seems taglike and trumpery, and does not even seem to cover a form which Leonardo would have been interested in for five minutes. . . . I feel sure that he would have spurned a thing of this kind, . . . it would have bored him."

Furthermore, Brockwell elaborated later on in his deposition, "the head shows no spiritual content such as is shown in the [Louvre painting.] . . . The parting of the hair is misleading; it is facetious; it is pettifogging; it is just what a parting is not; . . . the cheek is over round, almost swollen. It is unnatural, and I do not think that the right cheek matches the left cheek." The Hahn picture, concluded Brockwell, in no way reflects Leonardo's genius "except as a misunderstanding."

On psychological grounds—"the spiritual content and psychological correlation to other pictures"—this witness dated the picture in the eighteenth or nineteenth century. Pressed into specifics during Ringrose's cross-examination, Brockwell proceeded to the matter of the cracks. They, too, seemed modern. All the witnesses agreed, in fact, that the cracks in the Hahn painting indicated an artist other than Leonardo.

Much of the testimony involved lengthy discussions of the technical aspects of painting. Were Leonardo's pictures on wood and, if so, what kind? Did he use walnut oil? Did he prime his pictures with sepia, yellow, or purple pigments? In fact, Leonardo's technique is a matter that is fraught with controversy. Many of his paintings have undergone considerable restoration. The artist himself was a compulsive experimenter and he did not always follow his own advice as expressed in his famous *Treatise on Painting*. Each of these problems makes it extremely difficult to retrace the steps of Leonardo's technical working procedure.

On cross-examination, Ringrose took great pains to demonstrate that a qualified art expert must be thoroughly familiar with both the specific and general aspects of an artist's technique. Thus, when Sir Herbert Cook, the owner of Doughty House, testified to his total ignorance of, and lack of concern with, technique, Ringrose ran the point into the ground. "I pretend to be a connoisseur, but not a technical art expert," Sir Herbert snapped.

On the whole, the British witnesses were more sure of their judgment in matters of style than of technique and they genuinely believed, since they were not professional artists, that this was perfectly appropriate. "Flair," said Douglas, for example, was the one characteristic which most certainly qualified him as an expert: "I consider," he said, "that I have a flair for the likenesses of paintings. I mean by the use of the word *"flair,"* he explained, "a kind of instinct resembling the instinct for likeness in faces for members of a family which enables you to tell instantly whether a picture is by one master or another master. Of course, an artistic flair includes and must include a sense of quality. In order for a flair to be effective, the one possessing it must have a keen sense of quality. . . . A person's flair may be weakened and injured by absence from fine works of art or by looking at bad works of art. Flair is a difficult thing to define. It includes memory in a sense of quality as well as instinct for recognizing the quality of artistic efforts."

Having detected an obviously vague quality from a legal point of view in Douglas's criteria for expertise, Ringrose pounced. "The opinion which you have expressed that this Hahn picture was not painted by Leonardo da Vinci is largely put on what you call 'flair'?"

"A great deal of it," declared Douglas completely unfazed.

Despite some minor variations of opinion, the four witnesses whose depositions were taken in London were remarkably consistent in their observations. The Hahn portrait did not display the subtleties of light and dark, the almost imperceptible gradations of shading with which Leonardo defined his forms, his unique atmospheric effects of *sfumato*. The representation of the woman did not reveal that intensity of psychological mystery characteristic of Leonardo's women, nor was she painted with the anatomical knowledge one would expect from the artist.

Ringrose continually tried to rebut the consensus that Leonardo was an expert draftsman by pointing out defects in undisputed examples of the artist's work. Among the witnesses, there was further general agreement that Leonardo never copied his own work. Therefore the two pictures could not both be by Leonardo. Ringrose then seized upon the two well-known versions of *The Virgin of the Rocks*—one in London (fig. 10) and one in Paris (fig. 11). While not identical, these two paintings are strikingly similar, but, in view of Leonardo's compulsive perfection which frequently prevented him from even finishing his works and his extensive scientific investigation which severely limited and eventually blocked his artistic production, it seems highly unlikely on psychological grounds alone that both could be by Leonardo. Duveen's four British experts agreed that the Paris version was probably Leonardo's, while the London version was a product of his studio and executed under his direction. Today scholars are still discussing and revising their considerations of these two pictures; problems of style, attribution, commission, iconography and provenance remain. But in July 1922, Mrs. Hahn's attorney was determined to elicit statements to the effect that the London *Virgin of the Rocks* was badly drawn.

"Have you noticed the drawing?" Ringrose asked Brockwell.

"Yes, I have noticed it."

"Is it bad drawing in some respects?"

"No, I would not call it bad."

"Just fair? . . ."

"Quite fairly well drawn."

"Accurately drawn?"

"Quite fairly well drawn."

"Would you say as an art expert that it is well drawn?"

"One does not examine square inches, surely? One takes the whole thing as a net result."

"Did you notice the thumb of the left hand of the infant, Jesus?"

"I think I remember it vaguely."

"Is that frightfully drawn?"

"Its present appearance is unsatisfactory."

"It is shapeless, is not it?"

"Well, one might almost go so far as to say that."

"Is it not the thumb of an adult rather than the thumb of an infant?"

"Leonardo would not be concerned whether he was painting an infant or an adult."

Charles Holmes, director of the National Gallery, how-

FIGURE 10. Leonardo da Vinci, *The Virgin of the Rocks*, The National Gallery, London.

FIGURE 11. Leonardo da Vinci, *La Vièrge aux rochers*. Louvre, Paris. Cliché des Musées Nationaux.

ever, would not admit that any part of the picture in that museum was defectively drawn. What was more, in his view the London picture had been painted entirely by Leonardo. He had demonstrated this conclusively, he argued, by discovering Leonardo's own fingerprints on the painting and publishing his findings in the *Burlington Magazine*, a prominent English art journal.

Douglas, on the other hand, agreed that not only did the painting's draftsmanship leave something to be desired, but also that the flesh tones were ashen and corpselike. The implication was that Leonardo's figures were not uniformly "lifelike," as the experts had testified in excluding the Hahn painting from his body of work. However, Douglas pointed out, these defects in *The Virgin of the Rocks* were most likely due both to extensive restoration and to the painting's not being entirely by Leonardo.

Following this line of examination and cross-examination, both attorneys brought out the tantalizing fact that a great deal of Leonardo's work, like his own life and character, is shrouded in mystery and controversy. Holmes, for example, like Berenson, who would testify the following year, originally believed *La Belle Ferronnière* to have been painted by Boltraffio, a gifted student of Leonardo, but had later changed his mind. Even now, Holmes testified, "I, personally, am inclined to the Leonardo view, and I am pretty sure of it. Having spent a great deal of time upon this particular question I have no doubt it is by Leonardo, and not by Boltraffio. But if somebody proved it was by Boltraffio, I should be quite prepared to reconsider the subject."

The Last Supper in Milan had suffered extensive damage due to Leonardo's experimentation with oils on a plaster surface which demanded water-based paint. From a technical point of view, *The Last Supper* should have been executed in pure fresco, the application of water paint to wet plaster; as the plaster dries, it absorbs the paint which then becomes part of the wall. In order to do this, however, the fresco painters had to work relatively quickly, applying the paint before the plaster dried. Because of Leonardo's compulsive slowness, he tried to use oil paint which can be applied slowly and then retouched and reworked because it dries slowly. As a result, since the oil paint resisted absorption, it began peeling within a very short time after Leonardo applied it. Thus, argued Ringrose, Leonardo was quite capable of making mistakes and therefore might logically have made those which had been described in connection with the Hahn picture. Not so, persisted the experts, for Leonardo's mistakes in *The Last Supper* had been mistakes in preparation and technique and not defects of style.

And what of the *Mona Lisa* in the Prado in Madrid? Ringrose wanted to know. Were there not two versions of the *Mona Lisa*, both in leading European museums? The Prado *Mona Lisa* was unanimously and decisively pronounced a very inferior copy by all four experts.

Their testimony was officially recorded and added to the files. Many more years would elapse and even more experts would testify before the case would actually come to trial.

PARIS, 1923

Nearly a year later, on May 1, 1923, the attorneys entered into a second stipulation permitting expert depositions in London, Paris, and Amsterdam. Shortly thereafter, Duveen asked Louis S. Levy, from the same law firm, to represent him in Paris at what one New York paper would later refer to as "Duveen's dress muster of art connoisseurs." The dealer paid $2,000 for Ringrose's expenses and the transportation of Mrs. Hahn's painting to Paris. The expert witnesses would thus be able to make direct comparisons between the Hahn painting, the Louvre painting, and Leonardo's other, undisputed, works in the Louvre. The Hahn picture was in the custody of Conrad Hug who, together with Mrs. Hahn, was also present for the Paris depositions. Again Duveen paid most of the expenses, and again Ringrose declined to produce any witnesses for the plaintiff. As in London the previous year, he restricted himself to cross-examining Duveen's witnesses.

By September, Levy had prepared his case and was ready to proceed with his impressive array of experts.

On September 4 and 5, Bernard Berenson, who was to connoisseurship what Duveen was to the art business, testified in a lawsuit for the first time in his life. In addition to writing the still-authoritative volumes *Italian Painters of the Renaissance*, Berenson was a professional art counselor. He was on retainer to many of America's leading art collectors, including Isabella Gardner of Boston, John G. Johnson of Philadelphia, Henry Walters of Baltimore, the Wideners, and the firm of Duveen Brothers.

Berenson was Duveen's first Paris witness; his deposition lasted two days and was taken at the offices of the Guaranty Trust Co., 1 rue des Italiens. In view of Berenson's international renown as an art critic, Duveen's attorney opened the deposition with questions on the nature of expertise.

"You have to know the pictures," Berenson explained, "no matter how few or how many, and all the other works of art that practically nobody questions as being by that master. You then get a sense . . . this sort of sixth sense that comes from accumulated experience . . . a sense of the quality of the master, a sense of what that master is up to, what he is likely to do, able to do, and what he is not likely to be able to do. Then you control this by trying to find out what characteristics are recurrent in him and that do not occur in that one picture exclusively. For instance, a certain kind of ear, a certain type of hand, a certain lay of hair, a certain kind of eye, of chin, and so on; certain folds of draperies. When all these things go together in picture after picture, we conclude and are allowed to conclude by all people who allow for evidence, that that is the right kind of evidence; and if that occurs in the picture, then you say that it is a picture by the said master."

Later, under cross-examination, Ringrose launched into an attack on Berenson's description of his own expertise by bringing up the idea of the painter's unconscious. "Do you think it is possible for anybody to identify the unconscious characteristics of a painter?"

"Yes, it is the easiest thing in the world, because he was not trying to disguise them."

"The mystical characteristics?" Ringrose persisted, trying to discredit Berenson's technique by implying that it was vague, unscientific, even ridiculously magical.

"Not at all," asserted Berenson confidently. "It was what he was doing unconsciously; or what he was doing by rote—we all do most of our work by rote. What we do habitually, we always do in the same fashion."

"Didn't you use the word 'mystical' and say that you had ascertained the unconscious characteristics of Leonardo da Vinci by a sort of sixth sense?"

"I did not use it in that sense. I used it in expressing that the moment I see a picture my sixth sense tells me what it is; but not when I describe it. . . . You must distinguish in art criticism between the instantaneous impression, then the attempt to control it by all sorts of other detailed evidence and then the further effort to get the kind of evidence which would appeal to the other man, after you have convinced yourself. . . ."

"Is there any value at all in this so-called 'sixth sense'?"

"To me it is of the highest value, but I keep it to myself. I wouldn't give any value to it unless it was entirely vouched for by detailed counter-examination, counterproof. . . . It is a phrase which is accepted universally and may be called 'accumulated experience.' A man who has been working on a job for forty years gets an accumulated experience which gives him an instantaneous reaction within his field of competence. That is all I mean."

Berenson's use of a "controlled" experimental model would presumably have buttressed one of the weakest aspects of Duveen's case as seen by a jury completely untrained in art. The nature of expertise in nontechnical matters of art almost inevitably seems vague and unscientific when subjected to the demands of precise legal terminology. Qualities like "flair," "a sixth sense," or "an eye for likenesses" cannot be measured quantitatively. Nevertheless, these are extremely important qualities—even prerequisites—for true connoisseurship. At the same time, the very men who possess such qualities in the highest degree have made mistakes which often become evident only with the passing of time. Thus many of Berenson's own attributions have since been discarded.

Before testifying, Berenson had examined *La Belle Ferronnière* in the Louvre and the Hahn picture at Duveen's Paris office, located at number 20 in the fashionable Place Vendôme. During Berenson's deposition, the Hahn picture and a photograph of the Louvre picture were present along with the attorneys, Conrad Hug, and Mrs. Hahn herself.

In Berenson's view, the Hahn picture was "an honest but not a very good" copy of the Louvre picture. It had been painted, he thought, in France, toward the end of the eighteenth century. "In the Hahn picture," the critic said, "I feel the looseness, the pudginess, softness and uncertainty of a very good honest workman in the eighteenth-century French tradition . . . late 18th century. . . . There is a look there which is not Italian. It is a more bovine look, if I may say so without insulting the picture; I don't mean to; it is big-eyed, bovine." Here Berenson is partially referring to the different ideal of feminine beauty characteristic of France in the eighteenth century. The French taste for relatively fatter women is reflected in their late eighteenth-century paintings. Artists of that period preferred more rounded forms and broader curves than did the artists of Renaissance Italy. "You might say," Berenson concluded, "it is a fatter woman, more like a Boucher."

Asked to specify his reasons for rejecting the Hahn picture as the work of Leonardo, Berenson elaborated willingly. At this point in the proceedings, the Hahn picture was placed on an easel before the critic so that he could illustrate his conclusions by direct reference to the disputed work.

"Can you tell on the Hahn picture where that cheekbone is?" asked Levy.

"No, I cannot. I see no bones there. It is not even a mask. If I was really to tell the absolute truth, I get the impression of something like a child's balloon."

"The witness is not trying to be humorous, is he?" Ring-rose interrupted.

"No," protested Berenson, "I can only tell Counsel that it is extremely difficult to find the vocabulary to express oneself; I don't mean to be humorous. One feels this thing, but it is extremely difficult to put it into words. I would like nothing better than to pronounce this picture a Leonardo; unfortunately, I can't. I get all the impressions of a mask, of a child's balloon, from the Hahn picture."

If anything, Berenson stated, the Louvre picture could be distinguished from the Hahn picture by its excessive firmness; "if it has a fault, it is that it is almost too hard." Asked what he meant, the critic replied with a reference to his own famous concept of tactility in Renaissance painting. "You feel as if you could grasp [the Louvre picture] and shake the head and take hold of the shoulder; you feel almost as if the master had originally done this in terms of stone or terra-cotta." In other words, a painting by Leonardo—or any other major painter of the Italian Renaissance—would arouse those nerve endings of his fingertips, the response that became his trademark in recognizing a Renaissance work. For Berenson, writing in 1896, "painting is an art which aims at giving an abiding impression of artistic reality with only two dimensions. The painter must, therefore, do consciously what we all do unconsciously—construct his third dimension. And he can accomplish this task only as we accomplish ours, by giving tactile values to retinal impressions. His first business, therefore, is to rouse the tactile sense, for I must have the illusion of being able to touch a figure, I must have the illusion of varying muscular sensations inside my palm and fingers corresponding to the various projections of this fig-ure, before I shall take it for granted as real, and let it affect me lastingly."[6]

Since Berenson held the illusion of three-dimensionality in such high esteem, he tended to dismiss those artists among his contemporaries—like Matisse—who were moving more and more in the direction of the actual flatness of the picture plane. In his taste for convincing representation of the third dimension, however, Berenson was very much in tune with those artists he most admired, namely, the monumental painters of the Italian Renaissance. It is ironic, in view of the testimony presented so far in the Duveen case, that shortly after 1500 Leonardo himself commented on the results of painting from nature as opposed to painting from other artists: " . . . The painter will produce pictures of small merit if he takes for his standard the pictures of others, but if he will study from natural objects he will bear good fruit."[7] The Renaissance painters believed very much in the need to observe nature as a prerequisite for good art. They studied mathematics and mastered scientific perspective in order to create a three-dimensional illusion on the flat surface of a picture, and they studied anatomy in order to populate their illusory space with convincing figures. Leonardo's unquestioned mastery of both techniques lay behind much of the testimony given by Duveen's expert witnesses.

One of the most objective pieces of evidence in support of Duveen was the architectural feature of the two paintings. Berenson discussed this at some length, comparing the parapet in the Louvre picture with the horizontal band at the bottom of the Hahn picture. "In the Louvre picture," he explained, "you have a real parapet with the real cornice and the real copping under the cornice." He indicated the parapet on the photograph. "Now, in the Hahn picture," Berenson continued, "there is no architecture, nothing, just a band of something, a piece of wood, but it has no modeling or structure; whereas the Louvre picture has a structure. . . . The parapet in the Louvre picture is the parapet that we find frequently in the pictures of the Renaissance of the Italian artists of the fifteenth century. . . . It shocked their sense to cut a body off in twain, they wanted to give the illusion that the body was all there, but that it was sitting behind a parapet . . . the man who did the Hahn picture didn't understand the purpose of the parapet and therefore neglected it, paid no attention to it." Because the copyist had not observed the relationship between the figure and parapet directly and because he did not share Leonardo's cultural milieu, he could not render the image convincingly.

On cross-examination by Ringrose, Berenson admitted that he was not a painter and that he had worked for Duveen on several occasions. He also admitted to having changed his mind on the attribution of the Louvre painting. He had originally thought it the work of Boltraffio and later decided that Leonardo had painted it. Whereupon Ringrose asked, "Did you communicate with any of the authorities at the Louvre and tell them of your change of mind?"

"As we are all Americans here, I can tell you that there are no 'authorities' in the Louvre."

"Do you consider that there are any art experts connected with the Louvre?"

"Well, I don't want to go into that because it would not be friendly. I would rather not discuss that."

In another exchange, the frequent conflict between a painter's actual productions and his writing on art was exposed. Berenson made it clear that, in Leonardo's case, he believed the works themselves of considerably greater importance than the artist's literary comments.

"Do you remember, in the book *Trattato della Pittura* [*Treatise on Painting*] that Leonardo da Vinci himself said that one of his characteristics was to prepare a picture with the brush instead of the point?"

"No, I don't remember anything about it."

"Don't you remember his book?"

"I remember his book."

"You don't remember that statement by Leonardo da Vinci?"

"I don't regard his book as very important; I regard his *work* as very important. I am not a man of letters. I don't spend my time reading his books, but looking at his pictures."

"You don't consider that Leonardo da Vinci was as able a writer on art subjects, for instance, as yourself?"

"Not quite. " . . .

"Didn't he say . . . that he painted all his pictures with a mixture of walnut oil and not with linseed oil?"

"I will take your word for it; it is of no interest for me."

"Can you tell me the difference between a picture painted in walnut oil and linseed oil?"

"I certainly can't, and I defy you to do so, too. It is all perfect humbug."

"What is perfect humbug?"

"Perfect humbug whether anybody can tell whether a picture painted four hundred years ago was painted with walnut oil or linseed oil." And in the same vein, Berenson persisted, "It is not interesting on what paper Shakespeare wrote *Hamlet*."

Ringrose briefly interrupted his cross-examination to put Mrs. Hahn on the stand. She read the inscription on the back of her painting triumphantly—first in French and then in English: "Removed from wood to canvas by Acquin in Paris, 1777." The point of the inscription was clearly that—contrary to the testimony of every expert so far—the painting had originally been on wood. Hacquin was known for his unusual achievements in restoration work in the late eighteenth and early nineteenth centuries. About 1800 he transferred a Raphael *Madonna* and, in 1806, Leonardo's *Virgin of the Rocks* in the Louvre from wood to canvas. Berenson, however, was unimpressed. He had not heard of the famous restorer, and, as far as he was concerned, the cracks in the Hahn painting were not those which develop on wood. They were the "spider-web" cracks typical of an aged canvas and not the "little eruptions" that characterized wood.

Several days after Berenson's testimony, on Saturday morning, September 15, the Hahn picture was taken to a private room in the Louvre, where it could be compared first-hand with the Louvre painting. The French government had arranged for both versions of *La Belle Ferronnière* to be removed from their frames, placed side by side on an easel, and subjected to detailed examination by Duveen's experts. Needless to say, the French press devoted a great deal of attention to the whole affair.

Nor was it the first time that sensation surrounded a Leonardo in the Louvre. In 1911 the *Mona Lisa* herself had been lifted from the museum's walls by an Italian house painter. During the painting's absence from Paris, the French taste for romance combined with the *Mona Lisa*'s own mystery to inspire tales of the spell she had cast on the poor, helpless thief. When the culprit was arrested two years later in Florence with the painting tucked away under his hotel bed, he claimed that the *Mona Lisa* rightfully belonged in its city of origin. Upon its recovery by the authorities, the picture was first displayed in the Uffizi and was then accorded a heroine's reception when it was returned to Paris. Thus, with this new Leonardo affair, the French again rose to the occasion and the government itself intervened to facilitate the job of the expert witnesses.

Adolfo Venturi testified on the afternoon of the private viewing in the Louvre. Sixty-seven years old and a distinguished art historian with extensive publications and official honors to his credit, he had come from Rome to give his deposition. Venturi's reasons for rejecting the Hahn painting particularly emphasized questions of light and color. "Leonardo always has a quivering light in his pictures," he declared. The light in the Hahn picture did not quiver.

And the color? Above all, the color was not right. Venturi apologized for his faulty French and read from his notes. "In the flesh of the Hahn picture, we see that the color is very toneless; the flesh in Da Vinci's pictures always has a golden glow; it is flesh which is enveloped by a golden veil, almost bronzed. . . . As to the color in the corsage, we see an amaranthus red; Leonardo's red is a velvety red. . . . In the Hahn picture, on the contrary, the color is an opaque red; it is a red, how shall I express it?—the red of the tunic of one of the king's guardsmen; it is red without any vivacity; it is only the red of a banner, of a flag, of a standard; it is a red which has no depth, which is not velvety . . ." And, as for the yellow in the bodice, Venturi continued; "in the *Belle Ferronnière* in the Louvre, we do not see these crude yellows in the bodice; in the Hahn picture, everything is crude, the colors have no depth and they do not fuse together; they all remain separate."

Asked about Georges Sortais, the elusive French expert who had originally attributed the Hahn painting to Leonardo, Venturi dismissed him as being of no importance at all.

"Do you know Mr. Georges Sortais of Paris?" Levy asked.

"No, I do not know him."

"Did you ever hear him spoken of as an art expert or critic of international reputation?" . . .

"I have told you that I read everything which is written on Leonardo da Vinci. I know everything that is published about him. I have a complete library of it all. Yet Mr. Sortais' name has never reached me, and in all the works dealing with Leonardo, I do not remember that any literature of Mr. Georges Sortais has ever been quoted. If it had been, I should know it."

Ringrose tried to discredit Venturi's testimony—especially with regard to his comments on color—by questioning the precision of his eyesight. "You have defective eyesight, haven't you, professor?"

"No. At the present time my sight is very good, as good as it was in my youth. I have had an operation for cataract."

"If your sight is as good now as it was in your youth, why do you wear spectacles of darkened hue, bluish in color?"

"Because the oculist told me that in a strong light it is better." Venturi stuck to his guns in spite of his sixty-seven years and his cataracts and pronounced the Hahn picture a poor copy.

"The painter who did this," he said, pointing to the work before him, "probably copied from another copy. I do not believe he ever saw the picture by Leonardo. I think he simply laid on the color without endeavoring to understand . . . the very head itself is not properly placed on the shoulders . . . it is a poor, poor thing, this Hahn picture."

Roger Fry, the English formalist critic, also came to Paris to testify on Duveen's behalf. Before becoming a critic, Fry had been a painter and, in the belief that the Italians had discovered the "right" way to paint, he had studied their work from the point of view of craftsmanship. He had also had experience in restoration. By 1923, at the age of fifty-six, Fry was writing for the *Athenaeum*, an English journal devoted to literature, art, and archaeology; he was a director of the *Burlington Magazine*, and had once been the curator of paintings at the Metropolitan Museum. As curator, he remembered, Georges Sortais's name had appeared on a number of certificates of authenticity. None of these, in Fry's opinion, had proved accurate. He retained a decidedly bad impression of Sortais's judgment in matters of attribution.

Fry's famous theory of "significant form," in tune with the cubist developments of his time, substantially influenced his perception of Leonardo's style. For Fry, Cézanne and the cubist revolution represented an epitome of the painter's art. Since Fry's esthetic criticism was oriented more toward the formal than the iconographic problems of art, his criteria in judging between the Hahn picture and the Louvre picture focused largely on differences in "rhythms," "harmonies," the composition of planes. Thus, he testified, "the Hahn painter was a man of very small artistic and creative power, . . . I find throughout all the details of the so-called Hahn picture a want of rhythmic sense, such that I think it improbable that that painter could have conceived so rhythmic a general disposition."

From that general perception of the Hahn picture, Fry proceeded to a formalistic analysis of several details. Linguistically, there is little that is so removed from the precision of legal terminology as this kind of aesthetic description. For example, Fry explained, in the Hahn picture "there is a want of grasp, of imaginative grasp, of the meaning which the artist endeavors to express by the contours. . . . Whereas in the Louvre picture the contour which defines the back of the shoulder of the lady corresponds rhythmically with great exactitude to the line which defines her breast on the other side; I find no such exact correspondences of meaning in the lines on either side of the Hahn picture. . . . The movement of the head is very definitely missed in the Hahn picture, whereas we have it very exactly in the Louvre pic-

ture. . . . I should say that the Louvre picture had movement of planes; I should say that the Hahn picture lacked, altogether, movement of planes."

"Will you try to explain that, please?" asked Duveen's
lawyer.

Fry responded with an attempt to describe the distinction between the actual two-dimensionality of the picture and
the illusion of the third dimension in the figure represented.
"The picture is flat, both of the pictures are flat . . . but
they are both intended to represent a solid object, an object
which has not merely surface, but volume.

"In the Louvre picture, there is the most subtle perception of the structural planes of the head. Those structural
planes, although not marked out one from another by a
sharp line, as is done by the cubist, still, in spite of this very
soft and gentle gradation, are clearly present to the imagination of the painter. There results from that the feeling of
what I can only define as rhythmic relief, the appearance of
one plane passing into another in a beautiful gradation expressive of the whole form. When I turn to the Hahn picture
I find that none of these methods of expressing volume and
solidity are really seriously employed by the artist, because
he lacks plastic imagination to do so; compared with the
Louvre picture, this is flat."

As far as color was concerned, Fry found "no really
clearly established harmony of color" in the Hahn painting,
while in the Louvre painting there was "a very definite and
complete color harmony."

Nor did the Hahn painting reveal the artist's psychological insights as convincingly as did the Louvre painting. The
subtleties of facial expression as represented by the formal
characteristics of the painting in the Louvre "corresponded,"
according to Fry, "with Leonardo da Vinci's intense preoccupation with the psychological expression in his pictures."

"Have you found that Leonardo was intensely preoc-
cupied with psychological expression?" asked Levy.

"Yes, I think there is every reason to assume that."

"Do you find any evidence or trace of that psychology in
the Hahn picture?"

"Of course there is a trace, since it follows roughly the outlines of the Louvre picture; but if I were to express myself as I wish—I hope Mr. Ringrose will not mind—I should say it was a caricature of the expression in the Louvre picture, unconscious, of course; but I should say it missed altogether the essential expressiveness of the eyes and mouth of the Louvre picture."

Despite Fry's emphasis on formalism, he did comment on technique in so far as it influenced his judgment of the date of the Hahn picture. He referred to the technique employed in the Louvre picture as transitional: "that is to say, it belongs to the period of transition from tempera painting to the full oil technique. . . . When the Italian artists first began to use oil, they were familiar only with the tempera technique, so that all they did at first was to change the liquid in their pots from yellow of egg to some kind of oil. The main advantage of the oil over the yolk of egg was that it did not dry quite so quickly, and secondly, instead of one mass being separated from another by a sharp edge, the edges are fused. . . ."

Naturally, the relatively slow-drying oil paint would have appealed to Leonardo's compulsive working procedure. As he had been trained in tempera, like all Italian artists of the fifteenth century, he would have been among the first artists to make the transition to oil.

"Now," continued Fry, "the Hahn picture appears to me, on the other hand, to be painted in paste and not in washes." In other words, the Hahn painter's use of thick, opaque paint from the start, rather than thin paint applied in layers so that it was gradually built up, corresponded to a later stage in the development of oil technique than the period in which Leonardo worked.

On cross-examination, Fry agreed with Ringrose that in his case, the public seemed to appreciate his criticism more than his painting. This admission was followed by a lengthy exchange on art critics in which Ringrose attempted to discredit not only Fry's accomplishments, but also the infallibility of art critics in general. Fry, however, was undaunted.

"I understood you to say," Ringrose asked, "that in the

beginning of your career you had one definite opinion, and now you have a different one. Is that correct?"

"It is a technical question of methods," Fry replied. "What I noticed about the thick, opaque pigment of such modern artists as the Impressionists seemed to me, in power of expressiveness, not to compare with what the Italians had arrived at by more complicated and, I thought, also more methodical processes. At that time I really believed that there was a right way of painting and a wrong way of painting. I honestly confess that I have changed my mind. Now, I no longer think that there is a right way or a wrong way of painting, but every possible way. Every artist has to create his own method of expression in his medium and there is no one way, right or wrong, but every way is right when it is expressive throughout of the idea in the artist's mind."

"Did you ever read John Ruskin?" Ringrose asked, in order to demonstrate that not only do critics change their minds and are thus unreliable, but also that they disagree among themselves.

"Yes, in my extreme youth," Fry said.

"You do not agree with John Ruskin?"

"I think I agreed with him until I went to Italy for the first time, and after that time I do not think I have ever agreed with him."

"And you are still largely in disagreement with his criticisms of Italian paintings?"

"It is a very long time since I read him, but I should say he talked a great deal of nonsense."

"Well, it is a fact, is it not, that you great critics—great and small—differ among yourselves considerably?"

"Yes."

"You differed so much with Sir Charles Holmes," Ringrose pointed out, referring to another of Duveen's experts, "that you and he stood in front of *The Virgin of the Rocks* in the National Gallery in London and almost came to blows about it, did you not?"

"We never came to blows, nothing like that; we have always been very friendly. We discussed it, certainly, and did not agree about it. Really, Mr. Ringrose, it requires a picture of this Hahn quality to bring us all together."

In addition to Fry, Berenson, and Venturi, all men of international renown, Duveen called a variety of other witnesses. F. Schmidt-Degener, director-general of the Amsterdam Museum, testified that he had studied Italian art as a basis for his real area of expertise, seventeenth-century Dutch painting. Most of the seventeenth-century Dutch artists, like Rembrandt, Hals and Vermeer, he asserted, were considerably influenced by the High Renaissance in Italy. "You could not judge Dutch art," Schmidt-Degener said, "without knowing the Italian, too."

On cross-examination, as might be expected, Ringrose used the director's expertise in Dutch painting to imply that his knowledge of Italian art lacked substance. Nevertheless, Schmidt-Degener remained adamant in his rejection of the Hahn picture. It was "mechanical," it lacked finesse, and the figure had been "misinterpreted." "The man who made the Hahn picture did a job," he asserted, while "the man who made the Louvre picture was creating something."

Robert Langton Douglas and Sir Charles Holmes, both of whom had testified the previous year in London from photos, came to Paris for the comparison of the two paintings at the Louvre. Douglas made a few minor corrections in the transcript of his London deposition. He declined to change any of his earlier testimony, as seeing the two pictures together only confirmed his views. Douglas, however, elaborated on aspects of Leonardo's technique. He pointed out that the recommendations on painting which Leonardo made in his *Treatise* were problematical, because several of the manuscripts omit certain passages. Further, he believed, the *Treatise* was most likely compiled by Leonardo's students after his death.

After examining the Hahn picture in person, Sir Charles changed his testimony on only one point. While originally he thought it a nineteenth-century copy, he was now willing to date it as early as the seventeenth century. Other than that, he said, he stood by his London deposition.

Sir Martin Conway also came from London. Resident at Allington Castle, Kent, Sir Martin was a member of Parliament chosen as the representative of seven English universities. He had lectured on art, written on Italian and Flemish artists, and was presently a trustee of the Wallace Collection and the National Portrait Gallery.

Ringrose involved Conway in the question of the identity of the *La Belle Ferronnière*, but Conway was interested only in her style, not in her identity. "If I were writing or studying the life or history of Lucrezia Crivelli and was interested in her as a person," he explained his attitude, "then it would become a matter of very great interest; but as a picture, it does not matter two pins of whom it is a portrait. It is simply a picture."

"Is it not a fact," pursued Ringrose, "that Lucrezia Crivelli, according to your reading, was the mistress both of the duke of Milan and of Francis the First of France?"

"I am sorry to hear it; I was not aware of her peccadillos."

"Do you know anything about Lucrezia Crivelli?"

"I have not the smallest interest in the lady. I am only interested in art."

Not only did Sir Martin refuse to be dragged into a discussion of identity, he also would not enter into a technical analysis of the picture. He was more interested in general impressions—his own in particular—and the Hahn painting did not make a favorable impression on him. "The way I would put it is this," he tried to explain, "an artist is a person who gets some conception of beauty in the form, color and light, which he desires to make visible in a material form in order to transfer to other people that conception which has arisen in his mind. That implies that there exists in somebody else's mind a capacity for appreciation; so that you have in any work of art, on the one side, the creative faculty, and on the other side, the receptive faculty. . . . Now, there is a set of people, artists, whose business it is to work on that creative side, . . . on the other hand, there are the rest of us to whom the picture or work of art is intended to appeal. We have the receptive faculty; . . . my business is entirely on the receptive side; a picture or other work of art appeals to me, quite apart from how it was made; . . . as a completed whole, [it] produces a definite, receptive impression upon my mind. Do you follow?"

"Yes, a metaphysical reception?" Ringrose seemed determined to miss the point.

"When I look at a picture, if it is a real work of art, it produces an effect on me just as a piece of music affects me, and I can't play music, nor do I know how music is constructed; but I can appreciate music, painting, sculpture, advocacy in a court of law. I can appreciate any of these things which give me pleasure, but not from the point of view as though I stood behind the artist, the advocate or whoever it was, and realized how he went to work, how he produced this effect."

"That," pronounced Ringrose triumphantly, "I consider a very fine discourse on metaphysics."

But Sir Martin stood firm. Ringrose might try to denigrate his general impressions as mere metaphysics, but his general impressions were the result of fifty years of cultivation. "I have been endeavoring all my life long," he told the court, "to make myself a person whose opinion is worth something. . . . And if the jury were here they would see me and form their opinion . . . they would size me up."

Not to be omitted from Duveen's international court away from court, France, too, produced a witness. Marcel Marie Leonce Nicolle, presently an art dealer and located, like Duveen himself, in the Place Vendôme, had had extensive museum experience. For three years he had been the curator of the Musée Wicar in Lille, which had a good collection of Italian drawings; he was attaché of the Louvre in the department of paintings and drawings, a post that now was honorary, and he was a member of the Commission for the Conservation and Restoration of the National Museums of France. He had organized the Museum of Clermont-Ferrand, cataloged the Nantes museum and the Crespi collection in Milan which contained works by such artists of Leonardo's school as Ambrogio da Predis, Boltraffio, and Salario. On the whole, Nicolle's assessment of the two versions of *La Belle Ferronnière* corresponded with those of Duveen's other experts. In addition, he was able to shed some light on Georges Sortais, about whom no one else seemed to know much.

"You know Mr. Sortais very well, don't you?" Ringrose asked the witness.

"Yes," Nicolle replied. He had known Sortais for the last twenty years, during which time Sortais was an expert on paintings. But, Nicolle explained, "anybody can be an expert in France. All you have to do is rent a room and say: 'I am an expert.' You can be an expert, if you wish. At the same time he was a dealer, and I have done a lot of business with him. . . ."

Of Sortais's reputation, Nicolle said, "I consider Sortais to be an honest man, and I consider him to be a good connoisseur in generalities and in his own current business."

On redirect questioning by Levy, Nicolle would not admit that Sortais was an authority on Italian painters or on Leonardo. "Can you tell us," asked Levy, "whether you would accept Mr. Sortais's certificate as to a given picture being by Leonardo da Vinci as authoritative on the question of its authenticity?"

"That would not be sufficient reason for me to accept the picture as being by Leonardo. It would only prove that Sortais thinks the picture to be by Leonardo. I might have a different opinion, and I prefer my own."

When Levy asked Nicolle when he had first seen the Hahn picture, his response was most revealing: "I believe—in fact, I am practically sure—that the picture was offered to me for purchase a few years before the war. I was taken to a house in one of the quarters of Paris near the Étoile, and I was shown a picture which, according to my recollection, was this Hahn picture. What leads me to believe that it was this Hahn picture is this detail: that at the same time when the picture was shown to me, there was shown to me a letter on white paper, with *Cabinet de M. Sortais, Peintre, Expert* prés le Tribunal de la Seine, and the address; and two or three lines saying: "I consider that this picture is by Leonardo da Vinci." [signed] Georges Sortais." I know Sortais; I know his letterhead; I know his writing; and I believe that this letter was written by Sortais.

The people who brought the picture to me tried to get me to talk. They asked me whether I thought the picture was a genuine one. I never give my opinion on a picture. They said to me: "You do not think it is by Leonardo." I said nothing. They said: "But we have this certificate from Mr. Georges Sortais." I said: "That may be." They said: "Does this picture interest you?" I said: "It does not interest me." And that was all. That was the only time I saw the Hahn picture before last Saturday, when we saw it together with the Louvre picture at the Louvre Museum."

Aside from Nicolle's recollections and those of Roger Fry as a curator of the Metropolitan Museum, both of which were extremely damaging to Sortais's credibility, nothing more on the subject of the French expert would be heard in court for several years.

Duveen's final Paris witness was Arthur Phillans Laurie, the principal of Edinburgh's Heriot-Watt College. The dealer called Laurie in order to counteract the very impresion Ringrose had tried to make that art critics based their judgments on ethereal metaphysics. Laurie was a scientist; he lectured in physics, chemistry, and the history of pigments. He was the author of books on paints, pigments, artists' materials and artistic techniques. He was also very thorough in his attentions to the two versions of La Belle Ferronnière under discussion.

On September 8, in the presence of Conrad Hug, Laurie had examined the Hahn painting at Duveen's office. Because he found a standard magnifying glass insufficient, he went back to Scotland for more scientific instruments. When he returned to Paris in time for the Louvre comparison, he brought with him a high-powered microscope, which fit onto a traveling rod so that it could be passed across the surface of a picture.

Laurie's scientific assessment confirmed the aesthetic judgments of all the other witnesses. He repeated—in more technical terms—the transitional nature of Leonardo's period with respect to the use of oil paint. In the earliest stages of its use—contemporary with Leonardo—artists tended to remain under the influence of the older, tempera technique in which egg yolk was still the basis of the medium. The cracks of the Louvre picture ran in parallel lines and then at right angles with short, wriggly ones in between as one would expect of a picture on wood. Furthermore, Laurie said, since the *Mona Lisa* had cracked in a similar way, he concluded that the pictures had been painted similarly. The Hahn painting had cracked differently. The colors of the Louvre picture were low-toned, while those of the Hahn picture were painted in a higher key, although Laurie was unable to detect any dating pigments in either. Nevertheless, he was prepared to swear that the Hahn picture postdated the seventeenth century, and that, from a chemical point of view, both pictures could not possibly be from the same studio. "The one picture cancels out the other," he declared. With the conclusion of Laurie's deposition, Duveen's "dress muster" of international art experts was over.

With all the publicity accorded the case, the Hahns apparently wanted to hedge their bets with the French press. They did not wish to appear to be attacking the authenticity of the Louvre painting and at the same time to be proclaiming theirs to be an original Leonardo. The only possible rational explanation for such a stance is that *both* pictures were by Leonardo, a claim summarily rejected by all nine experts. On September 8, after Berenson's deposition and before the private viewing at the Louvre and Laurie's examination of their painting, a letter appeared in the French newspaper *Le Matin*. The letter was read in translation and placed in the record during Nicolle's deposition:

> Mme. Hahn, owner of the *Belle Ferronnière* that was brought back from America to France, wishes to correct the impression that seems to be existing amongst

the Parisian Reporters that she is trying to prove that the painting in question is authentic, whilst the *Belle Ferronnière* belonging to the Louvre Museum is not.

We can assure that, never at any time, have we doubted the authenticity of this marvelous painting, as we are certain that it is authentic and very fine. Our only objection is that our painting is equally from Leonardo da Vinci's brush and, when our case will come before the New York Courts, we shall have all the necessary proofs to corroborate our statements.

We must once more remind you that it is not on our own initiative that we have brought our picture to France for comparison with the similar picture which is in the Louvre; this suggestion has been made by Sir Joseph Duveen, and it is he who is responsible for the sending of our picture. We agreed to give satisfaction to Mr. Joseph Duveen whenever he should desire an expertise of our picture to be made. The former expertises that he has already made, have not proved that our *Belle Ferronnière* was such a flagrant copy as he was wont to declare. Our wish is to reestablish the facts through the intermediary of your excellent paper. We have never personally asked for our picture to be compared with that of the Louvre; we have never, at any time, doubted its authenticity or its value, and we do not wish the French public to think that we are in discussion with the Louvre authorities. Our only claim is that the *Belle Ferronnière* which we own, is authentic and Leonardo da Vinci's own handiwork, and that it is for Mr. Joseph Duveen only to prove the contrary.

[signed] Harry J. Hahn[8]

Needless to say, Ringrose was not pleased. The letter could well prove damaging to his case. He saw to it, therefore, that his own comments were also put on record: "Mr. Hahn," he said crossly, "has no more to do with this than Francis the First has. . . . Mr. Hahn may have written; . . . he should not have done so; he is a better soldier than a critic. . . . *Mrs.* Hahn has not written to any newspaper. . . . I discussed the matter both with Captain

Hahn and his wife . . . *she* did not write the letter . . . *he* did . . . her attitude was this: as a Frenchwoman she was not in her own country for the purpose of causing trouble for the Louvre authorities. . . . She loved France . . . I say that the article which Mr. Hahn fathered was very apt to mislead everyone as to Mrs. Hahn's attitude, and I am going to give him the mischief for it. . . ."

The following year, on March 28, the case of *Hahn* v. *Duveen* was marked off the New York County Supreme Court trial term calendar; it remained off the calendar for five years.

PARIS, 1927

Nearly three years later, on January 13, 1927, Duveen's attorney submitted a review of the witnesses to the court. Georges Sortais was about to surface, and Duveen blocked an attempt by Mrs. Hahn to have the court accept letters rogatory from Sortais. Duveen preferred to have Sortais's testimony taken orally so that he could be cross-examined.

From June 27 to July 27, Georges Sortais gave his deposition through an interpreter at a Paris law office. Levy was still acting for Duveen, and attorneys Manly and de Lacey for Mrs. Hahn. The Hahns and the Hugs—and the Hahn's painting—also attended.

Georges Sortais, sixty-seven years old, took the stand. He lost no time in pointing out that "if a man is to be able to judge paintings, he must be an artist and not a *littérateur*." Georges Sortais was a painter. Bouguereau was his master, and he had copied paintings in the Louvre. "I sold all these copies," he said, "and do not know where they are." As an expert, Sortais began his career at public auctions at the Galerie Georges-Petit and the Hôtel Drouot. In 1898, at the request of several "illustrious painters," notably Bouguereau, Sortais was appointed expert to the department of paintings at the Tribunal of First Instance of the Seine. In the course of his career, he had expertized thousands of pictures among which were many for the Newport home of William K. Vanderbilt as well as for Duveen himself. He had also had extensive experience as an expert witness in art lawsuits.

Turning to the Hahn version of *La Belle Ferronnière*, Sortais testified that he had first seen it on December 13, 1916, at the Paris home of the Marquis de Chambure. His first impression that the picture was a genuine Leonardo was confirmed, he said, by more detailed examination. "The construction of the figure," he maintained, "in conjunction with the correctness of its drawing are inattackable [sic]; everything in it is expressed with certainty. . . . Nowhere in the face does any weakness manifest itself, mastery is everywhere dominant." In addition, there was no doubt but that the picture had originally been painted on wood. This was evident from the "thousands of tiny, fine cracks which are to be seen from top to bottom, where the wood has worked through." He thus "conscientiously attributed the painting to the brush of Leonardo da Vinci." Now, nearly eleven years later, Sortais submitted his certificate of authenticity to the court.

Finally it was Levy's turn to cross-examine. Sortais became remarkably recalcitrant. He steadfastly refused to identify the Louvre painting from the photograph. "I have never been in the habit of judging any picture according to a photograph," he declared piously. Nor would he identify its museum label number, although he did pronounce it a student's copy of the Hahn picture.

Levy directed a set of questions toward Sortais's familiarity with the Louvre picture at the time he certified the Hahn picture. The French expert was not cooperative, but his answers were most revealing.

"Did you see [*La Belle Ferronnière* in the Louvre] in 1916?" asked Levy.

"I do not recollect; it was the war, you know," Sortais replied.

"At the time you gave that certificate, did you examine this picture in the Louvre called *La Belle Ferronnière*?"

"No, not at all; first of all, the pictures were in Toulouse, they were not in the Louvre."

"At that time, you had not recently seen the picture in the Louvre, had you?"

"I did not need to see it."

"When you saw the Hahn picture in December 1916, did it occur to you that there was any similarity between that picture and the Louvre picture with which you say you are so familiar?"

"A similarity of subject, yes, but I was not called upon to give any attention to the Louvre picture, in order not to be under the influence of any other impression than that which I had when looking at the Hahn picture; for when I am called upon to examine a picture, whatever it may be, I do not wish to be subject to any influence whatever, from any point of view. . . ."

"Has it never occurred to you, before or since," persisted Levy, "that one of these two pictures was a copy . . . ?"

"I am convinced that the similar picture which is at the Louvre is entirely inferior to the Hahn picture."

Asked if he were acquainted with the provenance of the Louvre painting, Sortais replied that he never occupied himself with such matters. "I rely above all on my own judgment. If there are favorable origins, royal or otherwise, so much the better. . . . I know more than one picture which has been sold and of which a copy has remained, made in order to replace the original, and the pedigrees have remained in the hands of the former owner."

Levy read him an account of the painting's history, from which it emerged that the two pictures were not exactly the same size. According to Sortais, this was because the Hahn painting had been cut in order to fit the interior decoration of the royal apartments.

Asked about the opinions of other art critics, Sortais was uninterested. "Generally speaking, I never read the literature of the art critics," he declared.

Did he read anything about the paintings he certified, asked Levy. No, Sortais did not.

"Then you do not believe in books, do you?"

"No, not in all books."

"Have you written any books yourself?"

"No, I have not written a book in my life. . . ."

"You say you know the critics' books perfectly well? Is that what you said, that you know the critics' books perfectly well? Did you say that?" Levy was exasperated.

"No, I know the spirit in which they are written." Sortais would not be ruffled. Furthermore, Sortais testified, he himself was "the only man that ever lived whose opinion as to the authorship and authenticity of an Italian picture of the fifteenth century" he would give weight to.

In view of such blanket self-confidence, Sortais's apparent ignorance of even the most famous Renaissance artists was colossal. He did not know the century in which Verrocchio lived, or that Leonardo had been his student. "I have only to consult my reference book or dictionary," he replied to all questions of fact.

"Do you know whether Leonardo da Vinci was a pupil of Verrocchio or not?" Levy repeated for the fifth time.

"That is of no importance to me," Sortais snapped impatiently. Nor would he discuss Baldovinetti, Perugino, Donatello, Piero della Francesca, or Raphael. His brain, he said, was not an encyclopedia. "This has nothing to do with this case," fumed the French expert, "I shall not reply. As far as I am concerned, I have said everything I have to say. I have nothing to add and nothing to withdraw, and I shall not return again."

Sortais did return, however, at the urging of Mrs. Hahn's lawyer, only to refuse to discuss any painting at all unless he stood in person before it. Did he remember Leonardo's *St. Jerome* in the Vatican Museum, Levy asked. Since Sortais had never been to Rome, he did not. Did he remember the artist's *Adoration of the Magi* in Florence? He did not; he needed only to consult his dictionary if he were interested.

Asked about the techniques of painting, Sortais replied like a custodian of the divine mysteries, "I do not wish, I will not, divulge the secrets of the processes of painting, which are personal to me, which belong to me."

And finally, Sortais announced in concluding his testimony, the whole lawsuit was a "frame-up" by Duveen, who was trying to discredit him, an act of revenge for Sortais's testimony against him in previous court cases.

NEW YORK, 1929

At long last, in the first weeks of 1929, the case of *Hahn v. Duveen* prepared to go to trial. By early February the jury had been selected; it consisted of twelve men who readily admitted to knowing nothing at all about Leonardo da Vinci. There were two agents, two real estate men, two artists, a hotel clerk, an accountant, a shirt manufacturer, a ladies-wear salesman, an upholsterer and one man who was unemployed. Parisians were reported to have been highly amused that the celebrated affair would finally be decided by a jury of nonexperts.

Most of the courtroom time in the eighteen-day trial was taken up with reading the experts' depositions. Presiding Justice Black pointed out the rarity of this type of case which was trying the law of "slander of title." Duveen's lawyers contended that a painting could not be slandered because it had no feelings. Mrs. Hahn's lawyer, S.L. Miller, argued that Duveen maliciously killed the sale of her painting because he was not the salesman. Furthermore, Miller pointed out, no one had tried to buy her painting since.

On February 5, the opening day of the trial, Duveen took the stand. He had never made a mistake since his youth, he asserted with characteristic self-confidence. As for Leonardo, the artist was not in the habit of making copies of his work. The Hahn version of *La Belle Ferronnière* spent her first day on trial wrapped in a paper bag, propped up against the court railing, awaiting the moment when she would be exhibited to her American jury.

The following day—the day before the bottom dropped out of the stock market—*La Belle Ferronnière* was unveiled and placed on an easel with a daylight lamp flooding her face. Unlike her viewing at the Louvre, however, she sat alone in the New York courtroom. The French government had denied permission for the Louvre version to be sent to New York, thereby making comparisons from photographs necessary.

Duveen was questioned extensively about his dealings in art. The works that he sold, he said, were always genuine. He told the jury that in his opinion the Louvre picture was by Leonardo, even though some experts had attributed it to Boltraffio. Duveen himself had once deferred to the Boltraffio attribution, but had later changed his mind. He discoursed on the chemistry of paintings, and on color, and demonstrated his ability to distinguish between Leonardo's two versions of *The Annunciation*. He felt that the Hahn portrait was too fat and most likely painted in eighteenth-century France. He explained the organic nature of Leonardo's style and pointed out that the right eye of the lady on the easel seemed pasted on her face rather than a natural, living form. Leonardo's works, he declared, are alive, but the Hahn picture had "one dead eye."

"How about the right eye?" he was asked.

"It's dead," he replied sadly shaking his head, "very dead." As for the $250,000 sale which had fallen through, Duveen scoffed. A genuine Leonardo would be worth $3,000,000.

"We're learning an awful lot about painting," the juror who was the accountant reportedly observed to the shirtmaker, as the court adjourned after the third day.

The press enjoyed itself thoroughly throughout the proceedings. On February 10, the Sunday edition of *The New York Times* predicted a hard week ahead for Duveen in the witness box. "It will be equally hard for *La Belle Ferronnière* herself," continued the report, "both in that version of her that decorates the Louvre and in that which daily looks frostily upon Justice Black's court and sets an example in composure for all."

Throughout Duveen's testimony, the art world urged him to fight for the freedom of art criticism. To his contention in court that he had not only a right but also a duty to comment publicly on paintings, Justice Black ruled that this did not exempt him from the practical consequences of doing so.

Immediately after Duveen stepped down, Conrad Hug took the stand. The Midwestern dealer was reported to have mortgaged his Kansas City home to support the continuance of the lawsuit. His small, frail, and sickly appearance—a sharp contrast to Duveen's vigorous arrogance—aroused considerable sympathy from the jury. Hug described his negotiations with one Jesse Clyde Nichols, former president of the Kansas City Art Institute. "I told him," said Hug, "that we had a chance to get a wonderful painting for Kansas City . . . it was by Leonardo da Vinci—and I had convinced myself that the expert, Georges Sortais, was qualified to expertise a painting of such great value . . . I told him that it would be a great acquisition to have Kansas City, the people of Kansas City, buy this painting for Kansas City. . . ."

"And did you name a price at which you would be willing to sell it to the Kansas City Institute?"

"Yes . . . two hundred and fifty thousand dollars."

"Now what did Mr. Nichols say to you, Mr. Hug?"

"He said, 'Yes, we will buy that painting if it is what you say it is, . . . and is by Leonardo da Vinci, we will buy it.' I saw Mr. Nichols the following Monday."

"And what conversation did you have with him?"

"When I came into his office he said, 'Mr. Hug, I guess your painting is not what you thought it was or said it was. The newspapers state that it is a copy, and of course, we could not entertain to purchase a copy for our art institute. . . . With that stain upon this picture, coming from an important art dealer in New York, we will not dare to be interested any further in it."

"Did Mr. Nichols say anything to you about what he would do if Mr. Duveen would retract his statement?"

"He said that if we could get Mr. Duveen to make a retraction, that they will buy the painting."

Clearly Hug's testimony seemed to confirm the damage done by Duveen's statements.

Mrs. Hahn rushed to join Hug's defense of her injured picture. She had spent nine years, she testified, collecting evidence to support her claims, and she referred the jury to Sortais's deposition, which was duly read in court. Much was made of his assertion that the Hahn painting had been cut to suit the proportions of the French royal apartments. Mrs. Hahn's counsel prepared to arrange for scientific testing of her picture. A Dr. William Diefenbach X-rayed the painting, and his results were compared with X-rays of the Paris picture. The comparison yielded little that was definite since the X-rays recorded only the density of paint rather than clearly recognizable objects.

Mrs. Hahn repudiated her husband's letter of 1923 to *Le Matin* and produced a new expert for the court. Vadim Chernoff was a Russian artist. Cracking numerous eggs, he demonstrated the technique of tempera painting to the jury. Ostentatiously bored, Duveen read the paper during the performance.

Duveen's experts' depositions were read. Only Captain Langton Douglas appeared in person. When he testified that there was a painting by Leonardo in a private collection in Ireland, Duveen waved his gold pencil in the air, as if bidding at an auction. "I must have it" he shouted across the courtroom. The jury, apparently more interested in the testimony than in Duveen, paid strict attention as Douglas discoursed on various aspects of artistic expertise. "The twelve jurymen," reported *The New York Times* on February 20, "followed his lecture so intently that their twelve faces were a study in parallel position." Meanwhile, *La Belle Ferronnière* was shuttled back and forth between Mrs. Hahn's attorney, Douglas, and the jury, with Mr. Hahn closely supervising her every move.

One key figure remained to be questioned in the case: Jesse Clyde Nichols, whom Hug had so lengthily quoted in demonstrating the damage done by Duveen's statements to the *New York World*. An affidavit signed by Nichols denying Hug's assertions was unacceptable to Mrs. Hahn's attorney. He thus obtained the court's permission for a delegation of court representatives to go to Kansas City and take an oral deposition from Nichols, who was sick in bed, unable to travel.

On February 23 Nichols testified in Kansas City. He had been president of the Art Institute from 1920 to 1928. In 1920, however, the institute, which today is one of America's finest regional art museums, was just getting started, and there was little money to spend on major acquisitions. Sometime in the summer of that year, Nichols said, Conrad Hug contacted him several times about the painting by Leonardo. He never at any time agreed to buy the painting for the institute. Nor did the institute have the funds or the credit to pay for the painting. Nichols did concede that he thought it would have been desirable for Kansas City to own such a picture and that he himself would willingly contribute to its purchase if it were genuine. He did not even remember reading or hearing of Duveen's remarks. Finally, Nichols testified, should the painting now prove to be authentic, he would still like to see Kansas City own it.

Further evidence from Kansas City bolstered Duveen's case. The art editor and music critic for the *Kansas City Star* testified to having voiced doubts about the painting as early as January 1920, five months before the publication of Duveen's comments in the *New York World*. A Kansas City restorer of old paintings confirmed the views of all of Duveen's experts, asserting that the Hahn picture had never been on wood.

Following the summations and denial of Duveen's second request for dismissal, Justice Black addressed the jury. It would have to decide whether Duveen made his statement in good faith, whether the Hahn painting was indeed by Leonardo da Vinci, and who was a reliable witness. "You are to determine just how much of an expert a witness is," Black charged, "and you will determine that by his knowledge, his experience, his study, and his ability to assimilate and apply this knowledge, study, and experience." This proved no small task for a jury completely ignorant of Leonardo da Vinci.

Nor did the art world sit silently by for the duration of the trial. Before the jury rendered its verdict, Forbes Watson, editor of *The Arts* magazine, who had himself been an expert witness in the Brancusi trial, wrote that New York's greatest exhibition during the month of February, 1929, took place not in an art gallery but in the Supreme Court.[9] His comments on Kansas City were not flattering. "At the time when the Hahn portrait was on exhibition in an art store in Kansas City," wrote Watson, "the Kansas City Institute was about the poorest excuse for a museum in existence." Was it the magic name of Leonardo da Vinci, he speculated, which had aroused the wealthy citizens of Kansas City who had hitherto been unwilling to acquire any pictures of consequence? Or was it the intrinsic beauty of the Hahn portrait? For, if so, she had not changed her appearance since 1920. Watson suggested that the painting be subjected to impartial tests. If the painting were to be certified a genuine Leonardo, the editor was certain that Sir Joseph himself would buy it at a far higher price than Kansas City. "I can't believe," he concluded, "that anyone would want to sell a picture unless it was exactly what the experts represented it as being. That would be such a wicked thing to do."

At 3:30 A.M., the jury emerged from seclusion and reported that it was unable to agree. Justice Black promptly sent them back and told them to try again.

On Sunday, March 3, after a fourteen-hour deadlock and with no resolution in sight, Justice Black dismissed the jury. The members of the jury had voted nine to three in favor of Mrs. Hahn. They agreed that Duveen had maliciously intended to stop the sale of the painting but disagreed on the credibility of his experts. One juror later reported believing that the experts testified in order to protect Duveen. Throughout the trial, Mrs. Hahn's attorney endeavored to create the impression that Duveen controlled an international art cabal which would respond to his every whim. Apparently most of the jury was convinced.

The art world rocked on its heels. Press comment on the outcome was widespread. *The New York Times* reported that the jurymen had become suspicious of the connoisseurs. The *New York World* wrote that "the law had not covered itself with glory," the issue of free speech was involved, and simply because Duveen's opinion proved to be worth more than anyone else's, was no reason to penalize him. In addition, the *World* pointed out, Mrs. Hahn may not have made her $250,000, but it could "be argued with equal cogency that [Duveen] prevented the Kansas City Art Institute from *losing* $250,000." The *Evening Post* thought Leonardo would have enjoyed the proceedings. "How can anyone outside of a comic opera expect the authenticity of an old painting to be settled by a lawsuit?" the paper queried. "Judgment upon masterpieces must be a final distillation of the taste and knowledge of generations of artistic opinion," it asserted wisely and concluded that "the jury did well to dodge all these questions, quit, and go home." Forbes Watson also had something to say. "The gentlemen of the jury," he declared, had been persuaded by Hug's pathetic appeal to their sympathies, by the impression that experts are "musty old scholars," and by an objection to experts being paid for the work they do. "The disagreement of the jury in the Hahn-Duveen case," Watson wrote, "demolished the possibilities of bringing to a hilarious conclusion the season's maddest extravaganza. It did not seen possible that a farce which had fascinated its audience for so long could go completely flat. . . . What must the ghost of Leonardo have thought if it visited Part VII of the Supreme Court! In fact, it did and behaved very badly. I heard it laughing when one of the lawyers was lulling the jury to sleep with an "expert's" long deposition. I may be mistaken. Perhaps it was crying."[10]

Justice Black, meanwhile, decided that the case would have to be retried. He held that there had been "sufficient evidence before the jury to enable them to render a verdict."

In art circles, Duveen's reputation had barely been scratched. On March 9, one week after the trial's uncertain conclusion, British Prime Minister Stanley Baldwin appointed Duveen a trustee of the National Gallery in London.

NEW YORK, 1930

The New York Supreme Court set the retrial of *Hahn* v.

Duveen for May 15. Tantalizing reports hinted at sensational new evidence gathered by Mrs. Hahn's family in France and Italy over the past year. It was rumored that the new facts would not only discredit Duveen's experts but also have a devastating effect on the international art business. "It would seem," declared the *Arts Digest* on April 1, 1930, "that the art world, to protect itself, might very well raise a fund of $5,000,000, if necessary, and use it to 'close' the case between these two stubborn antagonists."

Duveen changed his attorneys. He dropped his old firm and hired Max Steuer, reputedly New York's most successful criminal lawyer. Sir Joseph himself was recovering from a hernia operation, and complications had set in. He asked to have the trial postponed. A court-appointed physician, however, found the dealer "in excellent physical condition" and said he might appear in court in a month.

Conrad Hug, already in poor health during the first trial, was now dead.

Even the unsinkable Duveen seemed to lack enthusiasm for a new trial. Rather than sign on for a repeat performance, Duveen settled out of court on April 11. He paid Mrs. Hahn $60,000, and, as far as the law was concerned, the matter was closed.

EPILOGUE: KANSAS CITY, 1946

The Hahns were a persistent family. In 1946 Harry J. Hahn, the World War I aviator whose French bride had received a painting as a wedding present, became an author. He published *The Rape of La Belle*, a book which roundly accused none other than Duveen, now Lord Duveen of Millbank, of that crime. Dedicated to one "Conrad Hug, Sr. (1869-1929), A Loyal Friend, An Honest Art Dealer," the work was the culmination of fifteen years of Hahn's own research in the National Archives of France.

Hahn leveled a vitriolic attack at his wife's opponents during the trial. Duveen, he said, headed an international plot by art dealers to control the market, and Duveen's array of experts, no better than "fortune-tellers, clairvoyants and two-bit prophets" were mere puppets in his "defense clan." Berenson, declared Hahn, was the "major-domo of the Duveen clan."

Perhaps the most significant aspect of *The Rape of La Belle* was its introduction, written not by Hahn, but by Thomas Hart Benton, the American regional painter. Benton did not concern himself with the authenticity of anyone's *Belle Ferronnière*; he had another ax to grind. Benton joined Hahn in his tirade against the art business, dealers, rich collectors, and critics who hypnotize themselves "by stringing meaningless words together." But more particularly, Benton was interested in the state of American art. He was tired, he said, of Old Masters and European tradition; the worst of the art business was that it imported art from other cultures, thereby suppressing the reality of American art. In Benton's view Europe had not produced any art since 1850, and he denounced New York's famous Armory Show of 1913 as symptomatic of the failure of American art. He hoped that Hahn's book would reveal the commercialism of the American art world, dominated as he saw it by "tricky European marketeers," and thus liberate the American artist to develop a style of his own.

The Rape of La Belle concluded with Harry Hahn's outraged prophecy of the art world's end: "The art world will long remember the famous case of *Hahn* v. *Duveen* as the sorry instance of a clan of art experts resorting to every possible distortion of the truth and fair play in the futile defense of a rich, powerful and unscrupulous plush-art dealer whose hands were none too clean. The day Sir Joseph Duveen attempted to damn into oblivion a fine and beautiful painting by Leonardo da Vinci, which he had never seen, simply because of his egoistic desire to dominate everything and everybody in the art world, was indeed a significant day for the plush hook art business. It fatally marked the beginning of its end!"[11]

1947

A reviewer for *Art Digest* recommended *The Rape of*

La Belle as a thorough exposé of the art business. F.T. of *American Artist* wrote: "It should be required reading for every art student, gallery director, museum curator—and above all, for the prospective buyer of 'antique' art."

CHAPTER FOUR

TRAITOR OR / FORGER?/ "Van Meegeren v. Vermeer"

"Fools!" Han van Meegeren lashed out at his captors after six weeks of steady interrogation in an Amsterdam jail. "You are fools like the others! I sold no great national treasure—I painted it myself!" Van Meegeren's startling assertion on July 12, 1945, unleashed a whirlwind investigation that ended with the most intriguing forgery trial in Europe's history.

The circumstances surrounding Van Meegeren's arrest and subsequent trial were very much determined by conditions in Europe—and especially in Holland—immediately following World War II. The late spring of 1945 marked the end of a war which had devastated most of Europe. By May 1, the Germans were warning their own people of impending defeat. Dachau had been captured, the Soviet army was in Berlin, and Munich had fallen to the United States Seventh Army. In the next few weeks the Germans surrendered in Italy, Austria, Bavaria, Denmark, and Holland. The suicides of Hitler and Goebbels were announced, and Mussolini and his mistress were buried in unmarked paupers' graves in Milan.

The closing days of the war took their toll in Holland. Prince Bernhard reported incidents in three Dutch cities in which Germans fired at civilians celebrating the war's end.

Rotterdam suffered a breakdown of all facilities and reported scores of starvation victims. In Amsterdam, too, citizens were dying of malnutrition.

Meanwhile, Reichsmarschall Hermann Goering, the man who believed himself to be the most cultured of the Nazi leaders, was busy with his art collection. He had spent the month of April cataloging and packing his works of art; they had been kept in the Bavarian castle at Veldenstein some twenty-five miles northeast of Nuremberg. Seeing the writing on the wall, Goering ordered a special "art train" equipped with thermostats for proper temperature control. Paintings, hidden by day in a railroad tunnel, were loaded onto the train by night.

Goering's plans for the $200,000,000 art collection looted from Germany's defeated enemies were rudely interrupted by a United States Seventh Army task force. They stumbled upon a major art cache at Neuschwanstein castle, itself occupied in the nineteenth century by Mad King Ludwig of Bavaria. More art was found in a sealed, bombproof tunnel in nearby mountains. Here works of art, many of them from the French Rothschild collection, were housed on shelves of steel and concrete. Walter Hofer, Goering's chief art dealer, explained to members of the Seventh Army task force that the works had been obtained perfectly legally and for the benefit of the German people. Despite Hofer's assertions, it soon became evident that considerable pressure had been applied in the acquisition of Goering's collection and full value rarely, if ever, had been paid for a work. At Nuremberg the following year, Goering himself was to testify that he took the art—especially from Paris—in order to protect it from air raids.

So remarkable was the stolen art recovered that, on May 20, 1945, the American 101st Airborne Division mounted an exhibit devoted to Goering's "collection." Held at a requisitioned hotel in the small Bavarian town of Unterstein, near Berchtesgaden, the show included some fifty Cranachs, five Rembrandts, a Velasquez, Van Dycks, several Impressionists, and a spectacular array of gold and jewelry.

Also displayed at the exhibition was a Dutch painting, *Christ and the Woman Taken in Adultery* (fig. 12), signed I.V. Meer—Jan Vermeer of Delft. The seventeenth-century baroque painter and contemporary of Rembrandt lived and died in almost total obscurity. Like the others in the group known as "Little Dutch Masters," Vermeer's best-known paintings were small, exquisite interior, street scenes, and portraits. Vermeer, however, was by far the greatest of the Little Dutch Masters in his subtle representation of light and in the degree of psychological insight with which he endowed his figures. His interior scenes, in particular, are masterful studies of tension and introspection, nearly always projecting universal themes which seem to absorb the outer world into the picture (cf. fig. 13).

The Woman Taken in Adultery, though bearing the signature of one of Holland's most esteemed artists, was not a familiar example of Vermeer's oeuvre. Since the extant paintings by Vermeer were so limited in number, the discovery of an unknown example of his work naturally aroused a great deal of interest. Where had it been and how had Goering acquired it? An investigation led the Allies to Nazi records of the painting's acquisition. Three years earlier, in 1942, Goering had paid more than today's equivalent of $1,000,000 for this hitherto-unknown Vermeer. One of the Allies' aims in this early postwar period was to find and return works of art which had been looted by the Nazis. In their search for collaborators, the Allies also hoped to trace the provenance of the works which had fallen into Nazi possession. Naturally, the discovery of virtually any painting by Vermeer, an undisputed national treasure of Holland, would prompt the most rigorous investigation.

The Allies soon established the sequence of transactions that brought *The Adulteress* into Goering's possession. Walter Hofer had purchased the painting from a Bavarian banker, Aloys Miedl. Since Miedl had an Amsterdam office, he was likely to be aware of important events occurring in Holland. In due course he heard that a Vermeer had come onto the market and was in the possession of Dutch art

FIGURE 12. Han van Meegeren, *Christ and the Woman Taken in Adultery* (also, *The Adulteress*). Dienst Voor 'S Rijks verspreide kunstvoorwerpen, The Hague. Courtesy Rijksinspecteur voor Roerende Monumenten.

FIGURE 13. Johannes Vermeer, *Young Woman with a Water Jug.*
The Metropolitan Museum of Art. Gift of Henry G. Marquand,
1889.

dealer Rienstra van Strijvesande. The dealer, in turn, had received the painting from Han van Meegeren, a wealthy if eccentric figure on the Amsterdam scene. A reckless spender and a lavish entertainer, at the age of fifty-six, Van Meegeren was a heavy drinker and morphine addict. A property owner of some consequence, by the end of the war he had over fifty houses in Amsterdam. Known also as a sometime art dealer and collector himself, Van Meegeren had achieved a certain reputation as an illustrator and painter. His most popular picture was a portrait of Princess Juliana's pet deer (fig. 14). Van Meegeren was fully aware of the dangers of trafficking with the Germans and had specifically warned van Strijvesande against allowing *The Adulteress* to fall into enemy hands. Obviously van Strijvesande paid no attention because, as is well documented, the painting soon found its way into Goering's collection only to be recovered by the Allies when the war was over.

As a result of the Allied investigation, on May 28, 1945, two officers from the Netherlands Field Security Force called on Van Meegeren at his Keizergracht mansion. They were interested in *The Adulteress*, they informed him. Even though the painting had gone from van Strijvesand to the Germans, the officers had come to ask Van Meegeren about its provenance. Van Meegeren replied that he had obtained the picture from an impoverished but aristocratic Italian family; the seller did not want his identity disclosed. More than that Van Meegeren would not say. The story was not good enough for the Dutch authorities and, the following day, Van Meegeren was arrested for dealing with the enemy.

He spent six weeks in jail deprived of morphine and under continual interrogation before answering a single question. When he finally made the startling assertion that he and not Vermeer had painted *The Adulteress*, the police refused to believe him. Nor did Van Meegeren stop at *The Adulteress*. He mentioned several more paintings by Vermeer and de Hooch (also a Little Dutch Master) then in famous collections, which he said he had painted. All in all, he said, he had sold six forged Vermeers and two de Hoochs. Three other

FIGURE 14. Han van Meegeren, *Princess Juliana's Pet Deer.*
Courtesy Gerard Bywaard.

Vermeers, a Frans Hals, and a Terborch, had never been sold. Of these claims, the most outrageous was that he had painted the *Supper at Emmaus* (fig. 15) that the eminent Boymans Museum in Rotterdam had acquired as a Vermeer in 1937 for today's equivalent of over $500,000.

Nevertheless, the police X-rayed *The Adulteress* and found an underpainting described by Van Meegeren. With this piece of evidence supporting the prisoner's claim, the police challenged him to produce a convincing copy of Vermeer's *Emmaus*. Van Meegeren went them one better and offered to paint an original picture in the style of Vermeer, technically and intellectually a more difficult task than mere imitation. In addition to supplies of drugs, he would need to be provided with Vermeer's pigments and the other materials used in the previous forgeries. The police agreed and, under constant supervision, Van Meegeren returned to his studio and went to work. Toward the end of that July, having decided on a religious subject, *The Young Christ Teaching in the Temple*, and a large canvas, Van Meegeren began the painting which would take him two months to complete.

More than eight years earlier, in a villa in the South of France, a bitter but determined Van Meegeren was at work on another painting in the style and technique of Vermeer. This project, which reflected the vengeful, paranoid split in Van Meegeren's personality, was the result of a long process of failure, rejection, and real and imagined inadequacy in his self-image.

Han van Meegeren, born in 1889 in Deventer, was the son of a rigidly disciplinarian Catholic father and a more imaginative but unassertive mother. He alone, of his four brothers and sisters, showed an early inclination to draw. His father promptly set out to squelch what artistic talents Van Meegeren may have had and this, together with the boy's guilty awareness of his own frail build, did not bode well for healthy mental development. Once in high school, Van Meegeren found some encouragement for his creative ambitions from his art teacher, Bartus Korteling. As an artist, Kor-

GURE 15. Han van Meeg-
en, *Supper at Emmaus*.
useum   Boymans—van
uningen, Rotterdam.

teling was traditional, but well versed in technical skills which he imparted to his new pupil. Despite the persistent opposition of his father, who demonstrated his hostility by destroying his son's pictures, Van Meegeren determined to pursue an artistic career. Nevertheless, following his father's orders, at the age of eighteen Han entered the Institute of Technology in Delft to study architecture. Here he met the woman who would become his first wife, bear him two children, and urge him to become a professional artist.

Van Meegeren's early career as an artist netted him a certain amount of superficial recognition. He won medals in Delft and was offered a job as professor of art by the Hague Academy, which he declined. His critical successes, however, tended to be restricted to the fashionable and the social. Although technically competent, his style lacked conviction and direction. He left many canvases unfinished and soon turned much of his energy to commercial art and illustration. His personal life, too, began to deteriorate as he became increasingly promiscuous and alcoholic. In 1923 he and his wife were divorced; six years later he married Johanna Oerlemans, the former wife of an art critic, de Boer, and Van Meegeren's mistress of several years. Throughout this period of personal decline, Van Meegeren seems to have transferred his paternal hostilities onto one group of art-world authorities: the critics. They refused to acknowledge his importance, Van Meegeren decided, not only because they were incompetent, but because they were out to get him. He saw himself as a genius victimized by a critics' plot to banish him forever to obscurity and to deprive him of his well-deserved acclaim. Eventually he aired his antagonism, openly publishing his hostile views towards the critics.

The critics, in fact, were not wrong in their judgment of Van Meegeren's work. As a book of his pictures which he published in 1945 clearly shows, his competent draftsmanship —even his sense of color—was subordinated to a desire for shock and an inclination toward the grotesque and the pornographic (cf. fig. 16). Nevertheless, Van Meegeren was undaunted in his grandiose estimation of his own talents. He

FIGURE 16. Han van Meegeren, an example of his popular work, 1924. Courtesy Gerard Bywaard.

began indulging in practical jokes on the critics which took progressively serious turns until he finally made a permanent enemy of Dr. Abraham Bredius, Holland's leading art historian and critic.

By 1932, when Van Meegeren and his second wife, Jo, moved to the south of France, the painter had determined on a course of action designed to prove once and for all the incompetence of the critics. The overwhelming nature of Van Meegeren's obsessive hatred, his conviction that he was the target of a plot, is a clear indication of his paranoid mental condition. His own plan, besides being paranoid, required an intriguing kind of personality division. He would identify so strongly with another painter that, while painting, he must virtually transform himself into the other man. Having experimented with two Vermeer forgeries, a Frans Hals and a Terborch, Van Meegeren decided on Vermeer.

From a technical point of view, Van Meegeren proved highly competent. As a result of the extensive research necessary to carry out his obsession, he had become thoroughly familiar with Vermeer's pigments, various methods of falsely aging pictures, and the relevant chemical processes.

Psychologically, too, Van Meegeren acted with considerable historical insight. Vermeer's chronology is sparsely documented and, with one exception, the bulk of his oeuvre consists of interiors or street scenes with one or two small figures and a very few portraits. The exception, *Christ in the House of Mary and Martha* (fig. 17), now in the Edinburgh National Gallery, was first attributed to Vermeer by Dr. Bredius, the critic whom Van Meegeren had most thoroughly antagonized. This painting, totally unlike the others, is the only one with large figures and the only biblical scene. Bredius had postulated an early biblical period in Vermeer's development, of which the *Christ in the House of Mary and Martha* then became the only extant example. Once the attribution had been made, Bredius hypothesized the influence of Caravaggio's religious painting on Vermeer during Vermeer's youthful trip to Italy. In the light of what is known of the art of seventeenth-century Holland, the assumption of

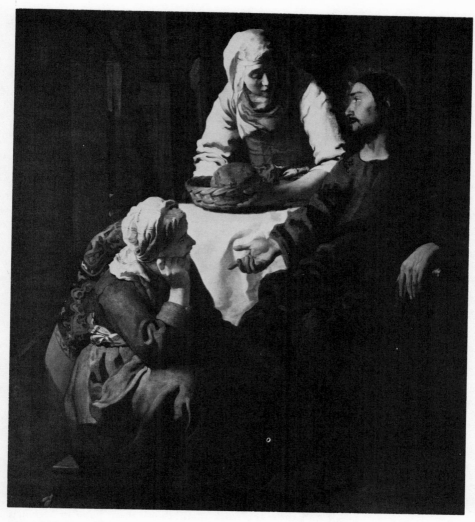

FIGURE 17. Jan Vermeer, *Christ in the House of Martha and Mary*.
Edinburgh, The National Gallery of Scotland.

Italian influence is plausible. Italian art had had a considerable impact on Rembrandt's work and, as Schmidt-Degener, director of Amsterdam's Rijksmuseum, had testified in his Paris deposition for Duveen, a study of Italian painting is a prerequesite to understand seventeenth-century Dutch art.

Van Meegeren's picture therefore, would add a second work to Vermeer's biblical period. He chose a subject of which Caravaggio had painted three versions: *Supper at Emmaus*. Certain aspects of Van Meegeren's painting resembled the Caravaggio version in Rome, while others recalled the painting in Edinburgh. Occasional touches could even be related to details of Vermeer's other, more certainly authenticated, works. When Van Meegeren completed the *Emmaus*, he forged one of Vermeer's various signatures, baked and varnished the canvas in order to induce the crackle of age, and transferred it to an old stretcher.

It was now the summer of 1937. Van Meegeren's next step would be to establish a background for the *Emmaus* and arrange to have its authenticity officially certified. After that, a sale would be a foregone conclusion. Van Meegeren proceeded to execute his deception in a systematic way. Dr. A.G. Boon, an old, influential friend of his, was spending the summer in Paris. He was a lawyer and member of Parliament who was also interested in art. Van Meegeren took his painting to Paris and called on Boon. He told the following story: His mistress belonged to a Dutch family then living in Italy. She had asked Van Meegeren to sell some of her family's art because she intended to leave the country. He, in turn, believing the *Emmaus* to be by Vermeer, agreed to take the painting out of Fascist Italy. If Boon would act as his agent and show the work to Bredius—then living in Monaco —he, Boon, would receive a generous commission. He would also, of course, be performing an act of patriotism in securing a new Vermeer, stolen from the enemy, for Holland. Van Meegeren further pointed out that neither his own identity nor that of his fictional mistress must be revealed to Bredius: his because of past antagonism between himself and the critic, and hers, because she did not want her financial distress to become publicly known.

Boon agreed that the painting was indeed by Vermeer and, at the end of August, contacted Bredius. By then in virtual retirement, the famous expert was over eighty and his eyesight had declined. Nevertheless, he examined the *Emmaus* carefully, although not scientifically, and immediately declared it to be authentic. In a certificate dated September 1937, Bredius enthusiastically hailed the emergence of a new, profound masterpiece by Vermeer.

The *Emmaus* spent most of the following October in Paris being shown to prospective buyers. Despite Bredius's certification however, the painting remained unsold. A number of experts, in fact, expressed doubts about its authenticity; among these was a representative of Duveen's firm. On October 4 he sent a cable dismissing the *Emmaus* as abruptly as Duveen himself had dismissed the Hahn version of *La Belle Ferronnière*: "Seen today at bank large Vermeer about four feet by three *Christ's Supper at Emmaus* supposed belong private family certified by Bredius who writing article *Burlington Magazine* November stop price pounds ninety thousand stop picture rotten fake."[1]

Fortunately for Van Meegeren, as far as Holland was concerned, a certificate from Bredius (reinforced by his article[2]), was sufficient. Boon succeeded in interesting Dr. D. Hannema, the director of Rotterdam's Boymans Museum, and D.A. Hoogendijk, a well-known dealer, in the painting. Money to purchase the new Vermeer was soon raised from prestigious sources, and the painting passed into the Boymans collection. The museum had it cleaned and restored; still no suspicions arose. Van Meegeren himself received today's equivalent of over $330,000 for the sale. Despite the forger's original intention to expose the experts—and this would have been the perfect time to do so—Van Meegeren said nothing. He publicly explained away his sudden wealth by saying that he had won the National Lottery, he spent the money lavishly, and soon returned to the south of France.

In the course of World War II, five more new Vermeers and two de Hoochs unexpectedly appeared on the market. The de Hoochs, although not inexpensive, were not the spectacular finds that the unknown Vermeers were. In 1939 Van Beuningen bought an *Interior with Drinkers* by de Hooch for more than $184,800 in today's money and in 1941, another collector, W. van der Worm, paid over $154,000 for de Hooch's *Interior with Card Players*. The same year, Van Beuningen acquired two Vermeers—a *Head of Christ* and a *Last Supper*—for nearly $1,500,000. In the course of the next two years, three more Vermeers—*Isaac Blessing Jacob, Christ and the Adulteress*, and *The Washing of Christ's Feet* —were sold: to Van der Worm, Goering, and the Netherlands State respectively. Together they brought nearly $4,000,000. In every case, the transactions went through the hands of some of Holland's most respected dealers and, aside from *The Adulteress*, all went to major Dutch collections.

The Vermeers—all depicting biblical subjects—seemed to belong to that hypothetical early period of the painter's artistic development of which, until World War II, the picture in Edinburgh was the only accepted example. Once the *Emmaus* had been authenticated and its official recognition determined when the Boymans acquired it, the next five Vermeers logically followed its lead. All represented relatively large figures, the facial types—long heads with downcast, almost drooping eyelids, prominent noses and thick lips—were extremely similar. The pigments, of course, were Vermeer's, and several of the small objects—pitchers, pewter plates, baskets, even certain details of light—could be easily identified from the artist's later, well-established pictures.

When, at the end of the war, Van Meegeren made his startling announcement, the complacency of the Dutch art world was jolted. Van Meegeren's execution of the *Young Christ* after his arrest succeeded in raising sufficient doubts about the other "Vermeers" to have the charges of collaboration dropped. When the story became openly known, a variety of reactions set in. For some, Van Meegeren's wealth throughout the war was a sign that he had indeed been involved with Nazi transactions. For the collectors—including the Netherlands State—who now owned the alleged forgeries and the dealers who had acted as intermediaries in their disposition, the whole affair proved as embarassing as it was financially disastrous. The police confiscated the paintings and refused to allow outsiders to examine them. For most people, however, Van Meegeren became a hero, as successful forgers and even art thieves often do. Whenever an individual dupes nearly any group of highly trained specialists, the layman tends to identify with the individual against the group. The art world is particularly prone to arouse the hostility of the nonspecialist for several reasons, not the least of which is a certain elitist arrogance.

In fact, despite Van Meegeren's confession, a number of people refused to accept his word. They maintained Vermeer's authorship of the paintings in question, especially the *Emmaus*. The most notable dissenter was a Belgian expert, Jean Decoen. In order to settle the matter once and for all, in June 1946, a year after Van Meegeren's arrest, Holland's Minister of Justice appointed a commission to investigate the paintings and determine whether or not they were fakes. Chaired by Judge G.J. Wiarda, the commission was known as the Coremans Commission after P.B. Coremans,[3] director of the Central Laboratory of Belgian Museums. For nearly a year, the commission, cheerfully assisted by Van Meegeren, painstakingly examined the evidence offered by the paintings themselves. Meanwhile the police conducted their own investigation. They searched Van Meegeren's French and Dutch studios for every piece of available evidence. Aside from a few oversights, the police discovered the chemicals used to produce Vermeer's pigments, the falsely aged canvases, the various objects which appeared in the forgeries, and the fake paintings which Van Meegeren had made before the *Emmaus* and which he had not sold. This evidence was handed over to the Coremans Commission which, its views substantiated by two outside experts from England, concluded its investigation by January 1947.

The remarkably brief trial which brought the Van Meegeren story to a close was finally held on October 29, 1947, over two years after his arrest. The government had spent the entire time preparing its case against the forger. The large Fourth Chamber of Amsterdam's District Assize Court was filled with spectators. The paintings which Van Meegeren had sold as Old Masters were displayed on the walls of the court room. Three judges, with Meester V.G.A. Boll presiding, heard the case. The official charges now leveled at Van Meegeren were that he had fraudently received money and that he had forged signatures on an unspecified number of paintings. A great deal less serious than the original charge of collaboration, these carried a maximum penalty of four years' imprisonment. A reporter covering the trial described Van Meegeren, dressed in a blue shirt and blue suit, eagerly posing for photographers as he entered the courtroom. Thin and frail from the poor state of health that would soon kill him, Van Meegeren's cheeks were hollow, his long, grey hair combed back over his bald spot. His apparent self-satisfaction—even delight—in the proceedings, was a facade that would soon fall away.

"Are you Henricus Antonius van Meegeren?" he was asked as the trial went into session. "Do you admit the charge?" asked Judge Boll.

"Yes."

"Then let us hear the experts' opinions."

The commission members were sworn in, each one testifying that the pictures were recently painted and "could be the work of Van Meegeren." Coremans described the commission's examination of the evidence. Slides projected on the courtroom screen revealed X-rays of various details of the paintings, X-rays of the stretcher of the *Emmaus,* and a corresponding piece of wood from Van Meegeren's studio. Coremans pointed out that the particles of lapis lazuli used in the "Vermeers" were identical with those found in the modern studio. The synthetic resin which was used to age the picture had not been known before the twentieth century. Finally Coremans produced the actual water bottle that appeared in two of the forgeries. It, too, came from Van Meegeren's studio.

"Do you accept the evidence of the witness?" the defendant was asked.

"Yes," he agreed with every statement. Van Meegeren was in the unique position of having to prove himself guilty in order to prove his innocence. If he had indeed painted the forgeries, then he had not sold a national treasure to the Nazis.

"Have you any questions to ask Dr. Coremans?" the judge asked Van Meegeren.

"No," replied the forger, "but I should like to say that I find these tests amazingly clever. It will never be possible to get away with forgery again. It seems to me that it is much more clever to carry out a test of this kind than to paint a Rembrandt—or the *Emmaus*—for example. That would be relatively simple."

Despite the amusement generated in the courtroom by these remarks, there is a great deal of truth in them. If the prospective buyers of an Old Master would run the proper scientific tests, they would soon be able to eliminate the possibility of modern forgery. While such tests may be quite costly—even difficult to obtain, aside from the cost—they would probably prove less expensive than a mistake. On the other hand, if the work is relatively modern, the buyer—although he may be paying a considerable sum—is even less likely to find or even think of finding scientific ways to prove authenticity. Van Meegeren's observation that the commission's tests were more clever than painting a Rembrandt or a Vermeer was quite appropriate. From the standpoint of investigative history, the work of the Coremans Commission was virtually unprecedented. Imitating Old Masters, however, is done every day by competent art students. The interest in Van Meegeren's case lies not so much in his ability to recreate old paintings, technically brilliant though he was at first, as in the peculiar twists of his personality and his ability to successfully market what were patently bad paintings.

Dr. A.W. de Wild, the next witness, was another important expert on the commission. His presence on the commission was not his first contact with the forgeries. In 1943 Van Meegeren told an old friend that he had come into the possession of an unknown Vermeer, *The Washing of Christ's Feet.* The friend agreed to help Van Meegeren sell the picture and went with it to the Amsterdam dealer, Karel de Boer, coincidentally the ex-husband of Van Meegeren's second wife, Jo. De Boer believed the painting to be a Vermeer; it reminded him of the *Emmaus* in the Boymans Museum. He contacted a number of experts connected with the Rijksmuseum in Amsterdam who, together with de Wild himself, eventually agreed to advise the government to buy the painting. They did so not because they liked it—one of them even said it was a forgery—but because they did not want the Germans to buy it. The price—nearly $1,000,000.

How—the public prosecutor asked de Wild—do you account for these events, particularly the fact that the painting was not X-rayed before you advised its purchase?

"Because," replied de Wild, "the art dealer de Boer refused twice to allow X-ray photographs to be taken of those Van Meegerens which he had in his keeping. Such a test would have certainly shown that the paintings were not genuine."

When de Boer took the stand that afternoon, he told his story. "In 1943 I was visited by a Mr. Kok. He offered to sell me an old painting. He said I would be able to tell the name of the artist right away. When he showed me the painting, I saw at once that it was by the same Master who painted the *Emmaus*. I added that probably it was unsigned. Then I examined the canvas more carefully and saw the signature of Johannes Vermeer."

"Did you have any doubts?" asked Boll.

"None."

"What happened to the picture?"

"It was sold to the State."

In addition to the transaction itself, de Wild explained his work on the Coremans Commission. "For me these tests were less difficult, for it soon became clear to me that the defendant borrowed a formula for the composition of his quasi-oil paints from my treatise on the subject of the methods of Vermeer and de Hooch. Even certain impurities which are found in originals were copied by Van Meegeren in his work." It was also not until de Wild was on the commission that the *Washing of Christ's Feet* was X-rayed and then, of course, the painting was at once exposed as a fake.

Two more commission members testified, one discoursing on the chemical aspects of the forgeries and the other— who had originally proclaimed *The Washing of Christ's Feet* a forgery—on their aesthetic and formal qualities.

The commission members were followed to the stand by dealers involved in the transactions. The first, R. Strijbis, was not even a professional art dealer, nor did he know anything about art. Employed as a real-estate agent, he may have been an old friend of Van Meegeren who would buy extensive amounts of property in Amsterdam during the war. In any case, for a substantial commission, Strijbis agreed to act as intermediary between Van Meegeren and the well-known dealer, Hoogendijk, in four different transactions from 1941 to 1942.

"Did you know that it was forged?" Judge Boll asked Strijbis about *The Head of Christ*.

"Certainly not," replied Strijbis. "Van Meegeren said it was a Vermeer. He never told me where he had found it. I sold three others for Van Meegeren to Hoogendijk: *The Last Supper*, a Pieter de Hooch, and *The Blessing of Jacob*. They were all supposed to be from the same collection."

"How much was paid for the pictures?"

"I no longer remember the prices paid. I kept no record." Nor did he know who had purchased the pictures. Following Van Meegeren's advice, Strijbis had been vague about the original owner and Hoogendijk, in turn, had not revealed the identity of the buyers. Thus, in typical art-dealer fashion, sources and clients were closely guarded; a standard practice which played conveniently into the hands of Van Meegeren's deception.

Hoogendijk openly admitted having been duped. "I was fooled," he said. "When I saw *The Head of Christ*, it made me think so strongly of the *Emmaus* that I was deceived."

"Did you not think it strange that more Vermeers were discovered?"

"No. The historians agree that there should be more

Vermeers, and that the *Emmaus* could not be the only one of its kind in existence. In 1941 I sold the *Head of Christ* to Mr. D.G. van Beuningen. Then it was in better condition than it is now." Several of Van Meegeren's forgeries began to deteriorate a few years after they were painted, which made their eventual exposure a certainty.

"And the others?"

"Van Beuningen also bought *The Last Supper*. My first impression is often the best, but I again allowed myself to be influenced by the *Emmaus*. It seems beyond understanding now; at the time, you know, all was done secretly. After *The Last Supper*, I sold two more paintings, including the strange one—*The Blessing of Jacob*."

"How did you account for your acceptance of that one?"

"Yes," Hoogendijk agreed, "it's difficult to explain. It is unbelievable that it should have fooled me. But we slid downward—from the *Emmaus* to the *Foot-Washing*, and from the *Foot-Washing* to *The Blessing of Jacob*; a psychologist could explain this better than I can. But the atmosphere of war contributed to our blindness. One should remember," he continued, "that the *Emmaus* was declared authentic by world-renowned experts. The rest were links in the same chain, thus making the sales easier. There was also the desire to keep the paintings in Holland."

In his response, Hoogendijk summed up the two major reasons for Van Meegeren's successes. Once the *Emmaus* had been accepted as a Vermeer, a precedent had been set for a particular stage in the artist's development. Thereafter, any work similar in style and subject, as all the forgeries were, would seem to fit into the mold. Not only were the subsequent pictures easier to sell; they would also have been easier to paint. For now, instead of inventing a style and period for Vermeer, Van Meegeren was merely turning out Van Meegerens. And they were getting progressively worse at that.

The second explanation offered by Hoogendijk's response is the patriotic aspect of the entire fraud. Throughout the war years, Dutch experts, officials, dealers and collectors were so overwhelmed with anti-Nazi sentiment that their usual discerning judgment declined considerably. Even a bad Vermeer, they seemed to say, was a national treasure which must be kept in the country. This view in itself may prove a result of wartime frenzy since it is doubtful that a painter of Vermeer's caliber could ever—even at his worst—have produced works as low in quality as the forgeries. While patriotism may be a laudable sentiment in times of war, the Van Meegeren case is a perfect example of the way in which patriotic fervor clutters up the most experienced and best-trained minds.

Dr. D. Hannema, director of the Boymans, echoed Hoogendijk's patriotic explanation as he commented on *The Washing of Christ's Feet*. "None of us liked it very much, but we were afraid that it would be sold to Germany."

"But you also bought it for its artistic value?" asked Boll.

"Certainly. After all, Vermeers are scarce."

"Was there no interest in the origin of the picture?"

"Yes, but it was all very vague."

After Hannema stepped down, the industrialist and collector Van Beuningen took the stand. He had acquired de Hooch's *Interior with Drinkers* and Vermeer's *Head of Christ*, and *The Last Supper*. He had never entertained any doubts about their authenticity, he testified. Dr. Boon and de Boer had been involved in the de Hooch sale, and Hoogendijk in the Vermeers, Van Beuningen informed the court. All were highly respected experts, and important collectors like Van Beuningen are known to rely heavily on expert opinion when considering a major purchase.

Van Meegeren was the last to testify, although he had made several comments in the course of the trial. He had agreed with the technical evidence offered by members of the Coremans Commission. When asked about the forged signatures, Van Meegeren replied, "I did that last of all, and it was much the hardest job. It had to be done all in one stroke. Once I had begun it, there could be no going back."

"You agree that you painted these forgeries?" the judge asked that afternoon.

"Yes, Mr. President."

"And also that you sold them, at a very high price?"

"I had to. If I had sold them at a low price, they would have been at once recognized as fakes."

"But you continued after the first forgery?" pointed out the judge, referring to Van Meegeren's claim that his intention had been to expose the incompetence of the experts.

"I enjoyed painting them so much. One comes to a condition in which one is no more master of oneself. You become without will, powerless. I was forced to continue." In this, Van Meegeren was implying that he had lost control of himself and was not entirely responsible for his actions.

"At least you made a considerable profit." Judge Boll went to the heart of the matter.

"I had to." Van Meegeren continued to protest that money had not been his motive. "I had been so belittled by the critics that I could no longer exhibit anywhere. I was systematically damaged by the critics, who knew not a thing about art." This rather paranoid testimony received some substantiation from the psychiatrist who had been asked for a report on the defendant. He presented his report during the morning session: "The character of this defendant leads to sensitiveness to criticism; fed by a revenge complex which explains his antisocial attitude. Mentally I must say that he is unbalanced but responsible for his actions; and without doubt he is an excellent craftsman." The psychiatrist advised against imprisonment on the grounds that isolation would be detrimental to Van Meegeren's mental health.

Judge Boll seemed more interested in the financial than the psychological motivation. "Perhaps the financial advantage had some kind of influence on your actions?" Boll asked.

"It made little difference." Van Meegeren would not be moved. "The millions I earned from the later pictures were added to the millions I had earned before."

"Did you act from a desire to benefit?"

"Only from a desire to paint. I decided to carry on, not primarily from a desire to paint forgeries, but to make the best use of the technique which I discovered." Actually, however, after the *Emmaus*, Van Meegeren did not make the best use of his new technique. It was as if he had become hypnotized by the ease of his deceptions as well as by their enormous financial rewards. Nevertheless, he did conclude with a promise never again to age his pictures or to offer them as Old Masters.

As the public prosecutor rose to speak, Van Meegeren's cool facade collapsed. "The defendant," declared the prosecutor, "hoped to prove to the world that he is a great artist. But by these falsifications he has in fact shown himself to be less of an artist than ever." He did not succeed in proving himself a misunderstood genius, argued the prosecutor; his motives had been financial. Many had made serious errors, but Van Meegeren had thrown the art world into a state of self-doubt and had damaged the State. Though he said there was no reason for leniency, the prosecutor asked for two years' imprisonment instead of the maximum four. At this, Van Meegeren visibly began to come apart. His eyes strayed without focus and his hands twitched in constant, meaningless motion. He blew his nose and dropped his face on his hands.

Van Meegeren's lawyer presented the defense summation that by now was anticlimactic. He explained Van Meegeren's character, his sensitivity to criticism, and argued that there had been no legal fraud in any of the sales. The forged signatures, he added, were the least significant aspect of the paintings and therefore, on this latter charge, "utmost leniency" should be shown.

The trial of Han van Meegeren was remarkable for what was omitted as well as for what was included. The *Emmaus* was barely considered; the statute of limitations had passed. No one involved in the sale of *The Adulteress* to Goering (the basis for the whole affair) appeared in court. The German banker Miedl and the Dutch dealer van Strijvesand could not be found. Nor could Dr. Boon who had participated in the *Emmaus* transaction and in the sale of de Hooch's *Interior with Drinkers* to Van Beuningen. Van Beuningen, along with many others, had lodged a claim for damages in the purchase of *The Last Supper*. He thus did not want Jean Decoen—the Belgian expert who still believed it and the *Emmaus* to be authentic Vermeers—to be called. It took just two hours for all seventeen witnesses to testify. The entire trial lasted five and a half hours.

Van Meegeren received the lightest possible sentence: one year in jail. He died in a hospital before ever going to prison. On his deathbed, he made one final attack on the established art world. One of his forgeries, he told his son, had still not been exposed.

POSTSCRIPT

In 1952 Van Beuningen brought a suit against Coremans for declaring his *Last Supper* a fake. In his dissent, Van Beuningen received the support of Jean Decoen. The case was continually postponed until the industrialist died in June 1955. His heirs offered to waive the suit and pay expenses. Coremans, backed by the Belgian government, refused and insisted on a judgment. Finally, on April 4, 1956, the Eighth Chamber of the Court of First Instance in Brussels ruled in favor of Coremans. Van Beuningen's statements were judged to be erroneous and libelous. His heirs were ordered to pay 750,000 Belgian francs, interest, and court costs, and the ruling was ordered published in five Belgian, three Dutch, two French, two English and two American newspapers.

CHAPTER FIVE

"OUR FLAG WAS STILL THERE" / The People of the State of New York v. Stephen Radich

"A national flag is the supreme totem around which the clans gather in times of danger or celebration, but it is much more than a totem. It represents the continuity of a people, their common purpose, their traditions, their way of looking at the world, their defiance against their enemies, but this is only the beginning."[1] So wrote Robert Payne in a 1964 Sunday Magazine article in *The New York Times*. Americans, like everyone else (and probably more so), have special feelings about their flag. The image of Betsy Ross devotedly and diligently sewing away on Old Glory is impressed upon every American schoolchild. In 1892, 400 years after Columbus's famous discovery, the *Pledge of Allegiance* became part of the American way of life.

The real flag fervor, however, seems to have developed in the twentieth century, and particularly in times of war. Although today every American state forbids flag desecration, most of the statutes were enacted during World War I. In the 1920s various groups—notably the D.A.R., the American Legion and the Ku Klux Klan—successfully organized a campaign to see the flag displayed in every American schoolroom. By 1941 the American Flag Association had been established and, the following year, the National Flag Code was enacted. The year 1946 marked the inception of the United States Flag Foundation, and in 1949 Americans observed National Flag Day for the first time.

In the 1960s and early 1970s, the United States flag became a crucial symbol in the political polarization caused by American involvement in Vietnam. Many of those who approved of the involvement aggressively displayed the flag, which began to appear on cars, on buttons, and in front of houses. Those who were opposed, on the other hand, tended to avoid the flag, associating its image with the hawkish patriotism of the war's supporters. The more active protestors used the flag in various ways to demonstrate their point of view. The country witnessed a rash of flag burnings and other symbolic protests against the war in Vietnam. One group of students at Hobart College in upstate New York ended an antiwar play by washing the flag in a bathtub. At the Rochester Institute of Technology, a photograph of a girl, wrapped in an American flag, adorned the cover of a student publication also protesting the war. In both cases, charges of flag desecration were brought against the offenders. Similarly, when certain artists wished to indicate opposition to the war, they incorporated the flag into the iconography of protest art.

On December 13, 1966, in New York City, the Stephen Radich Art Gallery at 818 Madison Avenue mounted a one-man show of protest art by Marc Morrel, a former U.S. Marine. The works, which included thirteen sculptures and three watercolors, were unmistakably aimed at the Vietnam war. Morrel had represented the United States flag hanging in a yellow noose (fig. 18), the flag in chains (fig. 19), and the flag as a crucified phallus (figs. 20a and 20b). Another piece represented a large cross with a bishop's miter on the headpiece; the arms of the cross were wrapped in ecclesiastical flags. The sculptures ranged in price from $250 to $1,200 and were consigned to the gallery on a one-third-commission basis. As part of the exhibition, taped antiwar songs played in the background. The show was reviewed by Hilton Kramer, art news editor for *The New York Times*; he was unimpressed.

Ordinarily one might expect that to be the end of the story. But a legal battle lasting seven years ensued instead, reflecting much of the nation's emotional investment in its flag.

The months preceding and following the Morrel show were full of war news which, like the legal battle, was to continue for years. A week after the show opened, seventeen members of the House of Representatives urged President Johnson to use the Christmas truce as a road to peace, the Chinese called the latest United States peace efforts a swindle, Ho Chi Minh toured Hanoi's defenses, and United States planes struck within twenty-five miles of the Chinese border.

On December 27, 1966, in New York City, Patrolman John P. Burns, badge 21038, Nineteenth Precinct, was on duty and in uniform. Finding himself "in the vicinity of 818 Madison Avenue," he noticed "what appeared to be the flag of the United States government in a shape of a human body, hanging from a yellow noose (fig. 18)." The following evening, around 5:00, Patrolman Burns returned to the gallery with a member of the N.Y.P.D.'s photo unit and a court summons. At the time, Stephen Radich was in the gallery; he informed the police officers that the artist came in only occasionally. Patrolman Burns served Radich with the summons, and the photographer took pictures of Morrel's sculptures. Also present in the gallery were "a member of the Borough of Special Service," "a sergeant from the Nineteenth Precinct," and "an unknown female."

On December 28, Radich was charged with violating what was then Penal Law (section 1425 subdivision 16, paragraphs d and f):[2] no person "shall publicly mutilate, deface, defile or defy, trample upon or cast contempt upon either by words or act", or "shall publicly carry or display any emblem, placard or flag which casts contempt either by word or act upon" the flag of the United States of America.

On December 30, the New York Civil Liberties Union announced its defense of the rights of artists to incorporate the flag into their sculptures. It called the prosecution of Stephen Radich "a form of cultural suppression." The president of the Flag Foundation disagreed. "You can't use the flag as a protest," *Life* magazine quoted him as saying. "It's

FIGURE 18. Marc Morrel,
The United States Flag in a
Yellow Noose. Courtesy
Richard Green.

FIGURE 19. Marc Morrel, *The United States Flag in Chains*.
Courtesy Richard Green.

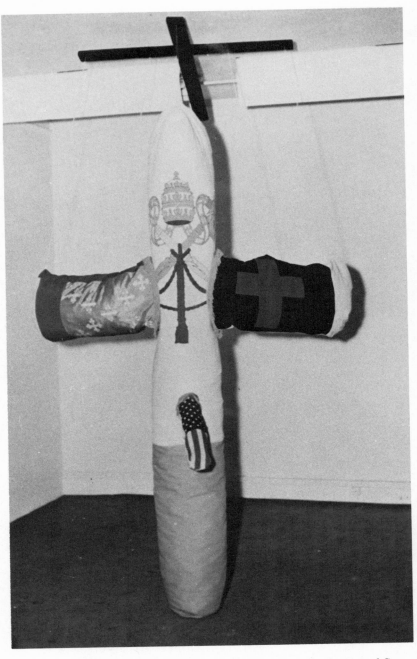

FIGURES 20a and 20b. Two views of Marc Morrel's *The United States Flag as a Crucified Phallus*. Courtesy Richard Green.

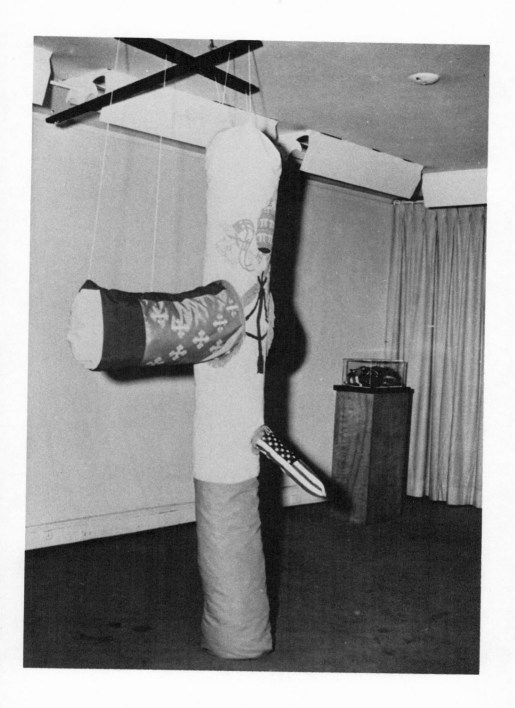

just like you wouldn't murder your grandmother. The American flag is so high above everything—it's on a pedestal—that nothing should touch it."[3]

Meanwhile both the flag and the war were much in the news. United States military officers were reported as calling the bombing of North Vietnam "effective, restrained, and essential." On February 4, Richard L. Roudebush, Republican of Indiana, announced that he had introduced legislation to establish June 14—Flag Day—as a national holiday. The holiday would commemorate the date in 1777 when the United States flag was first raised by the Continental Congress in Philadelphia. On the same day in San Francisco, the new bishop of the Episcopal Diocese of California criticized Cardinal Spellman for calling the war in Vietnam "Christ's conflict." A spokesman for Spellman replied that "the vast majority of Americans and their clergymen are in support of the efforts for peace being made through the American policy in Vietnam."

Over a month later, on March 29, 1967, the trial of Stephen Radich opened in New York City's Criminal Court with the testimony of Patrolman Burns. A three-judge bench —Honorable Amos S. Basel, Frederick L. Strong and James J. Comerford—heard the case. Gerald Slater, assistant district attorney, New York County, acted for the People while Richard G. Green, with Shirley Fingerhood present, acted for the defendant.

It is interesting that the United States has a rather extensive history dealing with aspects of its citizens' attitudes toward the flag. Most of the cases have had to confront the problem of a free society which tries to enforce respect and even veneration for the flag. This apparent contradiction has been a constant—if usually dormant—theme in American history. At times of national stress, however, these conflicts tend to resurface. The case of *The People of the State of New York* v. *Stephen Radich* became a political, moral, and artistic issue.

"How many flags did not represent the flag of the United States?" asked Judge Basel.

"The ones we didn't take a picture of," replied Patrolman Burns.

"How many is that?"

"Seven or eight. Some of them may be duplicates."

A discussion of which were actually United States flags and which only appeared to be flags followed. Burns eventually identified eight objects as containing the flag itself, or parts of it. One object—not displaying the flag—was nevertheless included in the complaint, a likeness of the president of the United States, Lyndon B. Johnson.

Richard Green, attorney for Radich, introduced a *Life* magazine article illustrated with pictures representing United States flags. This, he argued, constituted an exception to the statute that Radich was charged with having violated. Among other things, the statute excepted "an ornamental picture," and "an article of jewelry." Therefore, according to Green's logic, sculpture was implicitly included, together with pictures, as an exception and, if it was not, then the statute was discriminatory. Consequently Green moved to dismiss the case on the grounds that "neither the complaint nor the evidence that has been offered in support of it states any crime." He argued further that the legislature meant to except all opinions and artistic expressions from the statute, because otherwise it would be violating the right of free speech guaranteed by the First Amendment.

Assistant District Attorney Gerald Slater disagreed. In his view, no exception had been intended for sculpture; the flag had been dishonored and people viewing the "defilement of their national emblem might be aroused to violence." "The flag," he said, "is an emblem of authority, and the power to prohibit its use and the power to prevent its defilement is certainly within the power itself. If we were to allow individuals to show great disrespect to the flag, the People contend that the public would be aroused to the point where there would be possible riot and strike. . . . There is a certain amount of restriction on the power of free speech for the overall benefit of everyone. In this we contend the statute was intended for the benefit of society as a whole."

At this point, Judge Strong pressed Slater on the psychological distinction between two- and three-dimensional objects. "We have paintings of similar objects instead of three-dimensional sculpture," the judge observed, referring to the *Life* magazine article.

"I would say then the legislature took into consideration what objects would arouse the public wrath," replied Slater.

"Three-dimensional objects might and pictures might not?"

"Yes."

"Even though they are pictures of the same objects?"

"That's right. Well, for one thing, a photograph in a book is not an animated object and cannot be touched."

"Sculpture is animated?"

"It can be touched, it can be seen, and it is an object more likely to arouse the public wrath. I think this is what the legislature had in mind. It appears the legislature took into consideration which would arouse the public wrath and did not include them in the objects which would be excluded."

From an artistic point of view, distinctions of this kind between two- and three-dimensional objects raise a number of problems. There have always been, for example, styles of painting that are formally two-dimensional, like Byzantine or Gothic, while in the Renaissance painting gave the illusion of being three-dimensional. Therefore, on the grounds that three-dimensional objects are more likely to "arouse" the public in one way or another, one might wonder how this would apply to Renaissance painting. As all who are familiar with the writing of Berenson know, Renaissance painting did indeed arouse the nerve endings of that critic's fingertips. As a result, he developed the concept of "tactility" to describe his reaction to the characteristic three-dimensional quality of Renaissance pictures. Though painting may be considered three-dimensional from the stylistic or formal point of view, sculpture may be defined as two-dimensional if the object portrayed occupies a single plane of space. Such is typically the case in the sculpture of ancient Egypt, the pre-Classical art of Greece, and most pre-Renaissance Christian art.

In the late nineteenth and early twentieth centuries, when many traditional forms of art were being broken down, the distinction between painting and sculpture also became less precise than it had previously been. Judge Basel seems to have recognized this development when he asked Slater whether he was familiar with collage. "No," replied Slater.

"When you take forms and pieces and paste them upon a frame and then paint around it," explained the judge. "Do you think that would be excluded from the statute or included in the statute?" In some cases, collage is a medium which is transitional between painting and sculpture. As such, it is not covered by the statute at all.

"My opinion is strictly a personal one," Slater pointed out in a rather elusive response to Judge Basel's question.

"Based on a painting which is a very important form of art today, and then you took oil paint and painted around it, would that be in or out of the statute?" the judge persisted.

"I think that would be excluded by the statute since basically that is a painting, but here we do not have a painting."

"You get down to a very definite point of what is excluded and what is not excluded. I don't think your argument holds water—just because you could touch something, it's excluded from the statute."

Slater said that the statute did not apply to paintings. The power to limit free speech, he argued, is itself limited, and therefore the legislature would not act without justification. He assumed that Morrel's objects expressed his thoughts as well as those of Radich. The People thus contended that, in a case of this kind, "the power of free speech is abridged, and one cannot by word or act arouse the public to such a state that they will cause a riot and strike. . . ."

A lengthy discussion between the attorneys and judges ensued and, following a short recess, Judge Strong announced that Green's motion to dismiss had been denied. The trial proceeded and Stephen Radich, the defendant, was sworn in.

Radich testified that he had been an art dealer for about

fourteen years and had a degree in fine arts from Columbia, with a specialization in the nineteenth and twentieth centuries. His attorney then pursued the issue of the fading distinctions between painting and sculpture in modern art. "Could you tell us something about the use of materials in art—nineteenth and twentieth century art, particularly twentieth century art?" Green asked his client.

"The works of art that have been produced within the last fifty years have varied considerably," replied Radich. "Artists now use a various variety of materials in their work. The sculptors use wood, they use junk, they use cloth, they use glass, plastics and many materials that are coming into being through the advance of technology and products of new substances. The artists are finding these things valuable and are using them in their works of art."

"Now, there was a question raised before by one of the judges having to do with collage. What are the uses of materials on those?"

"Artists have used scraps of paper, fabric, plastic, chips of wood, and they have glued these together on wood, on canvas. There have been many objects."

In other words, Green observed, even though collages may be hung in frames like paintings, they are nonetheless three-dimensional.

"Yes," Radich agreed.

Turning to the inflammatory content of Morrel's sculpture, Radich's attorney introduced the question of protest art. "Would you describe protest art to the court?" he asked the dealer. Radich gave a summary history saying, "There have been many forms of protest art. For example, Michelangelo, we could say, protested against the church when he painted one of the cardinals who was the future Pope Paul III in a position which he considered Hell because he was upset by the actions and the behavior of the ecclesiastics. There was a great artist, . . . Goya, in Spain, who did many protest pieces. The famous thing was the disaster of war. He also protested against the corruption of the Spanish court. . . . Recently, Pablo Picasso did the *Guernica*, which is in the Museum of Modern Art, and this was a very violent and brilliant work of protest. This occurred during the Spanish Civil War. There are many others like this."

And what specific protest did Radich think Morrel's sculptures made? "Well, I felt there were many protests. There were protests of the war in Vietnam or war in general, destruction, protest against certain societies, and justice in this country, protest against the infringement of the people's rights to use freedom of speech."

"Did you consider, in exhibiting these works, you were being contemptuous of the flag of the United States?"

"No, I did not."

"Did you have any intent then to express yourself in contempt for the flag by exhibiting these sculptures?"

"No, I didn't."

On cross-examination, the assistant district attorney directed Radich to the sculpture representing the crucified phallus. "Please tell the Court what this object was expressing or protesting."

"Well, in my opinion," replied Radich, "this work is a statement by the artist showing or trying to depict that there is not a separation of church and state, that the government of this country is involved in aggressive acts of war. Perhaps the penis represents the sexual act which, by some standards, is considered an aggressive act. The figure represents a cross. Religion—organized religion is the symbol here—and it seems to suggest that organized religion is supporting these aggressive acts that are being made. It also suggests that this is a puppet, that the church or organized religions are either supporting or leading these actions of aggression or they are being led by it. That is my interpretation."

And on redirect questioning, Radich specified the aggressive actions being protested: "Aggressive actions of war, and they are being supported by organized religion, by the country and he [the artist] feels, it would seem to me, that he is showing disrespect for the people involved in these organizations rather than disrespect for the flag itself."

The defense produced only one more witness: Hilton

Kramer, *The New York Times* art news editor who had originally reviewed the Morrel show. Kramer was accepted as an expert witness and asked the inevitable question: What is art?

"I would define a work of visual art," he replied gamely, "as any physical object, specifically with visual properties specifically designed to communicate an aesthetic emotion."

"Is the communication of aesthetic emotion necessarily an emotion of pleasure or beauty?"

"No. It has been specifically a characteristic of the modern movement in art that aesthetic emotion is considered painful or a combination of pleasure and pain or any degree in between." Kramer added that, in his opinion, Morrel's sculptures were serious works of art.

"Would you say they give rise to an ecstatic emotion?" asked Judge Strong.

"Yes, I would," replied Kramer.

"Could you name what that emotion is?"

"Well, I would have to say that I think those are the only emotions they give rise to . . . I don't think they are a very high form of art, but I nonetheless think they attempt to come to grips with certain formal problems in sculpture that have a tradition of fifty years behind them. I don't think they do this extremely well, but I think their intentions are serious in that direction."

"You testified that in their aesthetic aspects you did not think these were so great. Do you mean in protest art?"

"Yes, as works of protest art I thought they were rather feeble because, in my view, the artist was much more engaged by the visual spectacles of his materials than by whatever social intent may have been laid with them."

"The fact that they failed, in your view, as works of protest art, did that make them any the less works of art?"

"Not at all; in fact, it made them more exclusively works of art. . . ."

Judge Comerford, like Slater, gravitated to the crucified phallus. Kramer described his own aesthetic emotions in connection with the object. "These sculptures," he said, "are clearly intended to be figures, clearly intended to show a male figure with his phallus erected."

"What do you mean by his phallus? Some people don't understand that word."

"With his male sexual organ erected." Kramer obliged the judge and defined his terms. "And I assumed when I first saw this work that the artist was making it quite similar to social military violence, to sexual excitement and to social excitement that one sees on numerous television shows and movies and novels and so on. However, as an art critic, that seemed to be a very minimal idea, and I was much more interested in the design of the figure, the fact that it was symmetrical, rearranged in the kind of cross form with this sort of textural effect as a kind of face and chest, a red cross on one sleeve, etc. These are more or less the aesthetic associations. With this figure, it seemed well done. I couldn't see that it had much substance. As an artistic idea I would place it low, but well in the category of artistic accomplishment."

"What," persisted Judge Comerford not to be sidetracked by formal analysis, "is it supposed to arouse in the public? You told me a lot, but you didn't answer my question."

"Well, I'm not sure it's possible to describe an aesthetic emotion being other than itself."

"Describe what an aesthetic emotion is."

"Aesthetic emotion," Kramer suggested, "is an emotion derived from the form rather than from the content of an object."

Under cross-examination, the assistant district attorney established that the sculptures were indeed sculptures and not "ornamental pictures," or "articles of jewelry." "Now, wouldn't you say," continued Slater, "it was your feeling that the artist who constructed these objects was more or less getting a kick out of doing this than trying to make some sort of protest or political protest, some sort of personal gratification rather than trying to express himself in a political vein?"

"I would have to answer that in two stages," replied Kramer, "one in terms of what I took to be the artist's intentions, and the other, what I took to be his success in realizing it. As to the first, I took it to be the artist's intention to be creating a form of art which was making a social commentary."

"How did you reach this conclusion?"

"Through my familiarity with this as an art medium."

"Now, as to what was conveyed, what was your idea?"

"As to my statement of his success in making the social commentary, I felt it was minimal. I felt as an artist he was much more engaged by the visual spectacle of the materials he was dealing with than in conveying any social commentary."

"Now, wouldn't you say that we would call almost any object on exhibit in a gallery an object of art?"

"Yes, anything specifically designed to be a work of art, whether it's poor or high quality, is a work of art."

On the flag hanging in a noose (fig. 18), Kramer testified as follows: "I didn't take the work of art to be one that communicated a message exactly. It seemed to me an attempt to make a certain kind of form suspended from the ceiling, which is a familiar modern sculpture device, and among such attempts this seemed to me not an interesting one."

"Then you didn't personally gain any particular protest from this object?"

"I felt it was the artist's intention to communicate something, but I personally did not feel politically stimulated by it." Furthermore, Kramer continued, he was more interested in the aesthetic nature of the objects than in their political message. In any case, neither struck him as particularly overwhelming. And finally, on redirect questioning, Kramer reiterated the contemporary tendency to dissolve the distinctions between such traditional artistic categories as painting and sculpture.

The defendant and the People rested, and Radich's attorney renewed his motion to dismiss the case on the grounds that the statute had not been violated beyond a reasonable doubt. The bench withdrew until May 5 to consider its decision.

The motion to dismiss was denied, and Radich was found guilty by a two-to-one vote. The majority held that Morrel's sculptures constituted "a contemptuous use of the flag of the United States and that the defendant by exhibiting them to the public cast contempt upon it . . . ." Judge Basel dissented, noting that many who protest the war are in fact loyal veterans who fought to defend the flag. This group— among which are the artist Morrel and the defendant Radich —protested that through our "persistence in this war, the image of the American flag as a symbol of freedom to lovers of liberty and a shining object to the oppressed is cast in contempt." Under the First Amendment, continued the dissenting opinion, laws must tolerate the expression of conflicting viewpoints, even viewpoints that bear on the most heated issues of the time. The ideals represented by the flag, according to Morrel's protest art, are enchained by Vietnam policy, "its inspiration publicly hangs in shame before the world, and the church and state are jointly to be charged as violators of the innocent. He makes that protest visible, it takes sculptural form." Is the artist, asked Judge Basel, "to be punished for his lack of manners and his vulgarity when his intention is a serious condemnation of our present foreign policy? . . . The motion to dismiss," concluded Basel, "should have been granted and the defendant found not guilty."

Radich received a suspended sentence. The maximum fine of $500 was imposed.

A little more than two weeks after the verdict against Radich, "Oh, Say Can You See . . . ," an article by Grace Glueck, appeared in the Sunday *New York Times*.[4] She reported that when Radich had first received his summons, he circulated a petition among members of the art community inviting support for his case. While support was forthcoming from critic Clement Greenberg, from the directors of the Yale

University Art Gallery and Harvard's Fogg Museum, and from the employees of Marlborough Gallery, the Art Dealers Association of America refused. According to Ralph Colin, vice-president and general counsel, the ADAA declined to submit a brief as *amicus curiae* (friend of the court) because of the low quality of art involved. Although a great many dealers, artists, and critics responded to Radich's appeal for support, official museum encouragement was weak, at best. A few museum directors and trustees were even actively opposed to Radich's point of view. Seven years later, Carl R. Baldwin, a professor of art history, would take Ralph Colin to task for his attitude toward the Radich case.[5] Colin, in turn, would reply that in his judgment as a lawyer this was a "hard case" and thus not likely to produce a victory for free artistic expression.[6]

From the public at large, Radich reportedly received a great deal of hostile mail; one letter from "one hundred patriotic Americans and Christians" threatened to burn "Jew Bastard" Radich (who is not Jewish) in ovens. The letter was signed "God Bless America!"[7] According to art historian Carl Baldwin, the Radich conviction was instrumental in furthering "the cause of the federal 'flag-desecration' bill passed by Congress on June 20 of that same year."[8]

Meanwhile the United States government was busy with Flag Day, the war, and other important matters. On May 31 the House of Representatives decided to observe Flag Day on June 14 for the first time in ten years. Alabama Democrat Bill Nichols backed the holiday as a means of "showing heartfelt thanks to the United States soldiers fighting and dying for Old Glory in Vietnam." The United States military command in Indochina had begun a campaign to improve the image of the faltering South Vietnamese army. American planes bombed two North Vietnamese oil depots at Haiphong, and the court-martial of Captain Howard Levy for refusing to train army medics in dermatology, was in progress.

Two days before Flag Day, President Johnson urged his fellow Americans to fly the flag on June 14. "Fly it from your home, and from your place of business . . . and fly it in your heart," he said. "Let us teach our children of its meaning by our proud and reverent example." When Flag Day finally arrived, the House joined the tribute with a military display, patriotic speeches, and songs. Democrat Jack Brooks of Texas, expressed sadness for those who thought it unfashionable to show patriotism.

Nor had the art world allowed Old Glory to fade away. On Sunday, October 29, 1967, Grace Glueck wrote another article on the Radich trial, "A Rally 'Round the Flag'".[9] It seemed, she reported, that art dealer John Myers of the Tibor de Nagy Gallery had asked the ADAA to reactivate the Radich case. The October 4 meeting of the ADAA, chaired by its president, Klaus Perls, issued a resolution expressing confidence in Radich's good faith and asserting the importance of free expression.

The case was being appealed in the courts. In Indochina, the war continued.

The following year, on June 10, 1968, President Johnson declared not National Flag *Day*, but National Flag *Week*. On Flag Day, June 14, the House of Representatives celebrated with a tribute to the veterans of the South Vietnamese outpost of Khesanh. In Boston, Dr. Benjamin Spock, world-famous author of *Baby and Child Care*, was found guilty of an antidraft plot.

In March 1969, apparently feeling a need to reassert "the basic principles that made our nation great," former President Eisenhower published a short statement in *Reader's Digest*. Reminiscing on his first day at West Point, he described the cadets' swearing-in ceremony. "As I looked up at our national colors and swore my allegiance," he wrote, "I realized humbly that *now* I *belonged to the flag*." Calling for a revival of flag display, Eisenhower concluded that "such a visible upsurge of respect for flag and country will do much to help bring about a new national solidarity, a renewed pride and faith in America."[10]

By June 5 President Nixon was urging the display of flags during National Flag Week from the Western White

House at San Clemente. "A flag is meant to be seen," he informed the nation. In November of the same year, Stephen Radich appealed his conviction in the New York State Court of Appeals.

Following a restatement of the case and a summary of the testimony which had been heard in 1967, five major points were advanced as grounds for reversing the conviction and dismissing the complaint: (1) The statute was not intended to apply to works such as the "constructions" made by Marc Morrel and exhibited by Radich. (2) If point 1 was invalid, then the statute arbitrarily discriminated against sculptors "in violation of the equal protection clause of the Fourteenth Amendment." (3) Radich was, in effect, punished for expressing his opinions, a freedom guaranteed by the First Amendment. (4) The statute was "unconstitutionally vague." (5) It had not been established that Radich *intended* to cast contempt upon the flag and proof of intent was necessary for conviction.

The People of the State of New York responded predictably that Radich had indeed cast contempt on the flag, and that his actions had been proved beyond a reasonable doubt. One had only to view the sculptures in question, the People argued, to understand that Radich intended to "hold the flag up to contempt, ridicule, and disgrace." The statute did not interfere with freedom of speech, since "the conduct of the defendant was fraught with danger to the public peace. In his gallery window, which faced a public street, defendant displayed for several weeks the flag of the United States, shaped in the form of a human body, suspended by a hangman's noose. The defendant's gallery, which was open to the public, was filled with works that similarly cast contempt upon the flag. His conduct was no less punishable than the burning of the flag." The People denied that the statute was unconstitutionally vague and concluded that "the statute does not violate the equal protection clause of the Fourteenth Amendment,"—that is, discrimination between painting and sculpture.

New York State Attorney General Louis J. Lefkowitz

submitted a brief as *amicus curiae*, urging that the conviction be upheld. On the issue of free speech, Lefkowitz cited the conviction that same year of antiwar activist Abbie Hoffman for wearing an American flag shirt and a button saying "Vote Pig Yippie in Sixty-Eight." Lefkowitz further argued that there were no real distinctions between painting and sculpture because the statute would not exempt *any* art form that defiled the United States flag. Since the statute expressly referred to "ornamental sculpture," and since, in Lefkowitz's view, Morrel's sculpture was not ornamental, the objects that Radich exhibited were not exempted. "Obviously," Lefkowitz stated, "the flag was draped over a phallus for shock effect and precisely because the sensibilities of most viewers would be offended." The constructions dramatized Morrel's views instead of informing the public in a precise way of his protest, thereby obscuring "the message in order to perpetrate a more dramatic and offensive act." Furthermore, continued Lefkowitz, even if Morrel's sentiments had been expressed in two-dimensional form, they would be contemptuous. And finally, he concluded, in the light of the wording of the Hoffman decision—"The term 'defile' encompasses conduct which dishonors the flag as well as the generally more accepted use of making something filthy or dirty" —the statute could not be considered vague.

On the night of December 9, less than two weeks after the appeal briefs were submitted in the Radich case, Nixon attended the National Football Awards Dinner at the Waldorf amid 3,000 antiwar demonstrators. The red flag was raised on a pole at Forty-eighth Street and Park Avenue. "Go in and secure that flagpole and get that flag down!" ordered a police inspector on the scene. Also present was a small pro-Nixon rally, including a singing trio in astronaut suits with little American flags on their helmets.

On February 18, 1970, the State Court of Appeals in Albany upheld the conviction of Stephen Radich by a vote of five to two. The court ruled that the right of free speech did not permit the use of the flag in "dishonorable ways" for protest. The crucified phallus (fig. 20), small though it was,

was apparently very eye-catching as it was again singled out for comment: "The flag of the United States of America," pointed out the court, was depicted "in the form of the male sexual organ, erect and protruding from the upright member of a cross." Such displays, in the court's opinion, were not protected by the First Amendment. "Insults to a flag," stated the court, "have been the cause of war, and indignities put upon it in the presence of those who revere it have often been restrained and sometimes punished on the spot. . . . This court has said our statute was designed to prevent the outbreak of such violence by discouraging contemptuous and insulting treatment of the flag in public."

All this talk about "violence" and "riot" resulting from misuse of the flag is quite remarkable since Morrel's sculptures were openly displayed for two weeks before anyone even noticed them. Nor did they arouse a single act of violence on the part of any American citizen.

Chief Judge Stanley H. Fuld dissented from the majority view on grounds that the sculptures were three-dimensional political cartoons and therefore should not be censored.

With this decision, the art world reacted once again to the machinations of the Radich case. Hilton Kramer produced a strongly worded article in the Sunday, March 1 *New York Times*.[11] Titled "A Case of Artistic Freedom," Kramer's article protested the decision of February 18. He pointed out once again that the art in question did not impress him; nevertheless, the trial was a "pretty bizarre experience. Suddenly complicated questions of aesthetic intention and artistic realization," the critic continued, "—questions that require a certain specialized intelligence and taste even to be properly phrased, let alone answered—were cast into an alien legalistic vocabulary that precluded the very possibility of a serious answer."

Commenting on the most recent decision, he wrote, "If you know anything about art—about either its creation, its exhibition, or the kind of response it elicits in the relatively small public that pays it any attention—the majority opinion of the Court of Appeals is full of strange and frightening details, and the strangest and most frightening of all is the notion that Mr. Radich's exhibition of Mr. Morrel's work offered 'the likelihood of incitement to disorder.' " Kramer concluded with the observation that the art world had been warned that anyone may be prosecuted for protesting government policies. And that, he noted, "is a frightening development—almost, alas, as frightening as the conspicuous silence with which our organizations representing art dealers, museum directors, art critics, and the artists themselves have greeted this curtailment of their freedom."

In *The New York Times* "Art Mailbag" of the following April 19, Sam Hunter, professor of art at Princeton University, wrote approving Kramer's comments but Ilka Chase wrote that she had read the article "with a shudder."

On October 19, 1970, the Supreme Court of the United States agreed to rule on the Radich case. It was the first time in American history that a case of artistic freedom had gone that far. Briefs and reply briefs were submitted to the court. Radich's reply included a compendium of the American flag in the works of contemporary artists in paintings, sculptures, collages, on buttons, posters, and in political cartoons.

Though the range of flag iconography presented in the reply brief was fairly comprehensive, none of the examples contained any sexual overtones. Radich's attorney brought out the fact that in the original trial there had never been any question of an obscenity charge. Nevertheless, it seems, on review of the various decisions, that the crucified phallus was the clincher. In that particular sculpture, the artist attacked not only the very war that Cardinal Spellman had called "Christ's conflict," but also the Church that had supported the war for so long. And hanging on the cross—not the savior Jesus Christ—but "the male sexual organ." And, to add insult to injury, the phallus was represented as the flag of these United States of America. The very same flag that Betsy Ross had lovingly labored over and that generations of soldiers had died for and were dying for even today in the American struggle for peace with honor in Vietnam. There it was, boldly displayed at a second-floor Madison Avenue art gallery, open to the public—the American flag, a crucified phallus.

With the advent of pop art, the American flag as an iconographic element became quite common. Perhaps the best-known painted flags are those by Jasper Johns (cf. fig. 21), one of which was illustrated in the defendant's reply brief. There are, however, several examples of the use of the flag in modern art in a directly sexual way, as in Tom Wesselman's series, *Great American Nudes* (cf. fig. 22). As an art form, the flag provides the artist with both formal (all those stars and stripes) and symbolic content. And, as is immediately clear from the Radich case, few national symbols have the emotive power of the flag, thereby making it an eminently suitable subject for various kinds of protest art.

The reactions to Morrel's sculptures—indeed the sculptures themselves—seem a long way from the nineteenth-century reactions to Whistler's impressionistic *Nocturnes*. Of course, an essential element in the difference lies in the quality of the works—but, as Hilton Kramer argued, that should not affect either the legalities or the principles involved. The nineteenth-century editorial that discussed the Whistler case concluded with a vehement call for protest against "flinging paint pots" in the name of cleanliness and propriety. Under a cloak of Victorian verbiage, this sounds suspiciously like anal-compulsive aversion to the sight of all that gooey paint.

In the Radich case, typical of its era, the sexual implications were out in the open. Even though the attorneys for Radich tried to play down the sexual impact of Morrel's sculptures, they referred to it indirectly pointing out the taboos associated with flag display. "It is well known," they said, "that in many primitive societies, symbols originally designed to represent a tribe and its values, gradually evolve into independent objects of veneration, existing apart from— and often at variance with—the values they were originally designed to represent."

What the attorneys did not point out is the sexual con-

FIGURE 21. Jasper Johns, *Flag*. 1954. Encaustic on newspaper on canvas. Collection, The Museum of Modern Art, New York. Gift of Philip Johnson.

FIGURE 22. Tom Wesselman. *The Great American Nude, 2.* 1961.
Gesso, enamel, oil and collage on plywood. Collection, The Museum
of Modern Art, New York. Larry Aldrich Foundation Fund.

tent implicit in the totemism they described. For, as Freud tells us, in those primitive societies, the totem is taboo precisely because it represents the tribal ancestor and thus is the object of unconscious oedipal incest wishes. The stronger the incest wish, the stricter the taboo and the more rigorous the punishment for violating the taboo.[12] The reply brief for Radich speaks of the flag as a totem on a social and historical—and therefore conscious—level.

At this stage in the lengthy proceedings, a new *amici curiae* brief was submitted—this time, at long last, by highly placed members of the art world: John Hightower, director of the Museum of Modern Art, Karl Katz, director of the Jewish Museum, and Kenneth G. Dewey of the New York State Commission on Cultural Resources. Motivated by a concern for free artistic expression and its public exhibition, the *amici* obtained permission to submit the brief.

Artists, they said, have traditionally used their media to communicate social, political and religious ideas. They cited Bosch's late Renaissance paintings which expressed his objections to "the gluttony and lasciviousness of the clergy," Hogarth's satires on the evils of eighteenth-century England, and Daumier's critical representations of legal abuses in nineteenth-century France. Antiwar protests have been part of artistic iconography from the Napoleonic wars to the present. Second, the *amici* pointed out that works of art are entitled to the same protection under the First Amendment as speech and writing. Further, since the artist communicates through visual rather than verbal images, the use of the flag's image "does not justify loss of First Amendment protection,." Finally, concluded the *amici*, the decision "makes the flag a fetish."

Another term with implicit sexual overtones is thus introduced; the flag is now a fetish. According to Frazer,[13] who defined the term anthropologically, a totem is a class of objects which embodies the god of the tribe, whereas a fetish is an isolated object. But again it is Freud who reveals the unconscious sexual content of the fetish, an object that has been substituted for the normal sexual object. The substituted object may vary widely according to individual cases; it may be a part of the body, like the foot, or an inanimate object such as a piece of clothing. Whatever the outward fetish may be, the source underlying its power to hold one's veneration is sexual.

The brief of the *amici curiae* also noted the religious aspects of flag veneration. Implicit in the decisions against Radich, according to the *amici*, is the view that the flag's presence alone would result in disorder—"making the flag more sacrosanct than religious objects." Thus, the *amici* submitted, "there is no reason either to treat paintings and sculptures differently from speech and writing, or to ban flag representation altogether."

In the March issue of *Commonweal*, political scientist Edward R. Cain elaborated on the religious implications of American flag worship. "The flag," he wrote, "has become a religious object."[14]

The United States Supreme Court upheld Radich's conviction by a vote of four to four. Justice William O. Douglas abstained.

Slightly over four years later, on November 8, 1974, after three more court decisions, a federal judge in New York found that Radich had been deprived of his rights under the First and Fourteenth amendments. The sculptures, Judge John M. Cannella ruled, were nonverbal communications intended to make a point and, he noted, disorder had not resulted from their exhibition.

In 1970 the United States extended the Vietnam war into Cambodia. In April 1975 *New York Times* correspondent Sydney Schanberg wrote the following in a report from Pnomh Penh: "After five years of helping a feudal government it scorned and fighting a war it knew was hopeless, the United States has nothing to show for it except a sad evacuation in which the Ambassador carried out the American flag in one hand and his Samsonite suitcase in the other."[15]

CHAPTER SIX

"THE MATTER OF MARK ROTHKO, DECEASED"

Mentally, physically, artistically, and perhaps even legally, Mark Rothko, the prominent American abstract expressionist painter, seemed to have announced his own death. He drank a fifth of vodka every day, took sleeping pills, and saw a doctor who prescribed Valium, the powerful tranquilizer. Despite an aneurysm of the aorta, he smoked heavily. Psychologically, he was given to melancholy and depression; he was obsessed with money and with the reception given his paintings. After the summer of 1968, Rothko withdrew from his family and his house into his studio, a converted carriage house in Manhattan's East Sixties. In that studio, he acted out his final withdrawal from life.

Reviewing some of the events that preceded Rothko's death, hindsight offers a picture of the artist's gradual but determined march toward his own departure from the world.

Rothko was born in Russia in 1903. Ten years later, his pharmacist father, Jacob Rothkovich, moved the family to Oregon. Rothko attended Yale but dropped out. Gravitating toward New York, as did all those who would later comprise the New York school of abstract expressionism, he studied for a short time at the Art Students League.

In the 1930s, along with Jackson Pollock and Willem de Kooning, Rothko worked in the W.P.A. He belonged to the Secessionist Gallery and "The Ten" and participated in various group shows. In the early 1940s he became involved with Peggy Guggenheim's artistic circle. Then married to surrealist painter Max Ernst, Peggy Guggenheim opened the Art of This Century Gallery, which specialized in abstraction and surrealism. In 1945 she gave Rothko his first one-man show.

Artistically, Rothko most esteemed Milton Avery and Matisse; intellectually, he was influenced by Nietzsche's existentialism and Jungian symbolism. At this point in his development, Rothko's paintings were surrealist, and judging from such titles as *Sacrifice of Iphigenia, Tiresias,* and *Syrian Bull,* much of his iconography derived from ancient mythology. In 1943 Rothko had described the artist's need to seek inspiration in the mythological past. Myths, he said, "are the eternal symbols upon which we must fall back to express basic psychological ideas. They are the symbols of man's primitive fears and motivations, no matter in which land or what time, changing only in detail but never in substance, be they Greek, Aztec, Icelandic or Egyptian. And our modern psychology finds them persisting still in our dreams, our vernacular and our art, for all the changes in the outward condition of life."[1] (Cf. fig. 23.) Reviewers of Rothko's first one-man show were impressed by the effects of his color, calling it "hypnotic," "subdued," and "subconsciously dictated."

From the late 1940s, Rothko's paintings followed the move to the nonrepresentational style which characterized the work of numerous other artists at the time. An exhibition at the Betty Parsons Gallery in 1947—the same year Peggy Guggenheim's gallery closed—reflected the beginning of Rothko's transition to nonobjective painting. Some recognizable forms remained, however, and the titles still provided clues to the artist's meaning. *Primeval Landscape* and *Votive Figure* suggested a preoccupation with the distant past and the mysterious rituals of primitive cultures. Textures and colors were typically muted, and the shapes were developing into the amorphous blurs that would later be referred to as "bio-morphs" (cf. fig. 24).

In the course of this process, Rothko's canvases, which

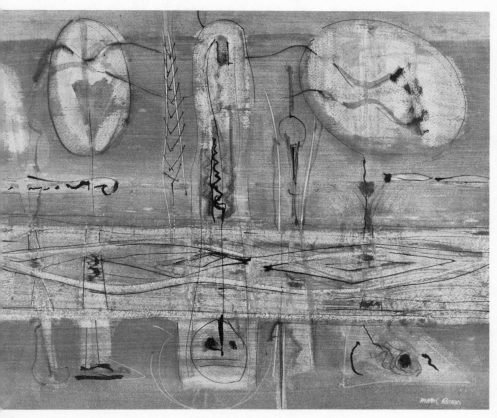

RE 23. Mark Rothko, *Baptismal Scene*. Watercolor, 1945. Col-
on, Whitney Museum of American Art, New York.

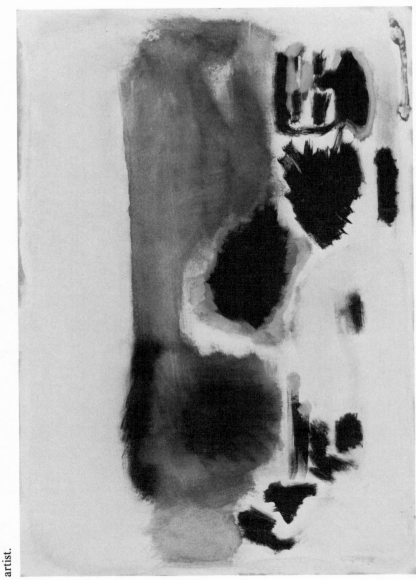

FIGURE 24. Mark Rothko, *Number 24* (c. 1947-48). Oil on canvas. Collection, The Museum of Modern Art, New York. Gift of the artist.

FIGURE 25. Mark Rothko, *Number 10*. 1950. Oil on canvas. Collection, The Museum of Modern Art, New York. Gift of Philip Johnson.

had been populated with the dreamlike images of surrealism, became progressively devoid of any human content. From the 1950s on, his individual style crystallized (cf. fig. 25). By January 1961 Rothko had arrived as a major American artist; the Museum of Modern Art mounted a retrospective exhibition of his work from 1945 to 1960. The fifty-four paintings that comprised the show revealed Rothko's development from surrealism to the style that became his trademark. Soft-edged rectangles of one color seemed to float over a background of another. Sometimes the floating rectangle was a different tone of the same color as the background. Shortly after Rothko's death, William Rubin, MOMA's chief curator of painting and sculpture, wrote that he "could set two reds together in a manner that would make your teeth chatter."[2]

Historically it is always problematical to separate the development of a single artist from that of his contemporaries, especially when the two are as interrelated as Rothko and abstract expressionism. Nevertheless, within the general movement defined as abstract expressionism, characterized largely by a combination of relative flatness with the absence of recognizable form, Rothko's style is among the most consistently and determinedly removed from natural existence. Having finally eliminated all form but the rectangle from his canvases, color became a primary focus of Rothko's art. He thus denied not only traditional iconographic content to the viewer but also virtually any forms of narrative associational value. Nor did he afford the observer the crutch of a title. Nearly all his pictures were now identified by number, date or color. Unlike Jackson Pollock's energetic drips, which eventually may suggest form to an observer inclined to find it, or Clyfford Still's craggy, rocklike patches of color, or Franz Kline's scratchy black brushstrokes, which have been referred to as "Chinese laundry tickets," Rothko tried to paint nothing which allowed for direct metaphorical association.

Compared with any other abstract expressionist works, Rothko's paintings are the least related to natural reality, whether it be imagery or the character of the paint itself. Pollock, Hofmann, and de Kooning all express the textural reality of paint. They never completely eliminate the associational titles either. Gottlieb's *Bursts* are immediately suggestive of a literal occurrence, and Motherwell—especially in the famous *Elegies to the Spanish Republic*—is downright literary. Barnett Newman, possibly the most reductive of the abstract expressionists, painted hard edges and flat planes which, together with his penchant for Euclidian titles, make direct reference to geometry. Even Josef Albers—as in the series *Homage to the Square*—resorted to a certain hard-edged mathematical precision that Rothko rejected by blurring the edges of his rectangles. Albers's squares played optical games with color and light as well as with space; thus, the squares advanced or receded in a tunnellike motion. By his own assertion, as early as 1949, Rothko sought to eliminate "all obstacles between the painter and the idea, and between the idea and the observer."[3] Obstacles, for Rothko, were memory, history, and geometry.

Thus devoid of iconographic content and geometric precision, Rothko's paintings seemed also to have been divested of gravity. In the works of Sam Francis, the paint itself acknowledges the reality of weight as it drips down the surface of the picture plane. The same may be said of Morris Louis. But, aside from an occasional drip, Rothko made virtually no concessions to the earthly laws of gravity. His rectangles just float, hover over the picture plane.

Minimal in form, lacking in gravity, Rothko's paintings were often described by critics as "religious" in spirit. Harold Rosenberg referred to Rothko as constituting "the theological sector of Abstract Expressionism."[4] Another critic, reviewing Rothko's 1954 show at the Chicago Art Institute, felt that the source of the artist's "religious" impact resided in the quality of his light. As a universal symbol, light has consistently been associated with aspects of divinity, spirituality, even inspiration and hope. Our saints are often distinguished in art by the halo, and philosophers—notably Plato and the Neo-Platonists—have constructed elaborate systems around the meaning of light. When inspired, we "see the light" and, to the hopeful, the light is always there at the end of the tunnel. Likewise, describing Rothko as the prophet who came down from the mountain, Hubert Crehan's review of the Chicago show finds his painting "*almost* a resuscitation of the ancient image of a vision . . . in the sense of the Biblical image of the heavens opening up and revealing a celestial light. . . ."[5] According to Max Kozloff, "Rothko has so etherealized the paint that it . . . gives . . . the unlikely but inescapable impression of light."[6] His paintings, says Kozloff, are neither light nor dark; they are "autoluminous," producing "a chromatic glow which no amount of visual inhalation will ever deplete." Comparing Rothko's light with Byzantine mosaics, William Rubin speaks of its emanation from the picture rather than its refraction from the spectator's environment.[7] For Peter Selz, writing in the catalog of the artist's MOMA retrospective, Rothko's "shivering bars of light" assume a function "similar to that loaded area between God's and Adam's fingers—on the Sistine Ceiling." Rothko, says Selz, "has given us the first, not the sixth, day of creation."[8]

Considering Rothko's determination to eliminate all means of metaphorical association from his pictures, critics have been remarkably eloquent in their associations. It would almost seem as though their need to be reminded of tradition is just as persistent as Rothko's desire to prevent them from doing so. Most of the associations have been religious in nature, although some critics have been reminded of such mundane forms as windows, passing clouds, and barren landscapes.

In the religious vein, Harold Rosenberg has called Rothko's blurred rectangles his "icons,"[9] and Peter Selz, detecting the influence of Fra Angelico's San Marco frescoes, likens his paintings to *Annunciations*. After 1958 Rothko's pictures remind Selz of "entrances to tombs, like the doors to the dwellings of the dead in Egyptian pyramids, behind which the sculptors kept the kings 'alive' for eternity in the *ka*." These "open sarcophagi" represent for Selz the door to the tomb opening "for the artist in search of his muse."[10]

Consistent with the critical tendency to emphasize the religious aspects of Rothko's art, his last major project was a chapel. In 1965 art patrons John and Dominique de Menil of Houston, Texas, commissioned a group of mural paintings for an interdenominational chapel, now part of the Texas Medical Center. The chapel itself is octagonal, the inside empty except for Rothko's fourteen large, somber paintings. The relatively small interior, together with the monumentality of the pictures, results in an effect of spatial compression. While Rothko was working on this commission, he constructed a replica of the chapel's interior in his New York studio. This enabled him to test the relationships of picture to architecture in advance of the final installation. Like the responses evoked in his admirers, Rothko produced his paintings after long, moody periods of meditation.

Three years after the Houston commission, in the spring of 1968, Rothko became seriously ill; an aneurysm of the aorta put a stop to his work for several months. Depressed and angry, he spent that summer in Cape Cod producing mainly small compositions on paper. From these works, Rothko's famous last works, recognizable as a cohesive body, emerged—the black paintings. In these, Robert Goldwater sensed "the mood that led to his tragic end."[11]

Artists' last works are frequently significant. Often they contain a kind of memorial signature, as if the artist were zeroing in on some desperate aspect of his own being. Michelangelo's last sculpture—the emaciated and elongated *Pietà* now in Milan—represents the artist as the dead Christ. Throughout his career, Michelangelo was plagued by an inability to finish much of his work. He had previously inserted his self-portrait into the figures of at least two saints— Bartholomew and Joseph of Arimathea. These two tendencies—saintly self-portraiture and reluctance to complete his works—are united with a unique force in his last sculpture. That Michelangelo associated the completion of this work with his own death is suggested both by his refusal to complete it and by his identification with the dead Christ. At the same time, the identification with the Redeemer, supported solely by his mother and enveloped by her cloak, reflects Michelangelo's desire for redemption. On his deathbed, the artist beseeched his friends to remember the resurrection of Christ. Titian's last work, also a *Pietà*, was painted for the artist's own tomb and contained a self-portrait in the figure of Joseph of Arimathea. More recent and more comparable with Rothko is Van Gogh, whose last painting is significant. The famous *Wheatfield with Blackbirds* is devoid of human figures. Instead Van Gogh painted the end of a road and a sky, populated by blackbirds, which is becoming heavy with dark, gathering clouds. Shortly thereafter, at the age of thirty-seven, Van Gogh shot himself.

In the last year of his life, Rothko, the determined abstractionist, took one final step in the direction of abstraction. For the most part, his paintings were stripped of their last vestige of reference to the natural world—color. Aside from occasional brown tones, Rothko's last pictures are black and grey; many of these are bordered by a thin edge of white. Though a preoccupation with black and white is characteristic of the abstract expressionist movement, no artist of that school was as unrelentingly oppressive in his use of black as was Rothko. Nor did any employ the white edge in the way Rothko did. Technically, black and white are not colors. White is light, or the sum of all the colors. Black is the absence of color. Black and white are thus opposites of sorts—each one an extreme of Rothko's two main formal qualities: light and color. He returned to a purity of light in the use of white and essentially eliminated color by using black. At the same time, he also removed his pictures' last metaphorical link with reality. In 1947 Rothko still thought in terms of everyday experience. He wrote: "I think of my pictures as dramas: the shapes in the pictures are the performers. They have been created from the need for a group of actors who are able to move dramatically without embarrassment and execute gestures without shame."[12] Describing Rothko twenty-three years later, Irving Sandler wrote: "His abstractions become a kind of stage set for a drama, before which the viewer is transformed into an actor who plays his solitary self."[13]

Following his determined march toward self-effacement, Rothko's stage became progressively devoid of actors. Eventually there was no longer a play—an ultimate absurdity—and finally the lights went out.

More or less concurrent with his production of black and gray paintings was Rothko's actual withdrawal from his home and family. He left his townhouse on East Ninety-fifth Street, his wife and two children—seventeen-year-old Kate and four-year-old Christopher—and went to live by himself in his studio. Donald McKinney, president of New York's Marlborough Gallery, described Rothko's life there in a catalog of his work: "The tiled walls of the carriage house . . . were masked off by great temporary walls on which paintings could be hung and moved via an arrangement of pulleys. The big painting room was lighted from a high, pyramid-shaped skylight in the center of a ceiling some thirty feet high. A bed, some chairs, a table and his record player completed the living arrangements. There was a total lack of any personal objects, and it was in this immense space that he would sit, sometimes for hours, looking at his paintings, thinking and meditating about them. He continued to live and work in his studio until his death."[14]

Despite this actual withdrawal—as if the direction of his art and his existence were merging into one—the artist made one final protest against his own determined rejection of color and possibly of life itself. Rothko painted a large, bright red on red. This was his last picture.

On February 25, 1970, Rothko committed suicide. He was sixty-six years old. His black paintings looming on the walls of his studio, Rothko swallowed a large dose of sleeping pills and slashed the veins in both his arms. He died in the early hours of the morning.

Nearly two years later, the estate of Mark Rothko became the subject of what was certainly the most complex trial ever involving works of art—*The Matter of Mark Rothko, Deceased*.

The trial, held in New York's Surrogate Court before Judge Millard Midonick, consisted of over 20,000 pages of testimony and some 3,000 more of briefs, reply briefs, and memoranda. No less than nineteen lawyers were needed to handle the various aspects of the case. It lasted years. In the process, a great many prominent art-world figures became caught up in the labyrinths of testimony, innuendo, and conjecture.

From the tangled web of issues in the case, two broad themes emerged which revealed a great deal about the inner workings of the art world and—above all—about its marketplace. On the one hand, there were allegations of wrongdoing, which were of a fairly straightforward legal nature and, on the other, there were the ever-elusive questions relating to art. There were, however, considerable areas in which these two main issues—the purely legal and the artistic—overlapped. In no other art trial had the financial motives of the art world been as starkly revealed as in the Rothko trial. And it was primarily in the area of finance that the legal and artistic elements of the case became virtually inseparable. Many unanswered questions were posed in the course of the trial, and, throughout, the ghost of Mark Rothko seemed to hover; many of his own actions—like his suicide—remained as inscrutable as the rectangles floating on his canvases.

During his lifetime, Rothko made several contracts and a will which partially set the stage for the events leading to the trial. After Rothko left the Betty Parsons Gallery, he joined Sidney Janis in 1954, along with other prominent abstract expressionists, and his prices went from the hundreds to the thousands. Two of Rothko's main concerns, which were to become matters of great discussion at the trial, were his international exposure as an artist and the way in which his paintings were exhibited. Commissioned in 1959 to paint a set of murals for the Seagram Building, he canceled the commission upon learning that his pictures would, in fact, hang in the commercial atmosphere of the Four Seasons Restaurant. Another characteristic was his insistence that his pictures be exhibited together—as a contemplative totality—rather than to hang among the works of other artists. The Seagram murals now belong to the Tate Gallery in London, where an entire room is devoted to their exhibition.

Eventually Rothko left Sidney Janis and began selling paintings from his studio. His next and final dealer would be Frank Lloyd, one of the most successful and controversial men in the world of art. Underneath a facade of Middle European charm, Frank Lloyd is something of a financial wizard. From a small business started in London after World War II, Lloyd has built up a network of twenty-one corporations—in the United States, Canada, Great Britain, Switzerland, Liechtenstein, Italy, and Japan—with galleries in New York, London, Zurich, Rome, Montreal, Toronto, and Tokyo. Members of Lloyd's family are the sole beneficial owners of the gallery group.

More than any other dealer, Lloyd openly admits that he is in the art business to make money. From his home on Paradise Island in the Bahamas, he controls the multimillion-dollar international network of Marlborough Galleries headquartered for tax (and other) purposes in Liechtenstein. Marlborough pays Lloyd a salary of $100,000 a year, plus expenses. For a variety of reasons, Lloyd has aroused intense hostility among rival dealers and among artists, critics, and collectors. Nevertheless, if Lloyd is not pure, neither are the others. Artists and collectors keep coming, and Lloyd continues to prosper.

In 1963 Rothko sold fifteen pictures to Marlborough A.G., a Liechtenstein-based company, for $148,000 on condition that they be marked up 40 percent. He also made a five-year exclusive agreement with Marlborough A.G. as his overseas dealer. Under the terms of this agreement, which expired in the summer of 1968, the gallery was responsible for the expenses of exhibitions, shipping, storage, and insurance. Marlborough was to receive a commission of one-third, with base prices to be reviewed annually.

Rothko was introduced to Lloyd and Marlborough by Bernard Reis, an accountant and art collector who acted both for Marlborough and for Rothko. Reis and Rothko became friends. The nature of their friendship and the course it took is crucial to understanding certain aspects of the trial. Was Reis the "loving friend of Rothko" or was he the "mastermind" behind a monumental "swindle of his estate"?

On September 13, 1968, at the age of sixty-four, Rothko made a will. It was drawn up not by an attorney, but by Bernard Reis. "Bernie," Reis quoted the artist as having said, "you know I hate attorneys, I hate going up in elevators. . . . Will you prepare something for me?" Rothko named three executors: Reis; Theodoros Stamos, a member of the New York school of abstract expressionism and a friend of the Rothko family; and Morton Levine, a professor of anthropology. Under the terms of Rothko's will, a tax-free foundation would receive most of his paintings. The foundation would have five trustees: the three executors of Rothko's will; William Rubin, curator of painting and sculpture at the Museum of Modern Art; and Robert Goldwater, a professor of art history at New York University and expert in modern and primitive art. By spring, Rubin had been removed and replaced by producer Clinton Wilder. Morton Feldman, a composer, and Rothko himself also became trustees. Other changes would occur later. To his wife, Rothko left $250,000 and the Ninety-fifth Street townhouse with all its contents. On his death, forty-four paintings remained in the house. The paintings that Rothko had originally made for the Seagram Building were left to the Tate Gallery.

In November of the same year, Rothko's 1963 exclusive overseas contract with Marlborough expired. Two prominent dealers, Arnold Glimcher of the Pace Gallery in New York and Ernst Beyeler of Basel, Switzerland, jointly offered Rothko $500,000 for a selection of eighteen paintings—an average of approximately $28,000 per picture. Although at first Rothko seemed prepared to accept, he rejected the offer after checking with Bernard Reis. Despite the 20,000 pages of testimony, the motive for Rothko's behavior in this instance has not been clarified.

The following February, 1969, Rothko made a new deal with Marlborough which, *prima facie*, seemed far less favorable than the Glimcher-Beyeler offer. He sold eighty-seven paintings to Marlborough A.G. for $1,050,000 (an average of approximately $12,000 per picture), payable over ten years without interest. A supplementary contract granted Marlborough an eight-year exclusive on condition that the artist could, at his option, sell an additional four paintings a year to Marlborough A.G. at 90 percent of the current selling prices. In effect, the supplementary contract guaranteed Rothko a yearly income equal to 90 percent of the price of four paintings. In December 1969 Rothko sold Marlborough another eighteen paintings for $396,000.

Two months later, Rothko killed himself.

Then the real trouble began. When Rothko died, he left 798 paintings, $330,000 in cash, and debts of $9,000. Marlborough A.G. in Liechtenstein owed him about $1,000,000. There was also the townhouse and its 44 paintings. Bernard Reis hired Frank E. Karelson, a seventy-eight-year-old New York lawyer to handle Rothko's estate. The will was probated, and the three executors, together with Karelson, entered into a set of agreements with Frank Lloyd and Marlborough that did not become known to either Rothko's family or the other trustees of the foundation until the end of June 1971.

In the meantime, in July 1970, Rothko's wife contested the will, claiming that half the estate should revert to herself; this was granted by the court. A month later, she died of heart failure. The children then had the house, its contents (including the paintings) and half the estate (including the 798 paintings). Nineteen-year-old Kate Rothko asked the executors for paintings instead of money. She did not receive a single picture. It was not until the following summer—June 1971—that the lawyers for Kate and Christopher were informed of the deals that the executors had made with Frank Lloyd and Marlborough.

The executors had entered into two contracts with Lloyd which prompted the first step toward litigation. First, on behalf of Marlborough A.G., Lloyd paid $1,800,000 for 100 paintings from Rothko's estate. Payments without interest would be made over thirteen years. This represented an average discounted price per painting of approximately $12,000, much less than the current prices for Rothko's work. A second contract gave Marlborough New York the remaining 698 paintings on a consignment basis at a commission rate of 50 percent if sold to clients and 40 percent if sold at a discount to a dealer. Thus, within a few weeks, the executors had handed over to Frank Lloyd nearly 800 paintings—the bulk of Rothko's estate—in return for an initial payment of $200,000 cash. By the end of 1970, 12 of the 100 paintings had been sold with an average markup of 800 percent. Both the sale of the "100" and the consignment contract were dated May 21, 1970, although the lawyers for Rothko's children alleged that the second contract had actually been made much later and backdated.

In November 1971 Kate Rothko's guardian filed a petition accusing the three executors of a conspiracy to defraud the estate and waste its assets. He sought to have the executors removed and their agreements rescinded. Two months later, the executors responded that they were bound by Rothko's own exclusive contract of February 1969 which left them with two choices. They could either deal only with Marlborough, thereby limiting their bargaining power; or resign themselves, under the terms of the exclusive contract, to selling only four pictures a year (at 90 percent of current prices.)

In June 1972 Surrogate Judge Midonick barred further sales of Rothko paintings pending the outcome of the litigation. Aside from strenuous objections to the two contracts of May 1970, petitioners in the case presented evidence of self-dealing on the part of the executors. Bernard Reis was by then a director and secretary-treasurer of Marlborough New York. Stamos had signed a contract of his own with Marlborough on far better terms than he and the other executors had obtained for Rothko's estate. Levine, at this time, split with Reis and Stamos, asserting that they had misled him. New York State Attorney General Louis Lefkowitz intervened in support of Kate Rothko as the representative of "the ultimate charitable beneficiaries of the Rothko Foundation." These beneficiaries were older artists who had not attained the success and financial security of Rothko.

The following year, new charges were filed. In addition to the executors, Marlborough was now accused of defrauding the estate. It was alleged that the gallery had sold paintings at high prices which were concealed from the estate in order to reduce its share of the proceeds.

Attempts by the executors and the foundation to retaliate included contesting the children's right to the forty-four pictures in the Ninety-fifth Street townhouse. Surrogate Judge Samuel DiFalco ruled that the pictures were part of the contents of the house and therefore willed to the family. This decision, however, was appealed by the foundation.

On February 14, 1974, the trial opened. Some 7,000 pages of pretrial testimony had been recorded, and 500 exhibits entered. At 10:30 A.M. seven sets of lawyers filed into the ornate, wood-paneled Surrogate's Court. From the first day, the trial was bogged down in extensive discussions between the lawyers over various legal technicalities. They began with arguments over witnesses.

From beginning to end, art and money have been the two main themes of this trial—and the amounts of money involved were staggering. John Corry, writing "About New York" in the February 15, 1974, issue of *The New York Times* observed: "The case involving Mark Rothko's paintings has nothing to do with art at all. It has to do with money and power in a very small world, and that is what so much of the art world has been about all along."[15] The financial proportions of the case were of such magnitude that they obscured its artistic aspects. But these were present nonetheless.

MONEY AND POWER

The financial aspects of the Rothko case were extremely convoluted, though for the most part they could be traced to the two contracts entered into by the executors with Marl-borough. Coincidentally, the bulk of the Rothko proceedings paralleled the height of the Watergate investigations. In the first week of the trial, special Watergate prosecutor Leon Jaworski sent a letter to the Senate Judiciary Committee as-serting that Richard Nixon was withholding White House tapes; former United States Attorney General Mitchell went on trial. While New York Surrogate's Court heard allega-tions seeking the dismissal of the executors of Rothko's es-tate, the House Judiciary Committee was discussing the grounds for the impeachment of a United States president.

Parallels with Watergate were not lost on observers of the Rothko trial. A *New York Magazine* article referred to it as "the art world's own little Watergate." Lawyers for Kate Rothko elaborated on the coincidence. "A basic lesson of Watergate," they argued, "is the . . . reluctant realization that persons of wealth and respectability, occupying positions of public prominence, trust and responsibility, are capable of fraud, dishonesty and deception. . . . Watergate's cleansing effect is a reminder that 'a trustee is held to something stricter than the morals of the marketplace.' " Lawyers for the petitioners illustrated this general observation by more precise parallels: in addition to the betrayal of a trust, fraud, and corruption, petitioners alleged efforts to "launder" paintings, backdating of important documents and obstruc-tion of justice by frustrating the discovery process, payments for silence and "sustained concealment." They even found a "Rose Mary Woods" on the loose in the vast machinery of the Marlborough complex. They said that Marian Moffett of the gallery's registrar office had altered various trial exhibits, records and documents and then was consistently unable to recall why or when she had done so.

Petitioners sought the removal of the three executors, legal costs, and the return of all unsold paintings. On all bona fide sales, they sought the actual prices paid, plus inter-est.

Retracing the actions of the executors in completing the two contracts with Marlborough, a certain pattern emerges.

Bernard Reis hired Frank Karelson to act as attorney for the estate. Karelson advised the executors that Rothko's exclusive contract of 1969 with Marlborough was binding on the estate. Reis urged Stamos and Levine to negotiate with Lloyd soon, adding that Karelson would stand in for him in order to avoid potential conflicts of interest. (Reis was then receiving a $20,000 per year salary from Marlborough.) Further, Reis informed the other executors that he had arranged for Daniel Saidenberg, an art dealer and member of the Art Dealers Association, to appraise the Rothko paintings "for estate tax purposes." Saidenberg's appraisal for the 100 paintings came to $750,000—an average of $7,500 each, although the current selling prices averaged between six and ten times that amount. In May, Levine, Stamos, and Karelson met with Lloyd and told him that the asking price for the 100 was $3,000,000. Lloyd offered $800,000. The economy, he said, was depressed. The Dow Jones was, at that very moment, at a new low. Eventually they all agreed on $1,800,000 and concluded the deal.

Objections to this sale ranged from allegations of self-dealing to wilful concealment. Reis, argued the estate, had acted improperly in a conflict-of-interest situation. It was alleged that he had used his position at Marlborough to increase the price of his personal art collection and had sold his own pictures one at a time for the highest possible prices. When dealing with Rothko's paintings, on the other hand, Reis rushed Stamos and Levine into a bulk sale on the basis of what petitioners called a fabricated crisis.

According to Reis, however, the estate needed cash and an executor was bound by law to liquidate an estate's assets as soon as possible. On the other hand, the estate did have $350,000 in cash. The executors could have exercised their right to sell four pictures a year to Marlborough at 90 percent of current prices. This, theoretically, would have produced at least $200,000 per annum. To this, the defendants replied that Frank Lloyd was threatening to cancel a Rothko exhibition in Venice to run concurrently with the Biennale. If Lloyd would go to all the expense of such a show, which the dealer argued, would ultimately benefit Rothko's reputation and his heirs, he wanted to buy 100 pictures outright. By doing so, however, Lloyd received an enormous discount. Compared with one of his own purchases of 44 paintings in 1969 at an average of $21,000 each, in 1970 (when prices were actually higher) he paid an average of $10,000 to $12,000 per painting. The estate claimed this was unconscionable, to which Lloyd replied that in the first place, he was entitled to a discount on a bulk purchase, and in the second, among the 100 were many paintings from Rothko's early surrealist period. These, said Lloyd, were virtually unsalable; he would have to create a market for them.

Lloyd's argument that there was no market for Rothko's early surrealist paintings raises an interesting point which is not unique to Rothko. Many artists, especially from the Impressionists on, did not attain their most advanced (and most individual) style until after a period of study and development had taken place. Often an artist's early style, reflecting its developmental character, will seem "old-fashioned" when compared with the later style. Thus, early Degas is influenced by the Neoclassical style, early Van Gogh by the Barbizon school, early Rothko and Pollock, by surrealism.

Very often the artist's most mature and most characteristic style is also his most popular. Given a perspective of time, on the other hand, the early style of an artist is likely to be of considerable historical and creative importance. Nevertheless, the popularity of the later style frequently makes it easier to sell. Frank Lloyd is in the art business to sell pictures, not to become involved in aesthetic history.

The Saidenberg appraisal also became a matter of much dispute at the trial, particularly among the expert witnesses. From the strictly legal point of view, the executors argued that his appraisal was low for two reasons. First, it was for estate tax purposes and, second, Rothko's own exclusive contract meant that there was no assessable market value for the pictures before 1977. Petitioners questioned the binding nature of Rothko's exclusive contract, asserting that the executors should have tested its legality in court before signing away the whole estate.

As for Stamos, the petitioners alleged that he had a secret understanding with Marlborough to the effect that, if he signed the sales contract, he would later be taken on as a Marlborough artist. Stamos did, in fact, become part of the gallery's stable several months later.

The petitioners alleged that Morton Levine knew of these conflicts of interest, and therefore his conduct as a trustee was "wasteful and improvident." They pointed out that Levine had borrowed $10,000 from the estate in 1971 and that he did not repay it until after the trial began. Furthermore, the petitioners alleged, Levine planned to write a book on Rothko, which Lloyd would subsidize, thereby compromising Levine's independence.

Levine, in turn, replied that he was a prudent man, but a layman in legal matters, acting on the advice of counsel. He was not told, he said, that he could retain his own lawyer, and alternative solutions to the estate's problems had not been disclosed to him. Although he was aware of the conflict of interest inherent in the situations of Reis and Stamos, Levine testified, he was advised not to "disrupt the harmonious coordination of the executors' actions, nor lose for the estate the benefit of Reis's and Stamos's expertise." Describing Levine as "the man on the flying trapeze," attorneys for Reis and Stamos accused him of sitting on the fence because of concern about his academic position.

Bernard Reis did not testify. He became ill after the litigation began, and his doctor advised against appearing in court. Thus, aside from his brief pretrial examination in February 1973, Reis, who seemed to hold the key to many of the trial's unresolved issues, had very little to say.

The negotiations for the consignment contract, unlike those for the bulk sale of the 100 paintings, remain shrouded in obscurity. The estate claimed it was made a year later and backdated. It also pointed out that it was not a favorable contract compared with estate contracts between other abstract expressionists and Marlborough. Attorneys for Reis and Stamos replied that the comparison with other estates was invalid. No other consignment agreement was negotiated in which the estate had to deal with the consignee for seven years. Others did not involve so many pictures (798), nor have so many that were unsalable (i.e. those painted before 1947). In any event, once the 698 paintings had been consigned to Marlborough, the estate lost control of their disposition, leaving Frank Lloyd free to do with them as he pleased.

Backed by the attorney general, the petitioners now charged Reis and Lloyd with a fraudulent scheme to manipulate the consigned paintings in such a way that Marlborough profited at the expense of the estate. As this scheme was outlined, estate paintings were transferred to Marlborough's foreign affiliates (notably those in Liechtenstein, where, by national law, the identity of a corporation's owners is not revealed), only to be reacquired by Marlborough at a later date (after the trial).

As a result of one transaction, Marlborough sold five pictures to a Bernini Gallery in Liechtenstein, seven to AEK (Allgemeine Europaische Kunstanstalt) also in Liechtenstein, and one to Galerie Flinker in Paris. Two of the pictures sold to Bernini were reacquired by Marlborough and sold to the Mellon family. The estate's share of the sale amounted to $248,000 for thirteen paintings (later amended to $321,000) while Marlborough received $420,000 just for the two paintings that the Mellons subsequently bought. Marlborough sold another twenty-two pictures to AEK and twenty-five more to Hallsborough, a London gallery.

These bulk sales became a subject of heated controversy during the trial. The identity of the Liechtenstein corporations is still obscure, but petitioners claimed that they were secret Marlborough affiliates and that Lloyd parked the paintings there pending the outcome of litigation. Marlborough would then reacquire them and sell them at great profit to itself, thereby leaving the estate with its much smaller share of the first sale. Should this prove to be the case, Marlborough would have violated its obligation to obtain the best possible prices for the estate. And Frank Lloyd left no doubt about who made the decisions on prices. From Paradise Island, he was in constant telephone contact with his galleries all over the world. "I make the prices," he asserted flatly.

In reply to the petitioners, Marlborough protested that its bulk sales were intended to establish a "secondary market" for Rothko abroad. In other words, by distributing large numbers of paintings in Europe, Lloyd would increase Rothko's international exposure, thus creating a demand for his pictures. To this, Attorney General Lefkowitz charged hypocrisy on the grounds that Marlborough sold in bulk only paintings from the estate and none of its own. He further pointed out the strange choice of client in creating this market, since AEK and Bernini were not dealers and did not have galleries. When questioned, Lloyd was unable to identify the owners of AEK and Bernini, nor would he admit to knowing what they planned to do with the pictures. As for Hallsborough, it specializes in Old Masters rather than modern art, and its location on the same street as Marlborough in London does not suggest a significant increase in international exposure. Finally, Lefkowitz argued, Marlborough had its own international network of galleries and could have used them for worldwide distribution. When petitioners pointed to Marlborough's insurance records for the paintings, they noted that the figures were much closer to actual prices paid for individual (rather than bulk) sales. To this, Marlborough replied that the paintings were insured for up to three times their value.

In addition to bulk sales to obscure Liechtenstein corporations, Marlborough sold groups of consigned paintings to wealthy collectors—also abroad. Accusations that these, too, were merely parked in friendly hands were hotly denied. Lloyd defended the sales saying he feared Rothko's market might suffer as a result of litigation (and the resultant public knowledge that 798 of his pictures were available). In order to raise money therefore—including funds for legal fees—

Lloyd offered the paintings for slightly less than usual.

These bulk sales were complicated by allegations of paintings being surreptiously exchanged, questionable and fabricated documents, backdating of transactions, coverups, omissions, and extensive "mistakes" in Marlborough's books.

By and large, Marlborough's employees were unable to recall the circumstances surrounding many of these "errors." Frank Lloyd professed astonishment at some of the mistakes, which he attributed to a variety of sources ranging from typographical and clerical errors and language barriers, to the negligence of a Paris museum. He, himself, he testified, was not familiar with accounting on a daily basis. He conducted most of his business orally, rarely signing anything because he was not a director. It was not until the end of each year that he received a balance sheet informing him how the galleries were doing. He could not be expected to concern himself with such details, Lloyd argued. He had bigger fish to fry and a lot of important business to worry about.

MONEY AND ART

Somewhere in the woodpile of convoluted legalities in the Rothko trial, amid allegations of self-dealing, violation of court injunctions, and dubious transactions, hide certain basic aesthetic arguments. Rothko's position as an artist permeated the entire case. Just how much were his pictures worth in May 1970? How predictable was his continuing reputation? And who—if anyone—was most qualified to make the predictions? It was on these questions that the experts entered the fray.

In the Rothko trial, the experts very nearly covered the spectrum of art-world activity, including academics, curators, and a variety of dealers. Because of the monumental amount of material covered in the trial, the petitioners agreed on a division of labor in which the New York State Attorney General would concentrate on expert opinion. His position was argued in court by Assistant Attorney General Gustave Harrow.

Harrow endeavored to establish that during his lifetime, Rothko had become part of the "fabric" of art history and that his recognized importance was reflected in his predeath prices. As the representative of the beneficiaries of Rothko's estate and of the public interest, Harrow proceeded to demonstrate Rothko's stature as an artist.

This proved to be a fairly simple matter. Not only did the experts characterize Rothko as an artist of unique vision, they also extolled him as a leader of abstract expressionism and an influential force for the future of art.

For Professor of Art History, H. Arnason, Rothko had been "universally recognized" as "one of the greatest American artists of the twentieth century." Mark Rothko, Arnason asserted, "was one of the three or four absolute leaders of the movement in American painting known as abstract expressionism which emerged during the World War II period." Abstract expressionism, he said, "is now recognized as the most significant single movement in the history of American painting. It is this movement that has made the United States the world leader in modern painting. . . . Thus, the intrinsic value of his work is found not only in its esthetic quality but also in its historical significance."

Thomas Messer, director of the Guggenheim Museum, had wanted to mount an exhibition of Rothko's black and grey paintings. The first witness of the trial, Messer described Rothko as a leader of the abstract expressionist movement. "Jackson Pollock and Mark Rothko," he testified, "could be said to occupy the opposite poles within this indistinct movement of abstract expressionism. Roughly, Jackson Pollock was concerned with spontaneous and linear forms, whereas Rothko was concerned with a single image, with what is called a field of painting in which the individual figuration was suppressed and subsumed. I would say that in his own way, Rothko is as important for the field fraction of abstract expressionism as Pollock is for his spontaneous figurations."

Sam Hunter, then a professor of art history at Princeton, consulting editor for art publisher Harry Abrams, and author of several books on modern art, went even further in his praise, placing Rothko "on a level of relative parity with the greatest masters such as Picasso, Matisse, Mondrian, etc."

Arnold Glimcher, president of Pace Gallery, explained his esteem for Rothko on a historical basis: "When you can point to an artist's ancestors and antecedents," he said, "and you can, with strong judgment, say that the antecedents [sic] would not have come after him, had he not existed, he's inextricable from the history of art. . . .." Glimcher elaborated on the specific nature of Rothko's stylistic contribution to painting: "In Rothko's works, the deliberate blurring of these rectangular images on this fuzzy field make it impossible to focus, as when a camera lens is out of focus. Therefore, the edges of the paintings diminish and the paintings become environmental and visual concepts of all the field, and become part of the subjects themselves. A very gradual occurrence in the history of art, and I think one of the great legacies of the history of art."

For Meyer Schapiro, the distinguished art historian and University Professor at Columbia, abstract expressionism was an extremely important development in American art because of its international impact. Asserting that Rothko was already recognized in the United States and abroad by the mid-1950s, Schapiro described the artist's appeal to innovative younger artists. He illustrated European response to Rothko's work by way of anecdote: "I was asked to go to London to give lectures on the occasion of a great show of American art at The Tate Gallery in the winter of 1955-56, and I was also invited to speak on the third program of the BBC Radio about new American art. The newspapers gave most importance at that moment to quite other painters, and made fun of and ridiculed the work of the new painters like Rothko and Pollock. The *Times* reviewer spoke of Pollock as 'Jack the Dripper.'

"But in the room with these American works, which were altogether new to Englishmen, most of the young art students got together, and I saw a young art student so excited by the paintings of Rothko and Pollock, that were together, that he rolled on the floor in joy to express his excitement and interest. That is one example. That was in the winter of 1955-56. And I regard that as prophetic of what happened."

Responding to questions about reactions to Rothko's work from critics, museum people, and dealers, Schapiro replied that when something new and strong emerges, only a few are quick to see it. In Rothko's case, however, "there was a continual growth of recognition, of appreciation, of his work." What was more, Schapiro added, in the 1960s which saw a stream of new styles (including pop art), Rothko maintained the high level of his reputation.

Schapiro's assertion that only a perceptive few realize when new and strong art emerges would seem to be borne out by some of the early negative reactions to Rothko's work. An *Art News* reviewer, commenting on a show at the Betty Parsons Gallery in 1947, wrote that on confronting "the crucial enigma of Rothko's symbolism," the spectator would "most likely walk out with a grandiose 'ho-hum' "[16] Two years later Rothko was compared to Whistler. Thomas Hess, also writing on a show at Parsons, compared Rothko's "Orientalism" with that of Whistler. Hess detected a "strength of composition which is almost Oriental in its reticence" underlying the emotional impact of Rothko's color.[17] A reviewer for *Arts Digest*,[18] however, was a trifle less flattering than Hess in noting similarities between Rothko and Whistler. Citing Ruskin's libelous attack on Whistler's Nocturnes, the writer thought that Rothko would be aptly described as having flung the proverbial paint pot in the public's face.

Some of Rothko's early reviews were merely lukewarm rather than negative: Robert Coates,[19] writing in 1955 after Rothko had moved to the Janis Gallery, admitted that his fondness for abstract expressionism was "minimal." On the other hand, he was impressed by the "brooding glow" and "totemic import" of Rothko's paintings—especially when viewed as a group. At the same time, Coates found himself disturbed by his own impulse to make associations between the formal rectangular structure of the paintings and reality —windows and landscapes, for example. This is a very honest reservation when considered in terms of Rothko's stated intentions to bar the viewer from metaphorical response. It is also a reservation that highlights the uncritical and occasionally self-indulgent abandon with which some have recorded elaborate literary associations evoked by Rothko's pictures.

In 1961 a scathing review of Rothko's Museum of Modern Art retrospective appeared in *The New Republic*.[20] The museum, argued Frank Getlein, in "The Ordeal of Mark Rothko," had illustrated the absurdity of Rothko's paintings by exhibiting so many of them together. Calling them examples of "mass-produced objects," Getlein found the only sign of Rothko's development as a painter to lie with the increasing size of his work. "The paintings," he wrote, "get bigger and bigger, like an inflating balloon. Similarly, in the work and in its worship, the surface gets thinner and thinner, the content gets purer and purer hot air." Comparing the formal similarity of Rothko's pictures to a stale joke, he added: "Rothko is getting on for sixty; if he doesn't pull out soon, the wallpaper people will get him, same as the linoleum men got Mondrian." Even more than Rothko, Getlein's review attacked the critics who praised the MOMA retrospective, particularly Peter Selz, the curator in charge of the exhibition and his catalog. Finally, Getlein concluded, "What the Museum's Rothko reveals is not that the emperor doesn't have any clothes, but that there isn't any emperor behind that enormous brocade."

On the witness stand in 1974, Frank Lloyd also had something to say about Rothko's international reputation in the 1950s and 1960s. As far as the dealer was concerned, Rothko's lucky day was the day he met Frank Lloyd. "A man like Rothko was a broken man in '63," he testified, "Nobody would touch his paintings in '64. . . ." Rothko "was a very unhappy person, and he was not encouraged by people, except by myself, by McKinney (president of Marlborough New York), and by Bernard Reis. All the others didn't encourage him in any way. We promised him exhibitions. . . . It gave him hope. He carried on working." Lloyd was unimpressed with claims of Rothko's European success. "They were made in basements of small museums," he scoffed at the exhibitions. "They were not really sponsored like an exhibition should have been sponsored. They were just forgotten exhibitions which had no effect on Rothko's prices, and I know only one thing—that the moment the Marlborough took over Rothko, it took us a lot of time, a lot of money, but it turned out to be for Rothko a blessing."

"Now isn't it a fact, Mr. Lloyd," queried a lawyer for the petitioners, "that from 1964 until 1970, you didn't arrange a single one-man show of Rothko paintings?"

"You don't know one thing," snapped the dealer whose courtroom manner shuttled between charming and irritable with frequent spells of not knowing and not remembering, "that if an organization like ours, even without exhibiting or making exhibitions, through the experienced sales staff which we have, will sponsor an artist, that creates an international market and an interest. . . . One-man shows we did not organize in this period, because we thought it would do harm for Rothko to make a one-man show. It is, in my judgment as head of that firm, and as an expert, to choose the right moment when, how, and where to do one-man shows of an artist. . . ."

Throughout his testimony, Lloyd addressed himself to finance, continuously distinguishing between Rothko's recognized importance as an artist and the market demand for his pictures. No other expert made the distinction between finance and aesthetics as precisely as Lloyd. He himself made this eminently clear when he stated that "art critics and museum directors are not art dealers. They are very removed from that." Money, in fact, was a basic factor in virtually every aspect of the trial.

Saidenberg's low appraisal ($750,000) of Rothko's 100 pictures set off a round of comparative appraisals from other experts. Peter Selz, a witness for Marlborough, estimated the May 1970 value of the 100 at around $4,000,000. Petitioners, on the other hand, relied heavily on the testimony of dealer and collector Ben Heller. Though a relative latecomer to full-fledged dealing in modern art, Heller had been noted in art circles for his distinguished collection of abstract expressionist paintings. It was Heller who sold Jackson Pollock's *Blue Poles* to the Australian National Gallery for $2,000,000, the highest price ever paid for an American painting. Heller provided the court with an appraisal of $6,420,000 for the 100 as of May 1970, and followed it up with a schedule of increases. Thus, according to his estimates, the 100 would be worth slightly over $8,500,000 by January 1972, and two years later over $14,500,000.

Heller thoroughly disapproved of the bulk sale to Marlborough on the grounds that paced selling was better and that control should remain in the hands of the executors. The bulk sales had prompted the attorney general to move for a court order restraining further sales. Since Rothko's works were particularly unique, he wanted to prevent their uncontrolled disposition, which might be damaging both to the beneficiaries and to the public interest.

Lloyd disagreed. If there is a big backlog of pictures, he countered (and 798 pictures is a sizable number of pictures), then the best thing for prices is widespread distribution. Thus, he would use the 798 for distribution, create a market, and then put up the prices. Picasso, Lloyd pointed out, "has high prices because he had the widest distribution."

Spencer Samuels, a witness for Lloyd, is an art dealer who had worked at French and Company, at Duveen's, and briefly at Marlborough, before setting up his own gallery. Asked what he thought the most prudent way to handle an estate of "800 pictures," he described one possible strategy:

> I would advise them to sell a group and to obtain a certain amount of cash for the heirs or the inheritors, and I would make every effort to market the other paintings at a pace which I considered adequate to distribute the paintings throughout the world while the artist was still popular. One would have to measure what the saturation point might be. It is important that a cer-

tain number of works are sold, because the more works that go into museums and fine private collections, the greater reputation and stature the works of the artist arrive at, and it would make other works more salable. One couldn't glut the market, on the other hand, it would require very careful judgment. I would plan exhibitions that would circulate to museums if the artist's work deserved to be shown in museums, and also try and sell them throughout the world, not concentrate just in one city or one country, if that's possible.

It would not have been prudent, in Samuels' view, to restrict sales to four pictures a year, holding onto the others until the exclusive expired.

Ben Heller—for the petitioners—did not agree. He would have restricted himself to the sale of four pictures a year, thus bringing in "a considerable source of income and preventing Marlborough from arranging significant shows." Hopefully, Heller testified, this strategy would have pressured Marlborough into a modification or even a release of the consignment agreement. Heller further contradicted Lloyd's assertion that taking control of so large a number of pictures (798) by one artist was a liability and that therefore the buyer was entitled to a discount. In the case of an artist of Rothko's stature, Heller argued, the "800" paintings were "a plum." Nor did Heller approve of the contract's twelve-year duration; in this Glimcher agreed. On similar grounds, Heller objected to Marlborough receiving a 50 percent commission on sales of the consigned pictures; it was much too high for works by a major artist. In general, commission estimates judged to be fair by all the experts ranged from 20 percent to one-third.

Lloyd was unimpressed and confident that his superiority as a dealer was well worth the full 50 percent. "Sometimes," he testified, "it's cheaper to pay 50 percent to Marlborough, as 10 percent to another dealer, who works from his apartment, with two rooms. If you want to make an international market, and if you want to benefit from an international organization, it's perhaps cheaper to pay 50 percent to us as 10 percent to a man who deals from his bedroom."

Lloyd and the executors made a considerable defense of economic conditions and the effect of a falling stock market on art prices in May 1970. Lawyers for Marlborough argued that high-priced art was not immune to the state of the economy; artists, they pointed out, were in great distress during the Depression. Dealer Spencer Samuels agreed: "I don't think the art market is immune to the economic fluctuations of any country. It perhaps responds more slowly than some other commodities, but it's basically a commodity, in a sense." When the market is down, Samuels testified later, art becomes more difficult to sell. "The prices did not fall so much," he said referring to the economic decline in 1970, "but the volume decreased tremendously."

Glimcher, on the other hand, believed that in times of economic depression there was a tendency to take money out of the stock market and put it into art. Selz said that from 1960 to 1969, prices of modern art increased 300 percent to 400 percent, becoming, for some buyers, a hedge against inflation.

When asked about this very point—art as a hedge against inflation—Frank Lloyd replied, "You cannot generalize that. I know of some people who put all their money in shares and said that it will never be as cheap as it is in 1974, you see. Others said that art is the only investment, and others said diamonds, and others said that gold is a good investment. . . ."

One gauge of art prices is auctions. Heller testified that even in a bad year like 1970 prices of good art rose at auctions. Rothko's prices, in fact, did continue to climb as the market fell. Nevertheless, Lloyd would not concede even this point, which he explained with a homily on the underhanded nature of the auction business. One cannot, he declared, rely on auction results, "because there is so much monkey business going on in auction sales that nobody knows what has been sold, what are the reserves, what are the conditions, and then the auctioneers buy themselves things and put them up for sale. . . . One has to check each sale . . . because in order to get high prices for the sales, they create an artificial market, and dealers are putting up paintings for sale, to establish high prices, which they buy back themselves."

A most ticklish question in connection with the art market is the degree to which it is predictable, whether in general or in the case of a specific artist. The subsidiary issue of the impact of an artist's death on prices is equally elusive. Schapiro discussed these matters on a broad historical scale, admitting, however, the difficulty of prediction in specific cases.

"We assume," Schapiro explained, "that the quality of the work of Rothko, the delight it has given to people who are serious about quality in painting, and in relation to many things that happened in the preceding ten to twenty years in the art world, which have declined in interest, in value—we would say that against that background Rothko in 1970 seemed to be an artist of lasting qualities. But, as I said, it is only in terms of that experience. We don't have any stronger, more precise way of gauging this."

Asked whether anyone could predict the market values of an artist, Schapiro replied; "The novelist George Moore, as a young man living in Paris in the 1880s wrote as follows: 'Buy Degas and your grandchildren will be millionaires.' That is an example of someone who made a prediction which has been confirmed. So, therefore, to answer your question strictly, 'Can anyone do it?' yes, people have done it. And many people have lost their shirts by doing it."

"And based on your experience, can you give us the probabilities of any such prediction?"

"No."

Ben Heller, on the other hand, had no such qualms about predicting Rothko's future. "He is a master," Heller declared confidently, "All masters' prices rise." Furthermore, Heller asserted, "Rothko's prices will go into the millions for individual works." And, in Heller's view, this escalation could have been predicted as early as April 1970, before the executors made the contracts with Marlborough. Even then, he said, "There was already a demand on the part of people who had not gotten quote their unquote Rothko's, the collectors or museums who had wanted to have Rothkos and hadn't been able, during the previous years, to get them."

Peter Selz was more cautious, "We do not know a man's place in history until a proper period of time has elapsed," he said. "By the 'proper period of time' I mean several generations."

And Spencer Samuels pointed out that an artist's prices may not necessarily go up after his death. An entire school, like the Barbizon, might go out of fashion, or a particular artist may be reevaluated, Samuels noted. Like Selz, Samuels would not guarantee an artist's reputation without the perspective of time. "I have seen the art scene long enough to know the changes and the whimsies in taste," he said.

It is interesting that artist and executor Stamos waxed more financial than any of the dealers. "How long Rothko is going to last?" he said. "I don't know how long Rothko is going to last. I hope he's going to last long enough for everybody to enjoy the best of the highest prices he can get."

Schapiro, however, believed that Rothko's reputation had already "outlived the moment of his novelty."

As might be expected, Frank Lloyd had something to say about all this. He scoffed at all predictions of the art market's future: "If somebody makes a statement here in court that Rothko or Klein or any American expressionist will be worth ten times, twenty times, or thirty times more than it is worth today, he is either a fool or a liar." Lloyd pointed to certain London and New York auctions that seemed to contradict Ben Heller's confidence in steadily rising prices.

As one illustration of the unpredictability of the art market, Lloyd's lawyers cited Monet's famous *Water Lilies*. It was unsalable when Monet died. They added that although the artist's *Argenteuil* was sold for $609,600 by Marlborough in June 1970, it failed to reach its reserve price of $170,000 in July 1974. What was more, Lloyd declared flatly, if Rothko's prices *did* increase after his death, it was thanks to the genius of none other than Frank Lloyd and his organization. "Of course," he testified, "the longer the time progressed, the more work we could put in in sponsoring the sales of Rothkos. Of course it beared fruit," said Lloyd, his accent and his grammar reflecting his Austrian origins, "our efforts which we made, you see. But I don't think it has anything to do with Rothko's death. I maintain that the death of an artist has no influence on his prices. However, if you give—he died in February. By September we had already time seven months to work on the market. The prices went up. It paid if you have a good selling force. Prices go up. It had nothing to do with his death."

Quite aside from the various expert opinions expressed in the course of the trial, there was the matter of Rothko's foundation and the related controversy over Rothko's intentions for his estate.

Rothko's will, drawn up during a period of mental depression but nonetheless a legal document, gave no indication of his intentions. As it stood, the Rothko Foundation was run by Bernard Reis (though with the assent of the other directors). Reis was thus in the prestigious position of controlling foundation funds and their distribution. Assistant Attorney General Harrow pointed to the will as yet another example of Reis's double-cross. Harrow argued that Rothko died owning 798 pictures, a clear indication that he was concerned about their disposition. This was apparently the impression that several of Rothko's friends had had as well. William Rubin expressed this very opinion in his affidavit. On the one hand—partly for legal reasons—the foundation would grant gifts to older, needy artists. On the other hand, Rubin's recollection was that Rothko had expressly indicated his wish to keep groups of paintings permanently together; nor did he want the bulk of his work placed on the open market. Even Bernard Reis, in his brief pretrial testimony, stated that Rothko had wanted his pictures displayed together. The artist, Reis said, envisioned "a series of paintings like an envelope . . . like in a structural envelope." At the same time, however, Reis also insisted that Rothko had wanted his paintings disposed of quickly in order to raise cash for the foundation.

Ben Heller was entirely certain about Rothko's plans for his estate. "The actions of the Estate," he declared, "are very far from the intentions of Rothko as expressed to me and to many others over the past many years." According to Heller, Rothko had three primary goals: the financial protection of his family; the arrangement of a significant body of his work so that it could be viewed and understood as a totality; and the support of older, unrecognized, or forgotten artists. "Anyone who knew him," Heller said, "knew how deeply he cared about protecting his work in a specific environment so that his deepest ambitions, which were mighty and high, could be felt, seen and understood."

The legalities, however, operated on another level. "His will," pointed out Judge Midonick, "isn't in terms of where he wants his paintings to end up. His will is in terms of money."

As for the foundation, it took a hard-line financial position in court, based primarily on self-interest. Lawyers for the foundation argued in support of the contracts, although they were quick to point out that this did not imply support of either the executors or Marlborough. In their view, the estate needed cash, Rothko's eight-year exclusive contract was valid and legally binding on the estate, and they preferred contractual assurances to a gamble on the future of the art market. "Paintings," they said, "are not like wheat or corn or listed securities. There is no established market for them in the sense of the Mercantile Exchange or the Stock Exchange." Nor did they see evidence of self-dealing on the part of the executors. Reis, they said, naturally attended to the accounting details because it was consistent with his previous experience. All three executors had been right to rely on the legal advice received from Karelson and his firm. As a result of that advice, Marlborough was in a superior bargaining position and this was Rothko's fault, not the fault of the executors. Such, in brief, was the stance adopted by the foundation.

At the same time, the foundation agreed with the petitioners that Marlborough's records were on the "spotty" side; it even went so far as to say that Marlborough breached the consignment contract. However, the foundation asserted, both transgressions were irrelevant as long as the estate was not damaged and, in their view, the estate was not damaged. If anything, the foundation believed that the greatest damage done to the estate had been done by the petitioners because "their wild claims of value" had brought the Internal Revenue Service into the case. "The I.R.S.," they alleged, "stands like the 'Sword of Damocles' over the hapless body of the Estate . . . ready to gobble up all funds that might become available through sales of the paintings. . . . The only escape now from I.R.S. destruction of the estate is for the Court to sustain the contracts as within the range of prudence."

One lawyer for the foundation summed up his views in a simple statement: "There's something wrong when this stuff's been palmed off as art," he said of Rothko's paintings. "We will take the money when we can get it." More clearly than almost any other, this statement highlights a very basic aspect of the Rothko trial. Underlying much of the financial wrangling was the question of Rothko's present and future importance as an artist. Those for whom Rothko was a great painter were outraged by what they saw as the plundering of his estate. For those who failed to discern his genius, on the other hand, while they might have acknowledged some irregularities in the handling of Rotho's estate, the enormously expensive trial was much ado about relatively little.

One mystery that the trial has not solved was the mystery of Rothko himself. Testimony regarding his intentions, his relationship to his art, was conflicting, to say the least. And it was compounded by some of his own agreements, executed during his lifetime.

William Rubin—not in court—was quoted by petitioners as having referred to Rothko as a remarkably consistent painter. Frank Lloyd said that, like his moods, even dependent on them, Rothko's style was very *inconsistent*.

Schapiro described Rothko as "an essentially spiritual nature with an ideal of art as a purifying and ennobling experience. He abhorred the exploitation of art for social prestige and found the self-interested form of publicity and promotion in the world of art exceedingly distasteful."

Bernard Reis said that Rothko was "a good bargainer" who liked "the idea of haggling."

Rothko has been quoted as having said one of his paintings was worth whatever he could get for it. "Today," he said, "my price is six thousand or better. Tomorrow it may be six hundred." In this, he sounds suspiciously commercial. He claimed to have hated the promotional machinery of dealers and the pomposity of the very critics who were instrumental in his success. At the same time, he entered into contracts with the most "commercial" of all art dealers, had the secretary-treasurer of one of the most "commercial" art networks draw up his will, and left his estate largely in that man's hands.

How many of these actions—like Rothko's suicide—were the result of mental aberration following a serious illness can only be surmised. What seems fairly certain is that during the last two years of his life, Rothko and Bernard Reis were close friends.

Reis's wife testified that Rothko had been a frequent visitor at their home. It was Rothko himself, she said, who had arranged for her husband to work at Marlborough, thereby knowing of the potential conflict-of-interest situation.

When Rothko was ill and in the hospital, Levine testified, Reis "hovered" over him.

Reis and Rothko were "like Siamese twins," said Frank Lloyd. "Closer than most married people," said Stamos.

In the eyes of Rothko's children, Bernard Reis, "the loving friend" of their father, masterminded the "swindle of his estate."

On December 18, 1975, New York Surrogate Court Judge Millard L. Midonick handed down his decision in *The Matter of Mark Rothko, Deceased*. Eighty-seven pages long, the statement summarized the case and presented the salient arguments for each side.

Of the three executors, Midonick focused first on the crucial role of Bernard Reis. Reis's position as director, secretary, and treasurer of Marlborough New York was found to be in direct conflict with his duty as fiduciary to the Rothko estate. As fiduciary, Reis was obligated to get the best terms possible for the estate. The contention that Rothko knew of Reis's conflict of interest did not, in Midonick's opinion, excuse the executor if he used his dual position for his own self-interest in dealing with Marlborough. Faced with the conflict-of-interest situation, Midonick continued, the executors should have submitted the contracts with Marlborough to the courts for approval. The judge spelled out a basic rule of conduct for trustees in Reis's position: "A fiduciary faced by a problem of conflict of interest should not use his dual position to deal for his own self-interest with the corporation to which he owes a conflicting duty as director and officer, in the disposition of estate or trust property without prior court approval (Matter of Scarborough, 25 N.Y. 2d 553). He cannot serve two masters, and if he has a conflict between his duty to his estate and his duty to his corporation, he must resign or seek the direction of the court in advance."

During the testimony, Reis's counsel had argued that personal "aggrandizement" had to be demonstrated in order to prove that a trustee was guilty of a breach of fiduciary responsibility. The implication was that a man of Reis's personal wealth was hardly likely to be tempted by the annual salary of $20,000 paid to him by Marlborough, out of which he paid the salary of his own secretary, amounting to $12,000 per annum. Judge Midonick tackled both the psychological and financial aspects of this question and expressed the view that "the prestige and status of Reis as a director, secretary and treasurer of Marlborough New York, apart from his salary . . . and his fringe benefits and perquisites, were quite important to Reis's life style. The court infers and finds that Reis was concerned and insistent on the continuation of this prestigious status. He was known and wanted to be known as a collector of valuable masterworks of many artists." On a more tangible level, Reis had been selling works from his own collection through Marlborough, netting him and his family nearly $1,000,000 over a period of eight years; the judge observed that Marlborough's efforts on Reis's behalf far exceeded what the gallery normally did on behalf of other collectors. Finally, Judge Midonick pointed to the air tickets to and from Venice and Houston supplied by Marlborough to Reis purportedly to help in the promotion of Rothko's work—amenities of a prestigious and undemanding nature which Reis did not wish to relinquish and, cumulatively, evidence of self-aggrandizement and self-dealing. While Judge Midonick felt that "none of the executors acted innocently," for Bernard Reis there was "no question as to his dual role and his planned purpose to benefit the Marlborough interests to the detriment of the estate."

The two other executors, abstract expressionist painter Theodoros Stamos and anthropology professor Morton Levine, were also found to have acted improvidently and negligently though their positions were less clear than Reis's. Within months of signing the estate contract, Stamos himself signed a contract with Marlborough which was more advantageous to the artist than that made for the Rothko estate. As a result of the contract, Marlborough was able to considerably enhance Stamos's artistic career. The judge also pointed out that it was to the advantage of Stamos, as a not-too-successful artist, to curry favor with Marlborough. Levine, as well as Stamos, knew of Reis's conflict of interest but made no effort to prevent it and "docilely lent his approval to a deal of which he was distrustful." Although an educated man, he failed to exercise prudence in the performance of his fiduciary obligations. Levine was found to have been a "candid witness" throughout the trial and because of his candor and lack of self-interest, the court would have preferred not to penalize him. However, Judge Midonick pointed out that such leniency rested with the appellate court and all that he could do was to set a lower level of damages in Levine's case.

Addressing some of the specific actions of the executors, Midonick found the twelve-year consignment period too long, the absence of minimum prices for individual paintings "startling," and the 50 percent commission rate unusually, if not grossly, generous to Marlborough in view of Rothko's recognized stature as an artist. Despite the respondents' arguments to the contrary, the judge considered Saidenberg's appraisal of the estate paintings far too low.

As a result of these and other arrangements, all three executors were removed as fiduciaries of the estate, denied commissions, and the contracts for the sale and consignment of the paintings were set aside.

Judge Midonick dealt separately with Frank Lloyd and the Marlborough Galleries (especially Marlborough New York and Marlborough A.G. in Liechtenstein). In view of Lloyd's admission that he alone controlled all Marlborough operations, the judge ruled that, for purposes of liability, Lloyd *was* Marlborough and furthermore that there would be no distinction between the various companies in the Marlborough network. Lloyd himself did not become a respondent in the Rothko case until he was accused of violating the temporary restraining order of June, 1972, and a subsequent injunction issued to prevent all further sales of Rothko's work. Midonick found that a violation of these orders had indeed occurred. Following the restraining order, fifty-seven paintings (twenty-eight canvases and twenty-nine works on paper) had been sold, presenting the court with the problem of assessing their worth at the time of the court's decision. Citing expert testimony on the value of Rothko's work, Midonick decided on an average figure of $90,000 for each canvas and $28,000 for each paper. Lloyd and Marlborough were thus fined a total of $3,332,000 for contempt in violating the court order.

Of the 798 paintings originally left at Rothko's death,

658 remained unsold at the end of the trial. These were ordered to be returned to the estate. Any of the 140 paintings already sold, if retrieved, was also to revert to the estate, thereby reducing the respondents' liability. This arrangement, the judge stated, would satisfy two major opposing contentions of the trial. On the one hand, Marlborough's insistence that the art market had become depressed would, if true, enable the gallery to recover the pictures at lower prices. The petitioners, on the other hand, were convinced that Rothko's values had increased significantly and thus, reasoned the judge, they should be pleased to receive pictures instead of cash.

In assessing penalties Judge Midonick drew a distinction between the various respondents. Levine, who was not acting out of self-interest, was liable to the estate (jointly with Marlborough) for the value *at the time of sale* of paintings sold. Reis and Stamos, on the other hand, were liable (also jointly with Marlborough) for the *present* value of paintings sold (i.e., including any appreciation since the date of sale.) Accordingly, in addition to the fine imposed on Lloyd and Marlborough for contempt, Judge Midonick found Levine and Marlborough jointly and severally liable for damages in the amount of $6,464,880 plus interest, while he assessed Reis, Stamos, and Marlborough for $9,252,000.

The Rothko trial opened a Pandora's box that revealed the art world of the 1960s and 1970s in its most commercial aspects. More than most trials involving works of art, the Rothko trial provided a stage where spotlights focused on the conflict between aesthetics and money. Less elegantly stated, it opened a very big can of worms.

AFTERWORD

We have seen that a strange thing happens when art goes on trial. Objects cease to be props and become central characters in the conflict. In every case, there is a distinct quality of the absurd permeating the courtroom. Somehow the lawyers always seem to get around to the question: what is art? Regardless of the original reason for the trial, one side or the other feels it necessary to apply verbal definitions to works of art. It is, in fact, impossible to define art to everyone's satisfaction. Nevertheless, four themes continuously recur in the course of the various sets of testimony which offer some comment on the nature of art. These themes, interrelated for the most part, are the aesthetic response, a certain kind of religious devotion, money and value and, oddly enough, patriotism.

In *Whistler* v. *Ruskin*, all these elements affecting the character of the trial, were present. Beyond the profesional conflict of artist versus critic and the historical conflict between Impressionism and academic painting, Ruskin simply did not like Whistler's musical titles or the works to which they were applied. Neither did those witnesses who testified for the critic. But, even more than aesthetic response, Ruskin's counsel stressed the critic's piety in matters of artistic production. This is clear in the opening statement for Ruskin, whose "love and reverence for art" was offered as a defense for his libelous personal attack on Whistler. Ruskin's very "love and reverence," the attorney general pointed out, amounted to "idolatry," thus converting the work of art into a religious object. The implication of this as a legal tactic is obvious enough. The court, suggested Ruskin's counsel, did not have the right to deny a pious man his religious beliefs.

Going from the religious to the patriotic in his opening statement, the attorney general foreboded an "evil day" for Britain when Ruskin ceased to define the beautiful. Burne-Jones, the Pre-Raphaelite painter who handled the case for Ruskin, carried this argument to absurd lengths when he testified that the art of England would be "degraded" if "lack of finish" in painting were to become customary. Aside from the strategic value of the patriotic argument, it highlights the cultural impact of works of art. An object's style is primarily the product of its maker, to be sure, but it is considerably qualified by its social context as well. Even though Whistler was an American, he had become part of the contemporary London scene, and the style of his pictures had been conditioned by the study of European—especially French—art.

Possibly Ruskin's counsel was attempting to cast aspersions on Whistler as a foreign influence. Such an attitude would not be inconsistent with the insular nature of English society which, even today, continues to characterize a large percentage of that nation. In any case, Ruskin's supporters never explicitly made an issue of Whistler's American origins. Rather, they approached the question from another angle, asserting that the high standards of English art must not be allowed to falter.

The self-righteous tenor of Ruskin's case carried over into the financial as well as the religious and social spheres. Consistent with the puritan view that one makes money through diligence and hard work, Ruskin's counsel did his best to foster the impression that Whistler painted in an uncraftsmanlike manner. In his published statement, Ruskin had created the image of a Whistler carelessly tossing pots of paint onto his canvases and then having the effrontery to charge real money as if he had done an honest day's work. In this financial stance, Ruskin was as hypocritical as in his pious devotions to the religion of Art. Unfortunately for Whistler, his counsel was unwilling or unable to impress upon the court that the artist had suffered financial losses as a result of Ruskin's remarks.

By modern standards, both the judge and jury seem unusually inept. It is clear from the judge's comments and charge to the jury that he thought the trial an unnecessary waste of time. Further, he virtually instructed them to find Ruskin guilty of libel. At the same time, he suggested that Whistler merited no more than a farthing in damages, thereby making it abundantly clear that he had little regard for his pictures. The jury did as it was told.

In the Brancusi trial, the issue of money and value was hardly raised at all. Likewise, moral and religious elements were absent. The question of aesthetic response, however, became the central issue around which the trial revolved. More directly than in any of the other trials, the case of *Brancusi* v. the *United States* dealt with whether or not a specific object was a work of art. Brancusi's *Bird in Space,* an abstract representation of an idea, had to stand up to the official taste of the United States. Thus, as in *Whistler* v. *Ruskin*, the Brancusi trial reflected the more general conflict between abstraction and naturalism although it occurred some fifty years later. Also reflected was the geographical movement of the avant-garde in art which, like the sculpture on trial, had entered American consciousness with considerable fanfare and had met with no little resistance.

In the brief for Brancusi, Steichen's attorneys wisely converted this process into a patriotic appeal to the court. America's cultural heritage would suffer, they argued, if the country closed its doors to free artistic expression. Considering that the nation's character—and its self-image—has been largely determined by waves of immigration and a relative acceptance of new and modern ideas, this appeal proved extremely effective.

Though patriotism played a definite role in the argument presented in the plaintiff's brief, the main issue of the

Brancusi trial remained clearly in focus. Even though the attorneys for the United States continually attempted to sidetrack the court with irrelevant discussions about the *Bird*'s title, the case would ultimately stand or fall on the aesthetic question—was the sculpture a work of art or was it merely a lump of nicely polished bronze? Throughout the trial, witnesses for both sides generally agreed that art was what aroused the sense of beauty. What was beautiful for the defense, however, was not beautiful for the prosecution. And therein lay the absurdity of the case: taste cannot be legislated nor beauty determined by a court of law.

Fortunately Justice Waite proved to be rather more enlightened than the customs officials who admitted the statue as a "kitchen utensil" or the spokesman for government taste. While not personally an enthusiastic admirer of the avant-garde, Justice Waite realized that the precedents set by previous cases, as well as the existing statutes, had been superseded by new developments in artistic style. He thus had a sense of historical process and this, together with his open-minded willingness to listen to the impressive array of witnesses for Brancusi, prompted him to make the only reasonable decision.

Such was not the case in the *Hahn* v. *Duveen* trial where the judge's decision, as well as his charge to the jury, was, at best, muddled. Despite the extensive time spent in obtaining depositions from abroad and the nine-year wait for the case finally to come to trial, the aesthetic question was obvious and clear-cut. As the first set of British experts for Duveen maintained, the quality of the Hahn painting was so patently inferior to the version in the Louvre that a comparison of the two photographs—let alone the paintings—should have provided ample legal justification for Duveen's remarks. The unwavering persistence of the Hahns against the virtually unanimous opposition of the established art world seems to have been sustained by a combination of the financial motive with the gambler's fallacy. That the jury—even though composed of laymen—voted nine to three in favor of Mrs. Hahn resulted from the poor psychological tactics employed by Duveen and his attorneys. Legally as well as artistically, the case should have been quickly decided in Duveen's favor. In the light of recent developments in American jury selection, it would be interesting to see how a modern jury for a similar trial would be composed. Even in 1929, the French press was highly amused that laymen would decide a case requiring specialized artistic training. In retrospect, their amusement was entirely justified.

Duveen and his lawyers completely misjudged the jury and thus lost every chance for the overwhelming victory to which they were entitled. Trying to impress the twelve jurymen with the most eminent art experts of the day, Duveen lost sight of the jury's "common man" mentality. As Forbes Watson wrote in one of his scathing editorials on the trial, Duveen would have been better advised—in the case of Bernard Berenson, for example—not to stress his international renown but rather his Horatio Alger background. The jury, on the whole, was not impressed by expertise (which Mrs. Hahn's lawyers cleverly derided) but they might have been swayed by the human interest aspect of Berenson who came to America as a poor Lithuanian immigrant and rose to prominence through talent and hard work.

Duveen's attorneys, in fact, ignored all of the several possible appeals to the patriotic instincts of the jury while, ironically enough, Mrs. Hahn lost no opportunity to exploit this avenue of attack. French though she was, she assumed the role of the injured Midwesterner who had suffered outrageous damage at the hands of an international cartel of devious art dealers and fraudulent experts. In this pose, she received considerable support from her American husband, a World War I flier, from Kansas and the pathetic Kansas City dealer, Conrad Hug. Duveen might easily have turned the tables on Mrs. Hahn had he portrayed her as a foreigner trying to con the American public. The hypocrisy of Mrs. Hahn's assertions that her painting—and not that in the Louvre—had been painted by Leonardo was revealed when her husband wrote his letter to the Paris newspaper, *Le Matin*. The letter denied that Mrs. Hahn intended to cast doubt on the authenticity of the Louvre painting (although that is precisely what she was doing). Her lawyer offered a feeble explanation for this contradictory behavior in which he extolled her patriotic feelings for France. In short, when Mrs. Hahn was in France, she would allow that the French painting was authentic and when in the United States, it was her painting alone (which also happened to be in the United States) that had been produced by the brush of Leonardo.

As for her "expert" witness, Georges Sortais, it is difficult to imagine a more ridiculous caricature. He fit the image of the unscrupulous European trying to defraud the naïve Americans so perfectly that Duveen's failure to exploit this aspect in his defense is remarkable. Judging from his own testimony, Sortais knew next to nothing about either Italian Renaissance art or Leonardo; he was a self-proclaimed expert with no objective credentials, no publications to his credit and inferior standing even in the French art world. Internationally, he was practically unknown. Sortais's refusal to take the elementary precaution of comparing the Hahn painting with the Louvre painting before certifying the former as a Leonardo was negligent to the point of outright dishonesty. His feeble justification for this oversight—that the Louvre painting was in storage because of the war—does not explain why he never made the comparison subsequently. To render Sortais even more unattractive, he was an extremely uncooperative witness. Nevertheless, his concluding statement to the effect that the whole trial was an act of revenge against him by Duveen played right into the hands of Mrs. Hahn's lawyers, providing more support for the impression that Duveen masterminded an international plot to control the art world.

Duveen, on the other hand, arrogant and powerful as he was, did have something of a monopoly on art dealing, particularly in sales from Europe to America. Far from being sweetness and light himself, Duveen's energetic and comprehensive muster of expert argument suggests that he thoroughly enjoyed demolishing his opponents' position. Unfortunately for him, his prominent witnesses made little headway with the jury. The fact that most of them did not appear in person at the trial probably made matters worse. Their depositions were no match for the performances of Mr. and Mrs. Hahn and the ailing Conrad Hug. Duveen's own courtroom behavior was extremely ill advised. He acted like a social and intellectual snob, not an attitude likely to appeal to the layman who, under the best of circumstances, tends to regard the art world with some suspicion. His apparent oblivion to the mundane proceedings taking place before him must have kindled the jury's desire to deflate his monumental ego while rushing to support the injured Hahns.

The Duveen case was remarkable among art trials because in the face of the overwhelming evidence in the dealer's favor, his psychological ineptitude lost him the trial. The out-of-court settlement of $60,000 (a considerable sum, especially in 1929), indicates that Duveen suspected he would lose the retrial and Mrs. Hahn's willingness to accept the money rather than to fight on suggests that a strong financial motive lay behind her incompetent aesthetics.

The Van Meegeren trial, although spectacular in many ways, was but the last step in the forger's artistic, mental, and physical decline. Since forgery is a kind of perversion of the creative process, the trial proceeded in a somewhat backward direction from the aesthetic point of view. Van Meegeren's brilliance—both in forgery itself and in his follow-up activities of creating a market and a provenance for the pictures—in no way lessened the basic perversity of his career. Because of his arrest on a charge of treason, Van Meegeren had to confess to forgery in order to save himself. His legal defense—a reversal of the more usual procedure—thus consisted of proving that his own pictures were not art (at least not the art they were thought to be). His confession left a great many disappointed collectors, dealers, and critics in its wake. Their original disbelief, however, had been sufficiently worn down by Van Meegeren's supervised production of a "Vermeer," so that by the time the forger went to trial, they were, for the most part, ready to acknowledge their own deception.

While Van Meegeren's original impulse to embark on his career of deception may have been set in motion by matters of aesthetic principle as he claimed, he soon became the victim of his own activities. The ease with which he was financially corrupted suggests that his hatred for the critics who failed to appreciate his early paintings had considerable pecuniary motivation. Once he realized how wealthy forgery would make him, Van Meegeren became as addicted to good living as he was to drugs. Van Meegeren perceived the critics as the barrier not to his creativity, but to his success, for adverse criticism has never yet stopped a sincere, important artist. Van Meegeren was no Gaugin impelled to escape bourgeois pressures in order to pursue his talents freely. Indeed, Van Meegeren adored such bourgeois pleasures as family life, lavish entertaining, owning real estate, and material success, generally. The completeness of his confession (he did not have to admit to all his forgeries in order to save his life—only to the one sold to Goering) attests to his drive for fame, perverse though his view of it had become.

By choosing Vermeer as the primary target of his forgery, Van Meegeren was able to achieve several of his ends at once. Unable to identify with an openly hostile father and unwilling to accept the judgments of contemporary art authorities, Van Meegeren subjected himself to the domination of an artist dead for nearly 300 years. Since next to nothing is known of Vermeer's life, Van Meegeren's identification with the master must have been mainly of an artistic nature. It would nevertheless be interesting to discover what impact the striking similarity of the names Van Meegeren and Vermeer (= Van Meer) made on the forger. Perhaps Van Meegeren was also attracted to Vermeer because recognition of his genius had not come until many years after his death, thus permitting Van Meegeren to identify with Vermeer's early neglect by the art world. Certainly, in seeking revenge against the art experts, Van Meegeren's choice of Vermeer was particularly appropriate. Not only would he feel that he had fooled the experts, he would also eventually be in a position to destroy sacred idols and with them the reputations of those who had adored them. This is essentially what he did when he confessed; having provided the world with paintings by "Vermeer," he could now take them away.

Financially, too, of course, Vermeer proved to be more than satisfactory. The prices for his paintings—now among the highest in Western art—were considerable even during Van Meegeren's lifetime and in spite of the economic hardships of war. As a reflection of the esteem in which Vermeer was held, both his prices and his fame were no doubt extremely attractive to the bitter and unsuccessful Van Meegeren.

Dutch reactions to Van Meegeren's activities—first the sale of a supposed Vermeer to Goering and then his confession—again highlights the cultural importance of certain art treasures. This impact was heightened by World War II, by the continual threat of Nazi plundering, and by Holland's determination to safeguard her works of art underground. In addition to facilitating Van Meegeren's forgeries—because the concealment of Vermeer's paintings left them unavailable for comparison—Holland's heroic attempt to protect her cultural heritage from the ravages of war further sensitized the situation. So much patriotic emotion was invested in works of art that they became national treasures. Offenses against these works, therefore, were offenses against the nation. As it happened, the Dutch court could not convict Van Meegeren of selling a national treasure to the enemy, but it did find him guilty of forgery. In this the court followed a strictly legal interpretation of treason for, in forging national treasures, Van Meegeren was certainly doing the country and its art a serious injustice. Ironically, Van Meegeren was a psychological and an artistic traitor to Holland, but he could not be proved a legal traitor.

A unique kind of patriotism—America's special brand of "flag fervor"—characterized the trial of New York art dealer Stephen Radich in the late 1960s. Aesthetic and financial questions arose to only a minor degree in this case, largely because the sculptures on trial were not considered to be major works of art. Even *New York Times* art critic Hilton

Kramer, the expert who testified for Radich, said that while he believed the artist to be serious and sincere, he was not impressed by his sculptures.

Nor was this view disputed in court. The defense made no attempt to establish that Morrel's sculptures were aesthetically significant. This aspect of the case probably explains why the established art world took so long to make a positive legal move for the defense. Aside from scattered votes of confidence, highly placed figures in the art world did little until John Hightower submitted his *amicus curiae* brief to the Supreme Court several years after the original trial. The trouble with the failure to rally around Radich's cause—free artistic expression—is the resulting implication that art must be good in order to merit equal protection under the law. This would play right into the hands of the absurd confrontation between art and the law when the law tries to establish that something is or is not art. Perhaps Judge Basel realized this when—in his dissenting opinion in the original trial—he argued that the artist should not be punished for vulgarity or bad taste. Or, in other words, an artist need only be serious —not important—to enjoy the protections of the First and Fourteenth amendments. In any case, on both formal and iconographic grounds, Hilton Kramer testified that Morrel's sculptures were works of art, and the prosecution did not refute his argument.

Support for the prosecution was nevertheless abundant and it derived from two interrelated sources: deep-seated American flag worship and a kind of sexual outrage which obviously viewed one sculpture in particular as pornographic. Even though Radich was not charged with obscenity in displaying Morrel's *Crucified Phallus*, that sculpture aroused the most overt hostility among several of the judges who heard the case. By modern standards however, the *Crucified Phallus* was rather tame and, since pornography is rarely art, the prosecution would have had trouble making such a charge stick. Attorneys for the People of the State of New York were thus better advised to concentrate on the issue of flag desecration, leaving the inherent preoccupation with obscenity to implication and innuendo.

Evidence of this tactic appears throughout the trial and numerous appeals which followed. Assistant Attorney General Slater's argument that because sculpture can be touched it is more likely to arouse the public wrath than paintings or photos is basically a sexual argument. Looking, he thus implied, is safer than touching—a concept which might as easily be applied to a child's moral training. Nor was Slater's logic altogether faulty since most of the tactile qualities of art (whether it is in fact two- or three-dimensional) do contain erotic aspects.

On the other hand, however, Slater's assertion that sculpture—particularly Morrel's flag sculptures—were likely to incite "riot and strike" was patently preposterous. While Hilton Kramer discussed such standard critical matters as form, texture and even symbolism, the prosecution focused on the content of the objects. Slater's insistence that the artist was "getting a kick out of this sort of thing" and succumbing to the pleasures of "personal gratification" drove his point home. Attorney General Louis Lefkowitz supported Slater's stance declaring that Morrel had draped a United States flag over a phallus for "shock effect." Such sexually tinged statements made the desired impact and derided the artist's claims to political and moral conviction. For some seven years this proved to be the wisest strategy.

The recent Rothko trial has highlighted several important aspects of the contemporary art world focusing attention on one of the latest problems connected with art and law—the artist's estate. The trial testimony was permeated by the four main themes of art trials—aesthetics, religious response, finance, and patriotism—with a new, energetic force reflecting a great deal about the contemporary art world.

The religious response to Rothko's paintings is evident in the many critical discussions and reviews of his work and in the Houston Chapel commission as well as in the artist's own meditative way of working. The aesthetic issue did not arise on its own, but rather in connection with finance. There was virtually no attempt made in court to prove that Rothko was or was not a great artist; most of the witnesses who testified agreed to his importance.

Part of Rothko's generally acknowledged importance constituted the patriotic aspects of the trial. Experts testifying for the petitioners stressed the international impact of abstract expressionism and Rothko's place as a leader in that movement. As such, his paintings became ambassadors from the American art world inspiring new directions in art abroad. Thus, it was widely believed, abstract expressionism put America on the artistic map. At the same time, the New York State Attorney General entered the case partly to keep the paintings in the United States. The opposite side of the patriotic coin; the Attorney General wanted to prevent indiscriminate transportation of the paintings abroad. This, he argued, would deplete the artistic wealth of the United States, thereby causing harm to the public interest which he represented.

Despite general agreement on Rothko's international importance, witnesses were at odds on the market value of Rothko's paintings at various points in time and the predictability of that value in the future. The petitioners felt impelled to enter this extremely problematic area of prediction in order to prove that the trustees had wasted the assets of the estate. Legally it would have been simpler had the petitioners been able to confine their efforts to the more straightforward questions of conflict of interest, self-dealing and alleged breaches of contract. Unfortunately, each of these matters seemed affected by the value of the works involved. The difficulty in separating an object's aesthetic and monetary value and the complicating effect of this fact on the Rothko trial was reflected in the judge's constant attempts to encourage an out-of-court settlement.

Despite the apparent incompatibility of legal definition and aesthetics, there is a strong need for further clarification and development of the field of art law, especially in America. American law, which is made either by statute or precedent, is remarkably sparse in matters of art. This situation has given fairly free range to unscrupulous dealers, collectors, frauds, and forgers of all kinds, and probably accounts for the rapidly growing instances of major art thefts. At the same time, the artist is left in a particularly vulnerable position.

Since the art market has become a prominent part of the financial world, and art itself is of such obvious cultural importance, it follows that a body of law must develop to deal exclusively with this field. In order to be effective, such laws must be so formulated that courtroom discussion focuses on that which is relevant and legally provable. They should exclude extraneous aesthetic discussion—amusing though it often is—which permeates the testimony of so many art trials.

With his usual perceptive flair and stylish turn of phrase, Whistler captured the essence of the problem: "Art should be independent of all claptrap, should stand alone and appeal to the artistic sense of eye or ear, without confounding this with emotions entirely foreign to it, as devotion, pity, love, patriotism, and the like."

NOTES

CHAPTER ONE

1. Timothy Hilton, *The Pre-Raphaelites*, New York, 1974, p. 35.

2. Denys Sutton, *Nocturne: The Art of James McNeill Whistler*, New York, 1964, p. 13.

3. Roy McMullen, *Victorian Outsider*, New York, 1973, p. 156.

4. "Americans in London," *The New York Times*, June 3, 1878, p. 3.

5. Quoted by Stanley Weintraub, *Whistler*, New York, 1974, p. 124.

6. Cited by Elizabeth Mumford, *Whistler's Mother*, Ann Arbor, 1971 (reprint of 1940 London edition), p. 234.

7. Cited by Roy McMullen, p. 119.

8. Philip Hamerton, *Saturday Review*, June 1, 1867.

9. James McNeill Whistler, *The Gentle Art of Making Enemies*, New York, 1953, p. 45.

10. H. Montgomery Hyde, *Their Good Names*, London, 1970, p. 69.

11. Elizabeth Mumford, *Whistler's Mother*, p. 229.

12. John D. Rosenberg, *The Darkening Glass, A Portrait of Ruskin's Genius*, New York, 1961, p. 113.

13. Quoted by Weintraub, pp. 199-200.

14. From Weintraub, *Whistler*, pp. 209-10, and Hyde, *Their Good Names*, pp. 81-83.

15. Quoted by McMullen, *Victorian Outsider*, p. 217.

16. From Hyde, *Their Good Names*, p. 88.

17. From Weintraub, *Whistler*, p. 10.

18. From Whistler's *The Gentle Art of Making Enemies*, p. 34.

19. Whistler, *The Gentle Art of Making Enemies*, p. 26.

20. *The New York Times* (Triple Sheet), December, 15, 1878, p. 6.

21. Ibid.

22. Ibid.

23. *The New York Times*, December 15, 1878, p. 4.

CHAPTER TWO

1. See Milton W. Brown, *The Story of the Armory Show*, New York, 1963, pp. 112-13. Brown quotes the last stanza of the poem:

Ladies builded like a bottle
Carrot, beet or sweet potato—
Quaint designs that Aristotle
Idly drew to tickle Plato—
Ladies sculptured thus, I beg
You will save your tense emotion;
I am constant in devotion,
O my egg!

2. Edward Steichen, *A Life in Photography*, New York, 1963, ch. 10.

3. Steichen, *A Life in Photography*, ch. 10 and cf. Sidney Geist, *Brancusi*, New York, 1968, fig. 70a.

4. Steichen, *A Life in Photography*, ch. 10.

5. Steichen, *A Life in Photography*, ch. 10, and Geist, *Brancusi*, No. 198.

6. Geist, *Brancusi*, p. 128.

7. Geist, *Brancusi*, p. 129.

8. Geist, *Brancusi*, p. 130.

9. Steichen, *A Life in Photography*, ch. 10.

CHAPTER THREE

1. S. N. Behrman, *Duveen*, New York, 1951, p. 3.

2. *New York World*, June 18, 1920.

3. Kenneth Clark, *Leonardo da Vinci*, Baltimore, 1963, pp. 55-57.

4. Duveen's reply to Mrs. Hahn's complaint.

5. Ibid.

6. Bernard Berenson, *Italian Painters of the Renaissance*, revised edition, Oxford, 1930, p. 62.

7. Jean Paul Richter, *The Literary Works of Leonardo da Vinci*, London, no date, p. 370.

8. *Le Matin*, September 8, 1923.

9. Forbes Watson, "Exhibitions Coming and Going," *The Arts*, Feb. 1929, vol. XV, pp. 110-12.

10. Forbes Watson, "The Gentlemen of the Jury," *The Arts*, March, 1929, pp. 153-54.

11. Thomas Hart Benton in Harry J. Hahn, *The Rape of La Belle*, Kansas City, 1946.

CHAPTER FOUR

1. Cited by Lord Kilbracken, *Van Meegeren: Master Forger*, New York, 1967, p. 67.

2. Abraham Bredius, "A New Vermeer," *The Burlington Magazine*, November, 1937, p. 211.

3. See P.B. Coremans, *Van Meegeren's Faked Vermeers and de Hoochs*, Amsterdam, 1949.

CHAPTER FIVE

1. Robert Payne, "What's in a Flag? Everything," *The New York Times* (Sunday Magazine), August 30, 1964, p. 30.

2. This was ammended in 1968 and recodified as section 136 (d) of the New York General Business Law (McKinney's Consol. Laws c. 20, 1968).

3. Lawrence P. Tower, cited by *Life* magazine, March 31, 1967, p. 66.

4. Grace Glueck, "Oh, Say, Can You See. . . ," *The New York Times*, (Sunday Arts Section), May 21, 1967.

5. Carl R. Baldwin, "Art and the Law: The Flag in Court Again," *Art in America*, May-June, 1974, pp. 50-54.

6. Letter written to *Art in America*, July-August, 1974, p. 112.

7. See above, note 4.

8. Baldwin, *op. cit.*, p. 50.

9. Grace Glueck, "A Rally 'Round the Flag,' " *The New York Times*, (Sunday Arts Section), Oct. 29, 1967.

10. Dwight D. Eisenhower, "The Day I Knew I Belonged to the Flag," *Reader's Digest*, March, 1969, p. 93.

11. Hilton Kramer, "A Case of Artistic Freedom," *The New York Times* (Sunday Arts Section), March 1, 1970.

12. See Freud, *Totem and Taboo*, New York, 1946.

13. See Frazer, *The Golden Bough*, New York, 1963, especially chaps. 19-23.

14. Edward R. Cain, "The Stars and Stripes Forever," *Commonweal*, March 27, 1970, p. 62.

15. Sydney Schanberg, "Indochina Without Americans: For Most, a Better Life," *The New York Times*, (Sunday News of the Week in Review), April 13, 1975.

CHAPTER SIX

1. From Gottlieb and Rothko, "The Portrait of the Modern Artist," mimeographed script of a broadcast on "Art in

New York," H. Stix, dir., WNYC, New York, Oct. 13, 1943. Cited by Irving Sandler, *The Triumph of American Painting, A History of Abstract Expressionism*, New York, 1970, p. 63.

2. William Rubin, "Mark Rothko 1903-70," *The New York Times*, Sunday, March 8, 1970, p. 21.

3. Mark Rothko in "The Tiger's Eye," No. 9, Oct. 1949, p. 114, cited by Sandler, p. 149, fn. 12.

4. Harold Rosenberg, "The Art World," *The New Yorker*, March 28, 1970, p. 90.

5. Hubert Crehan, "Rothko's Wall of Light," *Arts Digest*, Nov. 1, 1954, p. 19.

6. Max Kozloff, "The Problem of Color-Light in Rothko," *Art Forum*, Sept. 1965, pp. 39-44.

7. William Rubin, *op. cit.*, p. 22.

8. Peter Selz, *Mark Rothko*, (MOMA Catalog), New York, 1961.

9. Rosenberg, *op. cit.*

10. Selz, *op. cit.*

11. Robert Goldwater, "Rothko's Black Paintings," *Art in America*, March-April, 1971, p. 58.

12. Mark Rothko, "The Romantics Were Prompted," *Possibilities* I, 1947-48, p. 84.

13. Sandler, p. 183.

14. Donald McKinney, *Mark Rothko*, (Marlborough Catalog) New York.

15. John Corry, "About New York," *The New York Times*, Feb. 15, 1974, p. 18.

16. *Art News*, March 1947, p. 48.

17. Thomas Hess, *Art News*, April, 1949, pp. 48-49.

18. M.B., *Arts Digest*, April 15, 1949.

19. Robert Coates, "The Art Galleries," *The New Yorker*, April 23, 1955.

20. Frank Getlein, "The Ordeal of Mark Rothko," *The New Republic*, Feb. 6, 1961, pp. 28-30.

INDEX

Whistler trial, 14-34, 211-13